A-Z
HOTEL MANAGEMENT AND CATERING

A-Z HOTEL MANAGEMENT AND CATERING

Dr. Ram Naresh Mahaling

CENTRUM PRESS
NEW DELHI-110002 (INDIA)

CENTRUM PRESS
H.O.: 4360/4, Ansari Road, Daryaganj,
New Delhi-110 002 (India)
Ph.: 23278000, 23261597
B.O.: No. 1015, Ist Main Road, BSK IIIrd Stage
IIIrd Phase, IIIrd Block,
Bangalore - 560 085 (India)
Tel.: 080-41723429
Visit us at: www.centrumpress.com

A-Z Hotel Management and Catering

First Edition, 2009
ISBN 978-93-80106-99-1

PRINTED IN INDIA

Printed at Mehra Offset Press, Delhi

Contents

Contents

Preface

This book is about being a manager in the hotel and catering industry; it is about managing people and controlling the cost of labor. The book is both focused and comprehensive.

It is focused in the sense that it is concerned exclusively with one large industry and is written to explain the opportunities, the constraints, the problem and the solution that face management at any level in the industry. It is, to use the parlance of detective thriller, an inside job.

It is comprehensive in the sense that it is not just concerned with social physiological aspects of people management, but also with the economics of labor- labor cost, labor market behaviour and pay. These aspects are inseparable from the skills of people management, especially in labor-intensive industry.

It is hoped that this book will prove immensely useful to students and teachers of Management, executives, professional and practicing managers and the like. It is undoubtedly an invaluable reference book for anyone who comes into contact with the Hotel Management.

Author

Chapter 1

Hotel Industries and Related Services

NATURE OF THE INDUSTRY

Hotels and other accommodations are as diverse as the many family and business travellers they accommodate. The industry includes all types of lodging, from upscale hotels to RV parks. Motels, resorts, casino hotels, bed-and-breakfast inns, and boarding houses also are included. In fact, in 2004 nearly 62,000 establishments provided overnight accommodations to suit many different needs and budgets.

Establishments vary greatly in size and in the services they provide. *Hotels* and *motels* comprise the majority of establishments and tend to provide more services than other lodging places.

There are five basic types of hotels—*commercial, resort, residential, extended-stay,* and *casino.* Most hotels and motels are *commercial* properties that cater mainly to business people, tourists, and other travellers who need accommodations for a brief stay. Commercial hotels and motels usually are located in cities or suburban areas and operate year round. Larger properties offer a variety of services for their guests, including a range of restaurant and beverage service options—from coffee bars and lunch counters to cocktail lounges and formal fine-dining restaurants.

Conventions and business meetings are major sources of revenue for these hotels and motels. Some commercial hotels are known as conference hotels—fully self-contained entities specifically designed for meetings. They provide physical fitness and recreational facilities for meeting attendees, in addition to state-of-the-art audiovisual and technical equipment, a business centre, and banquet services.

Resort hotels and *motels* offer luxurious surroundings with a variety of recreational facilities, such as swimming pools, golf courses, tennis courts, game rooms, and health spas, as well as planned social activities and entertainment. Resorts typically are located in vacation destinations or near natural settings, such as mountains, the seashore, theme parks, or other attractions.

As a result, the business of many resorts fluctuates with the season. *Residential hotels* provide living quarters for permanent and semi permanent residents. They combine the comfort of apartment living with the convenience of hotel services. Many have dining rooms and restaurants that also are open to residents and to the general public.

Extended-stay hotels combine features of a resort and a residential hotel. Typically, guests use these hotels for a minimum of 5 consecutive nights. These facilities usually provide rooms with fully equipped kitchens, entertainment systems, ironing boards and irons, office space with computer and telephone lines, fitness centres, and other amenities.

Casino hotels provide lodging in hotel facilities with a casino on the premises. The casino provides table wagering games and may include other gambling activities, such as slot machines and sports betting. Casino hotels generally offer a full range of services and amenities and also may contain conference and convention facilities.

In addition to hotels and motels, *bed-and-breakfast inns, recreational vehicle (RV) parks, campgrounds,* and *rooming and boarding houses* provide lodging for overnight guests. *Bed-and-breakfast inns* provide short-term lodging in private homes or small buildings converted for this purpose and are characterized by highly personalized service and inclusion of breakfast in the room rate. Their appeal is quaintness, with unusual service and decor.

RV parks and campgrounds cater to people who enjoy recreational camping at moderate prices. Some parks and campgrounds provide service stations, general stores, shower and toilet facilities, and coin-operated laundries. While some are designed for overnight travellers only, others are for vacationers who stay longer.

Some camps provide accommodations, such as cabins and fixed campsites, and other amenities, such as food services, recreational facilities and equipment, and organized recreational activities. Examples of these overnight camps include children's camps, family vacation camps, hunting and fishing camps, and outdoor adventure retreats that offer trail riding, white-water rafting, hiking, fishing, game hunting, and similar activities.

WORKING CONDITIONS

Work in hotels and other accommodations can be demanding and hectic. Hotel staffs provide a variety of services to guests and must do so efficiently, courteously, and accurately. They must maintain a pleasant demeanor even during times of stress or when dealing with an impatient or irate guest. Alternately, work at slower times, such as the off-season or overnight periods, can seem slow and tiresome without the constant presence of hotel guests. Still, hotel workers must be ready to provide guests and visitors with gracious customer service at any hour.

Because hotels are open around the clock, employees frequently work varying shifts or variable schedules. Employees who work the late shift generally receive additional compensation. Many employees enjoy the opportunity to work part-time, nights or evenings, or other schedules that fit their availability for work and the hotel's needs.

Hotel managers and many department supervisors may work regularly assigned schedules, but they also routinely work longer hours than scheduled, especially during peak travel times or when multiple events are scheduled. Also, they may be called in to work on short notice in the event of an emergency or to cover a position. Those who are self-employed, often owner-operators, tend to work long hours and often live at the establishment.

Employment

Employment is concentrated in densely populated cities and resort areas. Compared with establishments in other industries, hotels, motels, and other lodging places tend to be small. About 91 percent employed fewer than 50 people; about 56 percent employ fewer than 10 workers (chart). As a result, lodging establishments offer opportunities for those who are interested in owning and running their own business. Although establishments tend to be small, the majority of jobs are in larger hotels and motels with more than 100 employees.

Hotels and other lodging places often provide first jobs to many new entrants to the labour force. As a result, many of the industry's workers are young. In 2004, about 19 percent of the workers were younger than age 25, compared with about 14 percent across all industries.

Table: Percent distribution of employment, by age group, 2004

Age group	*Hotels and other accommodations*	*All industries*
Total	100.0%	100.0%
16-19	5.3	4.2
20-24	13.7	9.9
25-34	22.4	21.8
35-44	23.7	24.8
45-54	20.2	23.3
55-64	11.4	12.4
65 and older	3.3	3.5

Occupations in the Industry

Service occupations, by far the largest occupational group in the industry, account for 65 percent of the industry's employment. Most service jobs are in housekeeping occupations—including maids and housekeeping cleaners, janitors and cleaners, and laundry workers—and in food preparation and service jobs—including chefs and cooks, waiters and waitresses, bartenders, fast food and counter workers, and various other kitchen and dining room workers. The industry also employs many baggage porters and bellhops, gaming services workers, and grounds maintenance workers.

Workers in *cleaning* and *housekeeping occupations* ensure that the lodging facility is clean and in good condition for the comfort and safety of guests. *Maids and housekeepers* clean lobbies, halls, guestrooms, and bathrooms. They make sure that guests not only have clean rooms, but have all the necessary furnishings and supplies. They change sheets and towels, vacuum carpets, dust furniture, empty wastebaskets, and mop bathroom floors. In larger hotels, the housekeeping staff may include assistant housekeepers, floor supervisors, housekeepers, and executive housekeepers. *Janitors* help with the cleaning of the public areas of the facility, empty trash, and perform minor maintenance work.

Table: Employment of wage and salary workers in hotels and other accommodations by occupation, 2004 and projected change, 2004-14. (Employment in thousands)

Occupation	Employment, change, 2004-14 Number Percent	Percent	2004
Total, all occupations	1,796	100.0	16.9
Management, business, and financial occupations	99	5.5	26.6

Table: Employment of wage and salary workers in hotels and other accommodations by occupation, 2004 and projected change, 2004-14. (Employment in thousands)

Occupation	Employment	Percent	Change
Top executives	16	0.9	25.8
Food service managers	10	0.6	16.2
Lodging managers	28	1.6	27.4
Meeting and convention planners	7	0.4	27.3
Service occupations	1,169	65.1	16.0

Security guards and gaming surveillance officers	34	1.9	-2.3
Chefs and head cooks	13	0.7	16.9
First-line supervisors/managers of food preparation and serving workers	22	1.2	16.5
Cooks, restaurant	56	3.1	16.7
Food preparation workers	23	1.3	27.1
Bartenders	39	2.2	13.1
Fast food and counter workers	27	1.5	25.2
Waiters and waitresses	133	7.4	9.5
Food servers, nonrestaurant	39	2.2	11.9
Dining room and cafeteria attendants and bartender helpers	43	2.4	9.1
Dishwashers	38	2.1	8.3
Hosts and hostesses, restaurant, lounge, and coffee shop	21	1.2	9.1
Supervisors, building and grounds cleaning and maintenance workers	37	2.0	26.6
Janitors and cleaners, except maids and housekeeping cleaners	49	2.7	20.2
Maids and housekeeping cleaners	405	22.5	17.0
Landscaping and groundskeeping workers	23	1.3	20.3
Gaming supervisors	11	0.6	10.3
Gaming dealers	35	2.0	25.0
Baggage porters and bellhops	25	1.4	21.5
Concierges	7	0.4	17.0
Recreation and fitness workers	13	0.7	22.1
Sales and related occupations	54	3.0	18.3
Cashiers, except gaming	16	0.9	14.3
Gaming change persons and booth cashiers	10	0.6	7.6
Office and administrative support occupations	320	17.8	15.0
Supervisors, office and administrative	22	1.2	7.7

support workers			
Bookkeeping, accounting, and auditing clerks	24	1.4	14.6

Table: Employment of wage and salary workers in hotels and other accommodations by occupation, 2004 and projected change, 2004-14. (Employment in thousands)

Gaming cage workers	5	0.3	5.7
Hotel, motel, and resort desk clerks	183	10.2	17.4
Reservation and transportation ticket agents and travel clerks	13	0.7	15.7
Installation, maintenance, and repair occupations	75	4.2	26.8
Maintenance and repair workers, general	64	3.6	27.2
Production occupations	39	2.2	19.0
Laundry and dry-cleanin g workers	32	1.8	18.0
Transportation and material moving occupations	24	1.3	7.0

Note: May not add to totals due to omission of occupations with small employment

Workers in the various food service occupations deal with customers in the dining room or at a service counter. Waiters and waitresses take customers' orders, serve meals, and prepare checks. In restaurants, they may describe chef's specials and suggest appropriate wines. In smaller establishments, they often set tables, escort guests to their seats, accept payment, and clear tables. They also may deliver room service orders to guests. In larger restaurants, some of these tasks are assigned to other workers.

Hosts and hostesses welcome guests, show them to their tables, and give them menus. Bartenders fill beverage orders for customers seated at the bar or from waiters and waitresses who serve patrons at tables. Dining room and cafeteria attendants and bartender helpers assist waiters, waitresses, and bartenders by clearing, cleaning, and setting up tables, replenishing supplies at the bar, and keeping the serving areas stocked with linens, tableware, and other supplies. Counter attendants take orders and serve food at fast-food counters and in coffee shops; they also may operate the cash register.

Cooks and food preparation occupations prepare food in the kitchen. Beginners may advance to more skilled food preparation jobs with experience or specialized culinary training. Chefs and cooks generally prepare a wide selection of dishes, often cooking individual servings to order. Larger hotels employ cooks who specialize in the preparation of many different kinds of food. They may have titles such as salad chef, grill chef, or pastry chef.

Training and Advancement

Although the skills and experience needed by workers in this industry depend on the specific occupation, most entry-level jobs require little or no previous training. Basic tasks usually can be learned in a short time. Almost all workers in the hotel and other accommodations industry undergo on-the-job training, which usually is provided under the supervision of an experienced employee or manager. Some large chain operations have formal training sessions for new employees; many also provide video or on-line training.

Hotel operations are becoming increasingly diverse and complex, but all positions require employees to maintain a customer-service orientation. Hoteliers recognize the importance of personal service and attention to guests; so they look for persons with positive personality traits and good communication skills when filling many guest services positions, such as desk clerk and host and hostess positions. Many hotel managers place a greater emphasis on customer service skills while providing specialized training in important skill areas, such as computer technology and software. Vocational courses and apprenticeship programmes in food preparation, catering, and hotel and restaurant management, offered through restaurant associations and trade unions, provide training opportunities. Programmes range in length from a few months to several years. About 800 community and junior colleges offer 2-year degree programmes in hotel and restaurant management. The U.S. Armed Forces also offer experience and training in food service.

Nature of the Work

A comfortable room, good food, and a helpful staff can make being away from home an enjoyable experience for both vacationing families and business travellers. While most lodging managers work in traditional hotels and motels, some work in other lodging establishments, such as camps, inns, boardinghouses, dude ranches, and recreational resorts. In full-service hotels, lodging managers help their guests have a pleasant stay by providing many of the comforts of home, including cable television, fitness equipment, and voice mail, as well as specialized services such as health spas. For business travellers, lodging managers often schedule available meeting rooms and electronic equipment, including slide projectors and fax machines.

Lodging managers are responsible for keeping their establishments efficient and profitable. In a small establishment with a limited staff, the manager may oversee all aspects of operations. However, large hotels may employ hundreds of workers, and the general manager usually is aided by a number of assistant managers assigned to the various departments of the operation. In hotels of every size, managerial duties vary significantly by job title.

Lodging managers experience the pressures of coordinating a wide range of activities. At larger hotels, they also carry the burden of managing a large staff and finding a way to satisfy guest needs while maintaining positive attitudes and employee morale. Conventions and large groups of tourists may present unusual problems or require extended work hours. Moreover, dealing with irate guests can be stressful. The job can be particularly hectic for front office managers during check-in and check-out times. Computer failures can further complicate processing and add to frustration levels.

Hotels increasingly emphasize specialized training. Postsecondary training in hotel, restaurant, or hospitality management is preferred for most hotel management positions; however, a college liberal arts degree may be sufficient when coupled with related hotel experience or business education. Internships or part-time or summer work experience in a hotel are an asset to students seeking a career in hotel management. The experience gained and the contacts made with employers can greatly benefit students after graduation. Most degree programmes include work-study opportunities.

HOTEL, MOTEL, AND RESORT DESK CLERKS

Hotel, motel, and resort desk clerks perform a variety of services for guests of hotels, motels, and other lodging establishments. Regardless of the type of accommodation, most desk clerks have similar responsibilities. They register arriving guests, assign rooms, and check out guests at the end of their stay. They also keep records of room assignments and other registration-related information on computers. When guests check out, desk clerks prepare and explain the charges, as well as process payments.

Front-desk clerks always are in the public eye and typically are the first line of customer service for a lodging property. Their attitude and behaviour greatly influence the public's impressions of the establishment. And as such, they always must be courteous and helpful. Desk clerks answer questions about services, checkout times, the local community, or other matters of public interest. Clerks also report problems with guest rooms or public facilities to members of the housekeeping or maintenance staff for them to correct the problems. In larger hotels or in larger cities, desk clerks may refer queries about area attractions to a concierge and may direct more complicated questions to the appropriate manager.

In some smaller hotels and motels, where smaller staffs are employed, clerks may take on a variety of additional responsibilities, such as bringing fresh linens to rooms, which usually are performed by employees in other departments of larger lodging establishments. In the smaller places, desk clerks often are responsible for all front-office operations, information, and services. For example, they may perform the work of a bookkeeper, advance reservation agent, cashier, laundry attendant, and telephone switchboard operator.

Hotels are open around the clock creating the need for night and weekend work. Extended hours of operation also afford the many part-time job seekers an opportunity to find work in these establishments, especially on evenings and late-night shifts or on weekends and holidays. About half of all desk clerks work a 35 to 40 hour week—most of the rest work fewer hours—so the jobs are attractive to persons seeking part-time work or jobs with flexible schedules. Most clerks work in areas that are clean, well lit, and relatively quiet, although lobbies can become crowded and noisy when busy. Many hotels have stringent dress guidelines for desk clerks.

Desk clerks may experience particularly hectic times during check-in and check-out times or incur the pressures encountered when dealing with convention guests or large groups of tourists at one time. Moreover, dealing with irate guests can be stressful. Computer failures can further complicate an already busy time and add to stress levels. Hotel desk clerks may be on their feet most of the time and may occasionally be asked to lift heavy guest luggage.

Hotel, motel, and resort desk clerks deal directly with the public, so a professional appearance and a pleasant personality are important. A clear speaking voice and fluency in English also are essential, because these employees talk directly with hotel guests and the public and frequently use the telephone or public-address systems. Good spelling and computer literacy are needed, because most of the work involves use of a computer. In addition, speaking a foreign language fluently is increasingly helpful, because of the growing international clientele of many properties.

Most hotel, motel, and resort desk clerks receive orientation and training on the job. Orientation may include an explanation of the job duties and information about the establishment, such as the arrangement of sleeping rooms, availability of additional services, such as a business or fitness centre, and location of guest facilities, such as ice and vending machines, restaurants and other nearby retail stores. New employees learn job tasks through on-the-job training under the guidance of a supervisor or an experienced desk clerk.

They often receive additional training on interpersonal or customer service skills and on how to use the computerized reservation, room assignment, and billing systems and equipment. Desk clerks typically continue to receive instruction on new procedures and on company policies after their initial training ends.

An Employee

A worker is a common law employee when the employer has the right to direct and control the manner and means of accomplishing the work. Types of employees that are typical in the restaurant and hotel industries are:

- Chefs
- Cooks
- Dishwashers
- Kitchen Helpers
- Bus Persons
- Waiters and Waitresses
- Maitre d's
- Hosts and Hostesses
- Cashiers
- Managers
- Delivery Persons
- Bartenders
- Valets
- Clerical and Office Staff
- Maids
- Switchboard Operators
- Laundry Persons
- Repair and Maintenance Persons
- Desk Clerks
- Bellhops

Other services that may be performed by an employee under common law rules include, but are not limited to, those of bookkeepers, janitors, and entertainers.

Wages

Wages are payments made to an employee for services performed during employment. The payment may be made in cash or some medium other than cash. Types of payments typically considered to be wages are:

- Cash
- Lodging
- Meals and Beverages
- Tips

Employer-provided meals and lodging are subject to Unemployment Insurance (UI), State Disability Insurance (SDI), and Employment Training Tax (ETT). Meals are subject to personal income tax (PIT) withholding and reportable as PIT wages unless furnished for the employer's convenience and on the employer's premises.

The Values of Meals and Lodging

The taxable values of meals and lodging should not be less than the reasonable estimated values stipulated by the contract of employment or in a union agreement. If the cash values are not stipulated in the hiring or union agreement, the taxable values are established by regulation. The taxable value of lodging is 66 2/3 percent of the ordinary rental value to the public up to a maximum per month and not less than a minimum value per week.

The taxable values of meals and lodging are listed below:

The cash values of meals and lodging are subject to change each calendar year. This information is published in the Employment Development Department's (EDD) quarterly newsletter.

Employees who receive more than $20 in tips in a calendar month must report all tips in one or more written statements to the employer on or before the tenth day of the month following the month in which they are received from the customers. Tips are taxable when the employee's statement is furnished to the employer.

A Survey Report

Using specially developed models of service management, the researchers looked at five key service sectors: retail, hotels and catering, health care, utilities, and professional and financial services. "We identified the top 10 companies that have set the standard for service quality in America over the past decade and uncovered the secrets of the global leaders,". "Each excelled by systematically linking the drivers of service excellence: leadership, people, processes and performance management. We discovered that delivering service quality goes beyond simplistic prescriptions about people issues, and instead extends to strategic factors, such as organizational design, leadership and market acuity, to orchestrate the entire service encounter."

The researchers found vast differences among the service sectors. The retail and hotel industries were the two highest performing sectors in the survey; the researchers found they follow best practices, achieving good results.

The hotel industry also paid more attention to customer service than any other sector, which paid off in hefty returns. Not all hotels are wonderful, but those that succeed manage the "evidence" of quality, such as how the hotel looks and how employees dress.

These hotels also manage customer interactions and continuously communicate their high standards to employees, according to the study.

Other pacesetter sectors in the study are industrial service and telecommunications companies.

The researchers found that financial-services companies satisfy customers, but they concluded that the institutions may be yielding good performance without being brilliant strategists.

Many are riding a wave of low interest rates and a favourable economy.

For example, some financial institutions seemed complacent about managing customer interactions, compared to their counterparts in other service sectors.

By stressing re-structuring and reducing their staffs at the expense of customer service, businesses like banks and insurance companies may be vulnerable to future market changes.

Professional services such as legal and architectural firms were found to be "surprisingly weak" in both practice and performance.

Of the top 10 service practices emphasized by senior executives, half are customer-focused: accessibility, listening to customers, competitive positioning, consistently meeting customers' needs and customer orientation.

Accessibility is the new "location, location, location" of service. It refers to a customer's ability to contact someone in a company easily, and at many companies, 24 hours a day.

The top 10 companies were described as having "global-service leadership," demonstrating world-class capabilities, regardless of the geographic market of a company's location.

Nordstrom, the retail chain, was cited as a classic example of a company that maintained world-class standards in both practice (such as how they control quality and handle complaints) and service performance (such as value, quality, satisfaction, business performance and customer retention).

Chapter 2

Globalization in the Hotel and Catering Sector

GLOBALIZATION AND CATERING

The issues of globalization, employment and human resources development in the hotel, catering and tourism sector are linked to the strategic objectives of the ILO that were decided at the International Labour Conference in June 1999: to promote and realize fundamental principles and rights at work; to create greater opportunities for women and men to secure decent employment and income; to enhance the coverage and effectiveness of social protection for all; and to strengthen tripartism and social dialogue. The report points to recent developments in the hotel, catering and tourism sector and highlights factors driving the internationalization of tourists' travel and of tourism services, including information technologies, as welt as the internationalization or hotel and tourism enterprises.

Without neglecting the huge subsector of small and medium-sized enterprises, it describes typical features related to the composition of the labour force and to working conditions. It raises questions concerning the difficulties faced by the sector in attracting and retaining skilled workers and in enhancing the skills of newcomers to the labour market in order to stabilize the sector's labour force, while increasing the productivity of enterprises and the quality of services. Particular emphasis is put on new forms of management entailing new skills requirements, with a general tendency towards increased worker responsibility in an environment of flat hierarchies, multi-skilling and teamwork.

As to social dialogue in this sector, a description is provided of certain institutions, achievements and shortcomings in this respect, but in a way that also points to opportunities for increasing its scope and effectiveness. The causal relationships between globalization, employment and human resources development are examined on the basis of the information available, and other factors such as advances in technology and training, and changes in tourism demand are also highlighted.

SOCIAL RESOURCES

Small-business ownership among persons of Asian ancestry grew quite rapidly in the U.S. during the 1980s. Gross revenues of Asian-owned small businesses, according to the Census Bureau, nearly tripled from 1982 to 1987, and the number of active firms grew from 187,691 to 355,331 – an 89.3% increase. Rapid Asian business growth has been immigrant driven: of the Asian small businesses operating nationwide in 1987 that were started since 1979, nearly 80% of them were immigrant owned.

This study examines the performance of recently formed Asian immigrant-owned small businesses, focusing upon owner characteristics as well as firm traits; survival of firms operating in 1987 is traced through 1991. Recent studies suggest that Asian immigrant entrepreneurs have achieved success operating in low-growth or declining industry sectors; inner city areas have been the site of considerable business activity and minority clienteles have often been the targeted customer base. Waldinger found extensive firm development and growth among Chinese immigrants in a declining industry segment -garment manufacturing in New York City. Bonacich and Light report that Korean-owned businesses in Los Angeles have established a major presence in low-income Latino and African American communities, particularly in smallscale retailing.

Stressing the relevance of cultural factors, Waldinger, Light, Bonacich, and others have treated immigrant firm ownership and operation as a group phenomenon, heavily dependent upon social resources available from group support networks. This view is contrasted to the perspective that owner "class" resources – human capital and financial capital investments – explain smallbusiness behaviour.

Recent studies of minority entrepreneurship have often focused upon immigrants operating businesses in one specific location – Koreans in Los Angeles or Chinese in New York. Among recent Korean immigrants, Bonacich and Light note the effective use of family resources such as unpaid labour to develop successful small businesses (1988). These immigrant entrepreneurs, however, also tend to be highly educated persons with white-collar work experience, and many of them possess substantial personal wealth.

Qualitative studies of immigrant entrepreneurs operating at one geographic location are often provocative and interesting, yet generalization of the resultant findings is difficult because these studies rarely use sophisticated statistical methodology to sort out and establish cause-and-effect relationships between individual or group traits and business performance. Data sources such as the Census Bureau's Characteristics of Business Owners (CBO) data base – examined in this study -provide evidence that is not consistent with specific social resources explanations of minority business behaviour.

Self-Employment Patterns

The focus of this study is upon a nationwide sample of firms formed by Asian immigrants over the 1979-87 period. Firms operating nationwide are owned by Asian immigrants; this sample is representative of the relevant universe of firms entered since 1979 that filed small-business income tax returns in 1987. Firms owned by nonminorities constitute the small-business norm in this country, in the sense that such firms account for over 90% of the small-firm universe by number and 95% by total sales. A representative sample of nonminority-owned firms is presented as a comparison group. Businesses formed between 1979 and 1987 by Asian immigrants and nonminorities and highlights underlying hypothesized causes of Asian business success. First, we see that 57.8% of the Asian entrepreneurs of Asian business success. First, we see that 57.8% of the Asian entrepreneurs were college graduates (bachelor's degree holders), versus 37.5% of the nonminority business owners. Professional services – the field in which both owner educational attainment and average self-employment remuneration are highest – accounted for 11.5% of the Asian business start-ups, versus 8.7% of the nonminority firm formations.

Second, the average financial capital investment at the point of business start-up was $53,562 among the Asian immigrants, versus $31,678 for nonminority firms. Owner equity investment – derived almost entirely from household wealth holdings – averaged $26,345 among the Asian immigrant business entrants, 88.0% higher than the corresponding nonminority figure of $14,014. Bates and Dunham report that self-employment entry is very strongly and positively associated with possession of household net worth exceeding $100,000. Further, a higher proportion of Asian households nationwide were in the $100,000 plus household net worth category than nonminorities.

Theories of entrepreneurship developed by sociologists have been rooted in their efforts to explain the success of Asian immigrants who pursue self-employment. The entrepreneur is seen as a member of supportive kinship, peer, and community subgroups. These networks, in turn, assist in the creation and successful operation of firms by providing such social capital as sources of customers, loyal employees, and financing. What precise forms do these social resources take and how do they assist business operation? Social capital in the form of a captive market, according to Light (1972), derives from the culturally based tastes of ethnic minorities that can only be served by co-ethnic businesses. Ethnic businesses offer co-ethnics the comfort and security of conducting transactions in their own language. Also, the information costs in ascertaining consumer preferences among co-ethnics are lower for ethnic entrepreneurs than they are for potential competitors from the "outside".

Of the various forms of social capital associated with immigrant entrepreneurs, the protected market concept has been the most controversial. The very low incomes of most recent immigrants constrain the attractiveness of this protected market. The immigrant business that limits itself to the ethnic market sharply reduces its growth potential. Fratoe reports, for example, that Asians are much less likely to sell to a minority clientele than black- or Latino-owned firms (1988).

Yet reliance upon co-ethnic markets may nonetheless be pragmatic during early stages of firm development, providing an operational base from which later expansion can begin. The co-ethnic market may support immigrant entrepreneurs "in assembling a skilled labour force and gaining efficiency and expertise, qualities that are gradually allowing them to edge out into the broader market".

The Asian immigrant entrepreneurs differ systematically regarding sales, profitability, owner financial investment, and discontinuance rates when they are divided into two groups: those serving a clientele that is 50% or more minority, versus those whose clientele is either racially diverse or largely nonminority. It is the very youngest among immigrantowned businesses that appear to benefit most from serving clients in the broader, largely nonminority marketplace.

Small-Business Longevity

Over the period from 1987 to 1991, 18.5% of the Asian immigrant firms described discontinued operations. Firms sold to a new owner, merged, or otherwise altered are not counted as discontinued if they continued to operate. Logistic regression equations are estimated in this section to explain small-business longevity. Independent variables used to explain longevity among Asian immigrant firms include measures of owner characteristics, firm traits, and social capital proxies. While longevity is the primary business viability measure under consideration, profitability is analyzed later in this study to test for the consistency (robustness) of the observed relationships between the explanatory variables and firm viability. Binary variables identifying major Asian ethnic groups are introduced into the log it analysis of firm longevity as control variables. An owner ethnicity frequency distribution reveals that three groups – Chinese, Korean, and Asian Indian – dominate the Asian immigrant entrepreneur sample described previously:

Ethnicity	*Per cent*
Chinese	26.7
Korean	22.6
Indian	20.5
Vietnamese	9.8
Filipino	8.5
All other	11.9

Finally, an agglomeration variable is introduced to test for possible impacts on firm longevity of the intense clustering of Asian immigrant businesses in several large metropolitan areas. Nearly 43% of the Asian immigrant firms analyzed in this study operate in either (1) the Los Angeles county, Orange country megalopolis, (2) the New York City metropolitan area, or (3) the San Francisco Bay region (including Oakland, San Jose, San Francisco, and surrounding suburbs).

The fact that human capital measures such as owner education and managerial experience are more consistent determinants of firm profitability and more erratic determinants of longevity may be noteworthy. High rates of Asian immigrant business ownership coexist with a narrow industry base as well as annual sales and profits that are low, on average, relative to those reported by the dominant nonminority small-business sector.

Asian immigrants are very heavily crowded into several industry groups -particularly retailing – and within industries, they are often overrepresented heavily in several of the smaller-scale lines of business. Manufacturing, for example, is one of the larger scale industries where small business is active. Yet Asian manufacturers are concentrated in several of the small-scale lines of nondurable goods manufacturing: garments, food processing, and printing. In retailing, Asian immigrants are overrepresented in restaurants and food stores but they are underrepresented (relative to nonminorities) in larger scale retailing fields such as building materials, new car dealerships, and appliance stores.

If applicable barriers to upward mobility can be overcome, many of these self-employed persons could achieve a fuller use of their human capital either by (1) moving into managerial or professional salaried employment or (2) shifting into more skill-intensive, larger scale lines of small business.

The social capital explanations put forth by Light, Bonacich and Light, Waldinger, Aldrich, Waldinger, and Ward (1990), and others to explain the success of the Asian immigrant-owned small-business community rest, in fact, on an uncertain empirical foundation. The term success may be inappropriate given that Asian immigrants generate substantially lower sales and profits than cohort nonminority-owned small businesses, in spite of their much larger investments of human and financial capital into their firms.

Success may indeed typify the firms owned by immigrant Asian Indians; Fratoe and Meeks (1988) in their analysis of self-employment among individuals associated with the fifty largest ancestry groups in the U.S., found that Asian Indians ranked highest, overall, in mean self-employment income. Asian Indian small business owners, however, are the Asian immigrant subgroup that is least oriented to serving a minority clientele and least likely to employ a predominantly minority labour force. That is, they are least likely to use the forms of social capital discussed above.

Vietnamese firms, in contrast, are the group that most heavily serves a minority clientele and relies most upon minority workers. Relative to their Asian cohorts, Vietnamese run the smallest firms and suffer the higher firm discontinuance rates. Among Asian Indian and Vietnamese firms active in 1987, 14.9% of the former and 22.1% of the latter had shut down their businesses by 1991.

Chapter 3

Role of Advertisement in Hotel Industry

A hotel is an establishment that provides paid lodging, usually on a short-term basis. Hotels often provide a number of additional guest services such as a restaurant, a swimming pool or childcare. Some hotels have conference services and meeting rooms and encourage groups to hold conventions and meetings at their location. Hotels differ from motels in that most motels have drive-up, exterior entrances to the rooms, while hotels tend to have interior entrances to the rooms, which may increase guests' safety and present a more upmarket image.

In India, the word may also refer to a restaurant since the best restaurants were always situated next to a good hotel. The word hotel derives from the French hotel, which referred to a French version of a townhouse, not a place offering accommodation (in contemporary usage, hotel has the meaning of "hotel", and hotel particular is used for the old meaning). The French spelling (with the circumflex) was once also used in English, but is now rare. The circumflex replaces the 's' once preceding the 't' in the earlier hostel spelling, which over time received a new, but closely related meaning.

Services and Facilities

Basic accommodation of a room with only a bed, a cupboard, a small table and a washstand has largely been replaced by rooms with en-suite bathrooms and climate control. Other features found may be a telephone, an alarm clock, a TV, and broadband Internet connectivity. Food and drink may be supplied by a mini-bar (which often includes a small refrigerator) containing snacks and drinks (to be paid for on departure), and tea and coffee making facilities (cups, spoons, an electric kettle and sachets containing instant coffee, tea bags, sugar, and creamer or milk).

In the United Kingdom a hotel is required by law to serve food and drinks to all comers within certain stated hours; to avoid this requirement it is not uncommon to come across "private hotels" which are not subject to this requirement. However, in Japan the capsule hotel supplies minimal facilities and room space.

The cost and quality of hotels are usually indicative of the range and type of services available. Due to the enormous increase in tourism worldwide during the last decades of the 20th century, standards, especially those of smaller establishments, have improved considerably. For the sake of greater comparability, rating systems have been introduced, with the one to five stars classification being most common.

Boutique Hotels

Boutique hotel is a term originating in North America to describe intimate, usually luxurious or quirky hotel environments. Boutique hotels differentiate themselves from larger chain/branded hotels and motels by providing personalized level accommodation and services / facilities. Sometimes known as "design hotels" or "lifestyle hotels," boutique hotels began in the 1980s in major cities like New York, London, and San Francisco.

Very often it is the Morgans Hotel in Murray Hill of New York, that is awarded with the title of first boutique hotel in the world. It was opened by Ian Schrager in 1984 according to a design by Andree Putman.

Typically boutique hotels are furnished in a themed, stylish and/or aspirational manner. Although usually considerably smaller than a mainstream hotel (often ranging from 3 to 100 guest rooms), boutique hotels can often have hundreds of rooms in major cities. Guest rooms and suites are fitted with telephony and Wi-Fi Internet, air-conditioning, honesty bars and often cable/pay TV. Guest services are attended to by 24 hour hotel staff. Many boutique hotels have on-site dining facilities, and the majority offer bars and lounges which may also be open to the general public.

Despite this definition, the popularity of the boutique term and concept has lead to some confusion about the term. Boutique hotels have typically been unique properties operated by individials or companies with a small collection. However, their successes have prompted established multi-national hotel companies to establish their own brands. The most notable is Starwood Hotels and Resorts' W Hotels.

Currently, there is one publication dedicated to the boutique hotel, boutique DESIGN magazine, which is published quarterly. Boutique hotel resources are more commonly available online. One such site dedicated to boutique hotels is Tablet Hotels. There are also a number of sytlized design and coffee table books highlighting various properties throughout the world.

Apartment Hotel

An Apartment Hotel is a type of accommodation, described as "a serviced apartment complex that uses a hotel style booking system". It is similar to renting an apartment, but with no fixed contracts and occupants can 'check-out' whenever they wish.

Apartment hotels are flexible types of accommodation; instead of the rigid format of a hotel room an apartment hotel complex usually offers a complete fully fitted apartment. These complexes are usually custom built, and similar to a hotel complex contain a varied amount of apartments. The length of stay in these apartment hotels are very varied with anywhere from a few days to months or even years. Prices tend to be cheaper than hotels. The people that stay in apartment hotels use them as a home from home therefore they are usually fitted with everything the average home would require.

Bed and Breakfast

A Bed and Breakfast often referred to as a B&B is a type of boarding house typically operating out of a large single family residence. Guests are accommodated at night in private bedrooms and breakfast is served in the morning - either in the bedroom or, more commonly, in a dining room or the host's kitchen. Bathrooms can be private or shared (with other guests or with the family in smaller establishments) or en-suite (where the ablutions are directly accessed from the guest's bedroom).

B&Bs may be operated either as a primary occupation or as a secondary source of income. Staff often consists of the house's owners and members of their family who live there. Guests are usually expected to pay for their stay upon arrival and leave before noon (or earlier) on the day of departure. A big advantage of this type of hosted accommodation is the local knowledge of the host.

Capsule Hotel

A capsule hotel, is a hotel system of extremely dense occupancy. Guest space is reduced in size to a modular plastic or fibreglass block roughly 2 m by 1 m by 1.25 m, providing room to sleep and little more, although facilities usually include a television and other electronic entertainment.

The first capsule hotel was the Capsule Inn Osaka, designed by Kisho Kurokawa and located in the Umeda district of Osaka. It opened on February 1, 1979 and the initial room rate was ¥1,600. These rooms can be seen in the movie The Fast and the Furious: Tokyo Drift. They were also used as a basis for sets in the film The Fifth Element.

Casa Particular

Casa particular is a phrase meaning private accommodation or private homestays in Cuba, very similar to bed and breakfast although it can also take the form of vacation rental. When the meaning is clear the term is often shortened to simply casa. A casa particular is basically a private family establishment that provides paid lodging, usually on a short-term basis. In general under this term you can find full apartment and houses, rooms inside people homes, mini-apartments or rooms with separate entrance (studio or efficiency type rooms). It is also considered a type of boarding house typically operated out of a single family residence where guests can be accommodated at night in private bedrooms (which may or may not be equipped with private baths) and where breakfast, sometimes continental and sometimes the full English variety, is served in the morning. The business may be operated either as a primary occupation or as a secondary source of income, and the staff often consists of the house's owner(s) and members of their family who live there.

Because they are usually small, rarely with room for more than about 5-6 guests, it is advisable for anyone wanting to stay at a particular casa particular during high season to make advance reservations. However, outside the season there is no need because there are often many such casas, causing competition and opening opportunities to strike a deal. Prices can then drop to 15 euro or even less for longer stays. During high season they can rise to over 30 euro. Many belong to associations, have a web presence, and are described in various books and travel guides. Casas particulares can be recognised by a small sign on the door, with two blue triangles ('roofs') against a white background, which the owners obtain after paying a fixed per-room annual tax.

Services and Facilities

All rooms are clean, safe and upgraded to tourist standards. It ranges from basic accommodation of a room with a bed, a closet, a small table to full furnished independent apartments upgraded to western standards. Other features found may be a telephone, an alarm clock, and a TV. Food and drink may be supplied by a mini-bar (which often includes a small refrigerator) containing snacks and drinks (to be paid for on departure). It is possible to have breakfast/dinner in the casa for price. Often breakfasts/dinners sold will decide if case owner will break even or not. So if it becomes clear that one plans to generally eat out, the price may go up because this is an important source of income. The cost and quality of casas particulars are usually indicative of the accommodation type and type of services available. Most of the casas particulars are rented for short term to travellers. Long term accommodation is also provided by some casas, especially for foreign students. In Havana, the casas particulares are usually family apartments and a smaller number of them are houses. In other cities, private accommodation is provided mainly in family houses.

Types of Casas Particulares rentals:

- Private Room: a room is rented out most of the times with private bathroom and a key to the apartment/ house is usually given to the guest.
- Private Room with independent entrance. Sometimes the house/apartment is split in order to allow this.
- Apartment: the guest can enjoy the privacy and independency of a full furnished apartment for his/ her vacations. Sometimes this apartment is part of house being split by a wall usually with a connecting door.
- Studio-type or mini-apartment: it is not an apartment with several rooms but just the bedroom, a kitchen-living-dining room and a bathroom.

Condo-hotel

A condo-hotel or a hotel-condo is a building used as both a condominium and a hotel. This type of residential building meets several needs that make it attractive. As development costs increase, the cost of hotel development can make developing new hotels difficult, especially in major cities. By selling the units as condos, the developer moves much of the development cost to the condo owners. By owning units that can be rented as hotel rooms, the owners are able to get a return on their investment allowing them the ability to own a residence in a resort or major city.

Destination Hotel

A destination hotel is a place of lodging whose inherent location and amenities attract visitors regardless of the route needed to arrive or the areawide features of interest. The destination hotel concept has existed at least since the 19th century and occupies a significant market share of all lodging in the world as of 2006. From the late 1980s to the present the extent of amenities and conference facilities has greatly expanded for many destination hotels. Destination hotels are also called destination lodgings and destination resorts. Considerable academic and business analysis has been conducted in the field of destination hotels. In the Arnold Encyclopedia of Real Estate a destination hotel is characterized as a place of lodging not chosen for convenience and not chosen for people in transit to other areas.

The following typically are characteristics of a destination hotel:

- Amenities which are quite complete and self-contained
- Upscale nature of the lodging operation
- Distinctive characteristics of the building, gardens or adjacent natural feature
- Activity set which makes leaving the property unnecessary

Since the 1800s, the traditional concept of a destination hotel has been based upon a venue which is typically remote and has a natural feature as its attraction. For example, the Kviknes Hotel in Norway is a difficult to reach remote location which provides visitors access to the scenic fjord at Balestrand. Historically there were certain built-in amenities such as gourmet cuisine, music recitals and shoreline trails; however, the amenities of modern destination hotels dwarf the scale of these earlier models. Many of the Las Vegas and Carribbean resort hotels have complete shopping malls, conference centers and large entertainment halls on site; thus, the contemporary version of a destination often features large on-site capital investment in activities, although the access to a local natural feature is still retained by many newer destination hotels.

Luxury Resorts

A luxury resort, sometimes referred to as an exclusive resort, is a very expensive vacation facility which is fully staffed and has been rated with five stars. Luxury resorts often boast many visitor activities and attractions such as golf, watersports, spa and beauty facilities, skiing, natural ecology and tranquility. Because of the extent of amenities offered, a luxury resort is also considered a destination resort. A luxury resort is an elite luxury property which exhibits an exceptionally high degree of customer service and hospitality. A flawless execution of guest services will be the resort staff's and managements main concern. A luxury resort will commonly also feature a superb architectural interior and exterior design as well as an interesting physical location.

The interior design will normally be elegant with stylish bedroom decor, exceptional dining facilities, and manicured landscaping and meticulous grounds. Luxury resorts will often also be in based in exceptionally desirable and strategic worldwide locations, from beautiful tropical islands, to snow caked mountains, to scenic lakes and rivers, to exhilarating cities. The locations wili often be famous for featured activities from skiing to golf, water spots, diving, fishing, sailing and nature walks to glamorous shopping and nightlife entertainment.

Extended Stay Hotel

Extended stay hotels are a type of lodging with features unavailable at standard hotels. These features are intended to provide more home-like amenities. There are currently 27 extended stay chains in North America with at least 7 hotels, representing over 2,000 properties. There is substantial variation among extended stay hotels with respect to quality and the amenities that are available. Some of the economy chains attract clientele who use the hotels as semi-permanent lodging. Occasionally, these budget establishments can be the scene of criminal activity.

Extended-stay hotels typically have self-serve laundry facilities and offer discounts for extended stays, beginning at 5 or 7 days. They also have guestrooms (or "suites") with kitchens. The kitchens include at a minimum usually: a sink, a refrigerator (usually full size), a microwave oven, and a stovetop. Some kitchens also have dishwashers and conventional ovens.

Extended stay hotels are popular with business travelers on extended assignments, families in the midst of a relocation, and anyone else in need of temporary housing. Extended stay hotels are also used by travelers who appreciate the larger space a typical suite provides. Residence Inn is credited with popularizing the "extended stay" concept. The chain was launched in 1975 in Wichita, Kansas by Jack DeBoer, and acquired by Marriott Corporation in 1987. As of April 2005, there were over 450 Residence Inn hotels in the United States, Canada and Mexico. Some extended stay hotels are coming up in United Kingdom and Ireland as well.

Flophouse

A flophouse or dosshouse is a place that offers very cheap lodging, generally by providing only minimal services. Occupants of flophouses generally share bathroom facilities and reside in very cramped quarters. The people who make use of these places are often transients, although some people will stay in flophouses for long periods of time—years or decades. Some people who live in flophouses may be just a step above homelessness. In the late 20th century, typical cost might be about US$6 per night. A typical flophouse might advertise its services with a sign such as "Hotel for Men; Transients Welcome".

Quarters in flophouses are very small, and may resemble office cubicles more than a regular room in a hotel or apartment building. A cubicle might only have wire mesh for a ceiling. In the past, flophouses were sometimes called "workingmen's hotels" and catered to hobos and transient workers such as seasonal railroad and agriculture workers, or migrant lumberjacks who would travel west during the summer to work and then return to an eastern or midwestern city such as Chicago to stay in a flophouse during the winter. This is described in the 1930 novel The Rambling Kid by Charles Ashleigh and the 1976 book The Human Cougar by Lloyd Morain. Another theme in Morain's book is the gentrification which was then beginning and which has led cities to pressure flophouses to close.

George Orwell also discussed flophouses in the UK in his book Down and Out in Paris and London. He described them as having rather poor cleanliness standards, often issuing unwashed and badly stained blankets, and sometimes renting beds in a large common room resembling barracks more than private rooms. He noted that at the time he wrote the book (1933) the term "dosshouse" was already falling out of use.

ORGANIZATION WITHIN HOTELS

Hotel Manager

The Hotel manager oversees all of a hotel's daily operations, from staffing to coordinating fresh-cut flowers for the lobby. Many, over time, are given long-term responsibility for negotiating contracts with vendors (such as maintenance supplies), negotiating leases with on-site shops, and physically upgrading the hotel. Hotel managers usually relish "the ability to put your own distinctive style on the [hotel] experience." While managing a hotel and giving it your unique flair are wonderful, they come with full responsibility for failure. "The better you are at what you do, the more responsibilities you are given, the more chances you have to fail," mentioned one hotel manager. When things fall apart, "no one is a hotel manager's friend."

Hotel managers can feel great about their positions, create strong relationships with regular customers, and maintain an amicable working environment. But should the bottom line waver and financial woes occur, the first neck on the chopping block is the hotel manager's. Those in the hotel management industry say that sometimes it seems that you need "to be born on the planet Krypton" to be a good hotel manager because only Superman could juggle the administrative, aesthetic, and financial decisions which constitute daily life on the job. Over 70 percent of the respondents said that tired was an understatement about how they felt at the end of the day or night.

Financial management - preparing budgets and marketing strategies and achieving targets for the business - plays a major role. The manager must strike a balance between customer satisfaction and effective business management, ensuring financial viability, and facilitate a smooth-running customer service, whilst ensuring staff work together as a team.

Typical Work Activities

Typical work activities vary depending on the size and type of hotel, but may include:

- Planning and organising accommodation, catering and other hotel services;
- Promoting and marketing the business;
- Managing budgets and financial plans;
- Maintaining statistical and financial records;
- Achieving profit targets;
- Recruiting, training and monitoring staff;
- Planning work schedules;
- Meeting and greeting customers;
- Dealing with customer complaints and comments;
- Addressing problems and troubleshooting;
- Ensuring events and conferences run smoothly;
- Supervising maintenance, supplies and furnishings;
- Dealing with contractors and suppliers;
- Ensuring security is effective;
- Carrying out inspections of property and services;
- Ensuring compliance with licensing laws, health and safety and other statutory regulations.

How to Become a Hotel Manager

- Ask yourself if you have excellent interpersonal, communication and organizational skills. They are necessary for a successful hotel management career.
- Obtain a college degree in hotel management or restaurant management. Remember that a food services department contributes greatly to the profits of a hotel; a successful restaurant manager can see his or her career advance quickly.

- Take advantage of work-study programmes offered by many colleges so that you will gain solid experience working in hotels.
- Expect to go through a hotel's training programme once you are hired after college. During the first couple of years you will be handling only relatively mundane duties, instead of providing your input on issues such as staffing, hotel decor or conventions.
- Understand that you might be offered a position as a front office manager, a food and beverage manager, a convention services manager, or any of a number of administrative positions after your training period. If you are successful at different managerial positions, your career will benefit in the long run.
- Be aware that a promotion might require you to relocate for a few years if you work for a hotel chain that has properties throughout the country.
- You will need to quickly become proficient with computers because of their widespread use in hotel reservations, billing and overall management operations.
- Consider working for hotels in warm tourist destinations or snowy mountains, depending on your preferred lifestyle.
- Be prepared for long hours, night and weekend work, and the occasional unhappy guest.

Different managerial personnel working as hotel managers –

Catering managers plan, organise and manage the food and beverage services of organisations and businesses, both inside and outside the hospitality industry, with the aim of achieving good quality at low cost and maintaining high standards of hygiene and customer satisfaction.

Typical tasks will include:

- Recruiting and training permanent and casual staff;
- Organising, leading and motivating the catering team;
- Planning menus in consultation with chefs;

- Ensuring health and safety regulations are strictly observed;
- Budgeting and establishing financial targets;
- Monitoring the quality of the product and service provided;
- Keeping financial and administrative records;
- Managing the payroll and monitoring spending levels;
- Maintaining stock levels and ordering new supplies as required;
- Interacting with customers if involved with 'front of house' work;
- Liaising with suppliers and clients;
- Negotiating contracts with customers (in contract catering).

In more senior posts, principal tasks will involve:

- Setting and agreeing budgets;
- Monitoring quality standards;
- Overseeing the management of the facilities, for example checking events bookings and the allocation of resources and staff;
- Planning new promotions and initiatives, and contributing to business development;
- Dealing with staffing and client issues, as they arise.

Food and Restaurant Manager

Fast food restaurant managers are responsible for the provision of standardised food and customer service in outlets based in the high street, motor service areas, stations, airports or multiplexes.

Drawing on all the operational functions of a business, the work involves applying financial, marketing and operational know-how, and supervising and training staff.

Managers plan, organise, and co-ordinate all resources and activities in a store. The work involves: setting targets, planning budgets, and controlling stock; recruiting, training and inspiring restaurant teams; creating and driving marketing campaigns; and building bridges with the local community.

Ultimately, it is the manager's ideas, initiative and personality that shape the restaurant.

Tasks typically involve:

- Organising the store in terms of products, equipment and people;
- Planning and checking work schedules;
- Carrying out audits to check health safety, food safety and quality of service in the restaurant;
- Making sure the fast-track audit is completed daily to check the safety of equipment and that food is properly cooked, only in-date stock is used, and all other products are discarded;
- Carrying out work outside the restaurant, including 'mystery shopping' at other restaurants within the chain;
- Attending weekly meetings with senior managers;
- Dealing with problems, queries, complaints, staff and customers in the store;
- Monitoring and maintaining high standards of food, service and hygiene;
- Ensuring the company's required standards of customer care are met;
- Administering payrolls;
- Checking and securing cash receipts;
- Budgeting to ensure maximum profitability;
- Achieving set profit and loss targets;
- Maintaining and securing equipment and buildings and all company assets contained within the unit;
- Publicising and marketing restaurants in the locality;
- Motivating restaurant teams;
- Recruiting, selecting and training new staff and fully inducting the restaurant team in accordance with company policy;
- Developing all team members to their fullest potential using the performance management/review system and identifying individual training needs;
- Ensuring the implementation and maintenance of legislation, company standards and procedures;

- Recognising new trends and implementing action plans accordingly;
- Acting as a communication link between senior teams and the restaurant team;
- Leading by example, acting as a role model for the restaurant team.

A successful manager will strike the right balance between creating both a good service for restaurant customers and a fun work environment for members of staff.

Typical Work Activities

The role varies according to the size and nature of the establishment: in a small operation, the catering manager has more of a 'hands on' role and will be involved in the day-to-day running of the operation; in contract catering, the catering manager will spend time negotiating with the client organisation, assessing its requirements and ensuring that it is satisfied with the service delivered.

Typical tasks will include:

- Recruiting and training permanent and casual staff;
- Organising, leading and motivating the catering team;
- Planning menus in consultation with chefs;
- Ensuring health and safety regulations are strictly observed;
- Budgeting and establishing financial targets;
- Monitoring the quality of the product and service provided;
- Keeping financial and administrative records;
- Managing the payroll and monitoring spending levels;
- Maintaining stock levels and ordering new supplies as required;
- Interacting with customers if involved with 'front of house' work;
- Liaising with suppliers and clients;
- Negotiating contracts with customers (in contract catering).

In more senior posts, principal tasks will involve:

- Setting and agreeing budgets;

- Monitoring quality standards;
- Overseeing the management of the facilities, for example checking events bookings and the allocation of resources and staff;
- Planning new promotions and initiatives, and contributing to business development;
- Dealing with staffing and client issues, as they arise.

Human Resources

Human resources has at least two meanings depending on context. The original usage derives from political economy and economics, where it was traditionally called labour, one of three factors of production. The more common usage within corporations and businesses refers to the individuals within the firm, and to the portion of the firm's organization that deals with hiring, firing, training, and other personnel issues.

Modern analysis emphasizes that human beings are not predictable commodity "resources" with definitions totally controlled by contract, but are creative and social beings that make contributions beyond "labour" to a society and to civilization. The broad term human capital has evolved to contain the complexity of this term, and in macro-economics the term "firm-specific human capital" has evolved to represent the original meaning of term "human resources".

Advocating the central role of "human resources" or human capital in enterprises and societies has been a traditional role of socialist parties, who claim that value is primarily created by their activity, and accordingly justify a larger claim of profits or relief from these enterprises or societies. Critics say this is just a bargaining tactic which grew out of various practices of medieval European guilds into the modern trade union and collective bargaining unit. A contrary view, common to capitalist parties, is that it is the infrastructural capital and (what they call) intellectual capital owned and fused by "management" that provides most value in financial capital terms. This likewise justifies a bargaining position and a general view that "human resources" are interchangeable.

In regards to how individuals respond to the changes in a labour market the following should be understood:

- Geographical spread - how far is the job from the individual? The distance to travel to work should be in line with the pay offered by the organization and the transportation and infrastructure of the area will also be an influencing factor in deciding who will apply for a post.
- Occupational structure - the norms and values of the different careers within an organization. Mahoney 1989 developed 3 different types of occupational structure namely craft (loyalty to the profession), organization career (promotion through the firm) and unstructured (lower/unskilled workers who work when needed).
- Generational difference -different age categories of employees have certain characteristics, for example their behaviour and their expectations of the organisation.

Human Resources within Firms

Though human resources have been part of business and organizations since the first days of agriculture, the modern concept of human resources began in reaction to the efficiency focus of Taylorism in the early 1900s. By 1920, psychologists and employment experts in the United States started the human relations movement, which viewed workers in terms of their psychology and fit with companies, rather than as interchangeable parts. This movement grew throughout the middle of the 20th century, placing emphasis on how leadership, cohesion, and loyalty played important roles in organizational success. Although this view was increasingly challenged by more quantitatively rigorous and less "soft" management techniques in the 1960s and beyond, human resources had gained a permanent role within the firm.

Facing mankind's problems it is opportune to mobilize as many intellectual resources as possible in order to resolve the emerging troubles. The students have to be trained to construct pertinent knowledge together (for example using the method. Learning by teaching). Students can be trained in constructing knowledge outside the classroom too. They have to adopt following attitudes:

- Be aware that they are bearing resources
- Be aware that they have to increase their own resources in order to be more attractive inside the community
- Be aware that they can increase their own resources if they communicate
- Be aware that they can increase their own resources if they share their knowledge with other people
- Ability to identify resource from other community members and to make this resource available for all the group
- Ability to search for pertinent resources outside the group
- Ability to connect people looking for proposing resources
- Ability to organize collective thinking in networks

Employee Engagement

Employee engagement is a concept that is generally viewed in terms of employees feeling a strong emotional bond to the organization that employs them. (Robinson) This is associated with people demonstrating a willingness to recommend the organization to others and commit time and effort to help the organization succeed. (Harter) It suggests that people are motivated by intrinsic factors (e.g. personal growth, working to a common purpose, being part of a larger process) rather than simply focusing on extrinsic factors (e.g. pay / reward). (Ryan) The concept has gained popularity as various studies have demonstrated links with productivity.

In 1999, The Gallup Organization published research that showed that engaged employees are more productive, more profitable, more customer-focused, safer, and less likely to leave their employer. The review stated that "engagement with employees within a firm has shown to motivate the employee to work beyond personal factors and work more for the success of the firm." (Harter) Watson Wyatt found that high-commitment organizations (one with loyal and dedicated employees) out-performed those with low commitment by 47% in the 2000 study and by 200% in the 2002 study. (Wyatt) In a study of professional service firms, the Hay Group found that offices with engaged employees were up to 43% more productive, based on a comparison of revenue generation.

As employee productivity is clearly connected with employee engagement, creating an environment that encourages employee engagement is considered to be essential in the effective management of human capital.

Employee engagement will be influenced by:

- Employee perceptions of job importance. This study has found that "...an employees attitude toward the job['s importance] and the company had the greatest impact on loyalty and customer service then all other employee factors combined."
- Employee clarity of job expectations. "If expectations are not clear and basic materials and equipment not provided, negative emotions such as boredom or resentment may result, and the employee may then become focused on surviving more then thinking about how he can help the organization succeed."
- Career advancement/improvement opportunities. "Plant supervisors and managers indicated that many plant improvements were being made outside the suggestion system, where employees initiated changes in order to reap the bonuses generated by the subsequent cost savings."
- Regular feedback and dialogue with superiors. "Feedback is the key to giving employees a sense of where they're going, but many organizations are remarkably bad at giving it." (Hay Group) "'What I really wanted to hear was 'Thanks. You did a good job.' But all my boss did was hand me a check."
- Quality of working relationships with peers, superiors, and subordinates. "...if employee's

relationship with their managers is fractured, then no amount of perks will persuade the employees to perform at top levels. Employee engagement is a direct reflection of how employees feel about their relationship with the boss."

- Perceptions of the ethos and values of the organization. "'Inspiration and values' is the most important of the six drivers in our Engaged Performance model. Inspirational leadership is the ultimate perk. In its absence, [it] is unlikely to engage employees."

Human Interaction Management

Human Interaction Management (HIM) is the set of principles and patterns for structuring, supporting and controlling human work practices proposed by Keith Harrison-Broninski in his 2005 book "Human Interactions".

Current mainstream techniques and tools for work support, whether categorized as Workflow or as Business Process Management (BPM), deal only with "mechanistic" business processes. In such business processes, human involvement is limited to key data entry and decision points. Workflow/BPM techniques and tools deal with only the externally-observable aspects of work - tasks, that are visible from outside.

HIM extends this to include support for "human-driven" processes focused on human creativity and collaboration. To achieve this, HIM deals not only with tasks, but also with those aspects of work visible from inside - information, interaction and innovation.

The main focus of HIM is currently on the integration of organizational objectives with human work practices, in order to implement strategy/tactics and fulfil requirements for compliance. However, HIM has application beyond the improvement of organizational efficiency, since it provides a rich set of patterns for structuring and managing collaborative work that are also finding application in spheres such as social/political negotiation, law enforcement and healthcare.

Accounting Management (Business) is the practical application of management techniques to control and report on the financial health of the organization. This involves the analysis, planning, implementation, and control of programmes designed to provide financial data reporting for managerial decision making. This includes the maintenance of bank accounts, developing financial statements, cash flow and financial performance analysis. Accounting management is a mandatory knowledge module of any MBA programme.

Cost management has a broad focus. It includes - but is not confined to - the continuous reduction of costs. The planning and control of costs is usually inextricably linked with revenue and profit planning. For instance, to enhance revenues and profits, managers often deliberately incur additional costs for advertising and product modifications. Cost management is not practiced in isolation. It's an integral part of general management strategies and their implementation. Examples include programme that enhance customer satisfaction and quality as well as programmes that promote blockbuster new product development.

Customer Relationship

Customer relationship management (CRM) covers methods and technologies used by companies to manage their relationships with clients. Information stored on existing customers (and potential customers) is analyzed and used to this end. Automated CRM processes are often used to generate automatic personalized marketing based on the customer information stored in the system.

Customer relationship management is a corporate level strategy, focusing on creating and maintaining relationships with customers. Several commercial CRM software packages are available which vary in their approach to CRM. However, CRM is not a technology itself, but rather a holistic approach to an organisation's philosophy, placing the emphasis firmly on the customer.

CRM governs an organization's philosophy at all levels, including policies and processes, front-of-house customer service, employee training, marketing, systems and information management. CRM systems are integrated end-to-end across marketing, sales, and customer service.

A CRM system should:

- Identify factors important to clients.
- Promote a customer-oriented philosophy
- Adopt customer-based measures
- Develop end-to-end processes to serve customers
- Provide successful customer support
- Handle customer complaints
- Track all aspects of sales
- Create a holistic view of customers' sales and services information

There are three fundamental components in CRM:

- Operational - automation of basic business processes (marketing, sales, service)
- Analytical - analysis of customer data and behaviour using business intelligence
- Collaborative - communicating with clients

Operational CRM provides automated support to "front office" business processes (sales, marketing and service). Each interaction with a customer is generally added to a customer's history, and staff can retrieve information on customers from the database as necessary.

According to Gartner Group operational CRM typically involves three general areas:

Sales force automation (SFA): SFA automates some of a company's critical sales and sales force management tasks, such as forecasting, sales administration, tracking customer preferences and demographics, performance management, lead management, account management, contact management and quote management.

Customer service and support (CSS): CSS automates certain service requests, complaints, product returns and enquiries.

Enterprise marketing automation (EMA) : EMA provides information about the business environment, including information on competitors, industry trends, and macroenvironmental variables. EMA applications are used to improve marketing efficiency. Integrated CRM software is often known as a "front office solution", as it deals directly with customers.

Many call centers use CRM software to store customer information. When a call is received, the system displays the associated customer information (determined from the number of the caller). During and following the call, the call center agent dealing with the customer can add further information. Some customer services can be fully automated, such as allowing customers to access their bank account details online or via a WAP phone.

Analytical CRM

Analytical CRM analyses data (gathered as part of operational CRM, or from other sources) in an attempt to identify means to enhance a company's relationship with its clients. The results of an analysis can be used to design targeted marketing campaigns, for example:

- Acquisition: Cross-selling, up-selling
- Retention: Retaining existing customers (antonym: customer attrition)
- Information: Providing timely and regular information to customers

Other examples of the applications of analyses include:

- Contact optimization
- Evaluating and improving customer satisfaction
- Optimizing sales coverage
- Fraud detection
- Financial forecasts
- Price optimization
- Product development
- Programme evaluation
- Risk assessment and management
- Strategic Marketing
- Operational marketing

Data collection and analysis is viewed as a continuing and iterative process. Ideally, business decisions are refined over time, based on feedback from earlier analyses and decisions. Most analytical CRM projects use a data warehouse to manage data.

Collaborative CRM

Collaborative CRM focuses on the interaction with customers (personal interaction, letter, fax, phone, Internet, e-mail etc.)

Collaborative CRM includes:

- Providing efficient communication with customers across a variety of communications channels
- Providing online services to reduce customer service costs
- Providing access to customer information while interacting with customers

Driven by authors from the Harvard Business School (Kracklauer/Mills/Seifert), Collaborative CRM also seems to be the new paradigma to succeed the leading Efficient Consumer Response and Category Management concept in the industry/ trade relationship.

In its broadest sense, CRM covers all interaction and business with customers. A good CRM programme allows a business to acquire customers, provide customer services and retain valued customers.

Customer services can be improved by:

- Providing online access to product information and technical assistance around the clock
- Identifying what customers value and devising appropriate service strategies for each customer
- Providing mechanisms for managing and scheduling follow-up sales calls
- Tracking all contacts with a customer
- Identifying potential problems before they occur
- Providing a user-friendly mechanism for registering customer complaints
- Providing a mechanism for handling problems and complaints
- Providing a mechanism for correcting service deficiencies

- Storing customer interests in order to target customers selectively
- Providing mechanisms for managing and scheduling maintenance, repair, and on-going support
- Scalability: the system should be highly scalable, as the volume of data stored in the system grows over time
- Communication channels: CRM can interface with a variety of different channels (phone, WAP, Internet etc.)
- Workflow - a company's business processes need to be represented by the system with the ability to track the individual stages and transfer information between steps
- Assignment - the ability to assign requests, such as service requests, to a person or group.
- Database - the means of storing customer data and histories (in a data warehouse)
- Customer privacy considerations, such as data encryption and legislation.

Improving Customer Relationships

CRM applications often track customer interests and requirements, as well as their buying habits. This information can be used to target customers selectively. Furthermore, the products a customer has purchased can be tracked throughout the product's life cycle, allowing customers to receive information concerning a product or to target customers with information on alternative products once a product begins to be phased out.

Repeat purchases rely on customer satisfaction, which in turn comes from a deeper understanding of each customer and their individual needs. CRM is an alternative to the "one size fits all" approach. In industrial markets, the technology can be used to coordinate the conflicting and changing purchase criteria of the sector.

The data gathered as part of CRM raises concerns over customer privacy and enables persuasive sales techniques.

However, CRM does not necessarily involve gathering new data, but also includes making better use of customer information gathered as a result of routine customer interaction.

Financial Management

New business leaders and managers have to develop at least basic skills in financial management. Expecting others in the organization to manage finances is clearly asking for trouble. Basic skills in financial management start in the critical areas of cash management and bookkeeping, which should be done according to certain financial controls to ensure integrity in the bookkeeping process. New leaders and managers should soon go on to learn how to generate financial statements (from bookkeeping journals) and analyse those statements to really understand the financial condition of the business. Financial analysis shows the "reality" of the situation of a business — seen as such, financial management is one of the most important practices in management. This topic will help you understand basic practices in financial management, and build the basic systems and practices needed in a healthy business.

If your small business is a corporation, you would do well to find someone experienced in financial management and encourage them to be your board treasurer (your board chair has this responsibility to find someone suitable, as well). Therefore, it's important to understand the role of the board treasurer.

New, more "organic" forms or organizations (self-organizing organizations, self-managed teams, network organizations, etc.) allow organizations to be more responsive and adaptable in today's rapidly changing world. These forms also cultivate empowerment among employees, much more than the hierarchical, rigidly structured organizations of the past.

Many people assert that as the nature of organizations has changed, so must the nature of management control. Some people go so far as to claim that management shouldn't exercise any form of control whatsoever. They claim that management should exist to support employee's efforts to be fully productive members of organizations and communities —therefore, any form of control is completely counterproductive to management and employees.

Administrative Controls

Organizations often use standardized documents to ensure complete and consistent information is gathered. Documents include titles and dates to detect different versions of the document. Computers have revolutionized administrative controls through use of integrated management information systems, project management software, human resource information systems, office automation software, etc. Organizations typically require a wide range of reports, e.g., financial reports, status reports, project reports, etc. to monitor what's being done, by when and how.

Delegation is an approach to get things done, in conjunction with other employees. Delegation is often viewed as a major means of influence and therefore is categorized as an activity in leading (rather than controlling/coordinating). Delegation generally includes assigning responsibility to an employee to complete a task, granting the employee sufficient authority to gain the resources to do the task and letting the employee decide how that task will be carried out. Typically, the person assigning the task shares accountability with the employee for ensuring the task is completed. Evaluation is carefully collecting and analyzing information in order to make decisions. There are many types of evaluations in organizations, for example, evaluation of marketing efforts, evaluation of employee performance, programme evaluations, etc. Evaluations can focus on many aspects of an organization and its processes, for example, its goals and processes, outcomes.

Financial Statements

Once the organization has establish goals and associated strategies (or ways to reach the goals), funds are set aside for the resources and labour to the accomplish goals and tasks.

As the money is spent, statements are changed to reflect what was spent, how it was spent and what it obtained. Review of financial statements is one of the more common methods to monitor the progress of programmes and plans. The most common financial statements include the balance sheet, income statement and cash flow statement. Financial audits are regularly conducted to ensure that financial management practices follow generally accepted standards, as well.

Performance management focuses on the performance of the total organization, including its processes, critical subsystems (departments, programmes, projects, etc.) and employees. Most of us have some basic impression of employee performance management, including the role of performance reviews. Performance reviews provide an opportunity for supervisors and their employees to regularly communicate about goals, how well those goals should be met, how well the goals are being met and what must be done to continue to meet (or change) those goals. The employee is rewarded in some form for meeting performance standards, or embarks on a development plan with the supervisor in order to improve performance.

Quality Control and Operations Management

The concept of quality control has received a great deal of attention over the past twenty years. Many people recognize phrases such as "do it right the first time, "zero defects", "Total Quality Management", etc. Very broadly, quality includes specifying a performance standard (often by benchmarking, or comparing to a well-accepted standard), monitoring and measuring results, comparing the results to the standard and then making adjusts as necessary.

Risk, Safety and Liabilities

For a variety of reasons (including the increasing number of lawsuits), organizations are focusing a great deal of attention to activities that minimize risk, avoid liabilities and ensure safety of employees. Several decades ago, it was rare to hear of an organization undertaking contingency planning, disaster recovery planning or critical incident analysis. Now those activities are becoming commonplace.

Evaluation Activities

Evaluation, in the context of management activities, is carefully collecting information about something in order to make necessary decisions about it. There are a large number and wide variety of evaluations that can occur in businesses, whether for-profit or nonprofit. Evaluation is closely related to performance management (whether about organizations, groups, processes or individuals), which includes identifying measures to indicate results. Evaluation often includes collecting information around these measures to conclude the extent of performance.

Advertising and Promotions

Before you learn more about advertising, you should get a basic impression of what advertising is. Advertising is a major "phase" of overall product or service development and management. Advertising is specifically part of the "outbound" marketing activities, or activities geared to communicate to the market, eg, advertising, promotions, public relations, etc. Inbound" marketing activities are geared to communicate from the market, and include, eg, market research about the market.

Although your use of the latest hot marketing and sales strategies may improve the bottom line of your business, you may get into hot "legal waters" if you do not exercise the proper restraints. This article discusses the boundaries beyond which you do not want to stray lest you run afoul of the laws governing false advertising.

Two conflicting principles are involved in advertising law. On the one hand, the First Amendment, which is part of the U.S. Constitution and grants us the right of free speech, protects all forms of communication, including advertising (referred to by lawyers as "commercial speech"). On the other hand, the U.S. Constitution gives the federal government the power to regulate interstate commerce. Most state constitutions similarly give state governments the power to regulate commerce conducted solely within that state. In exercising its power over interstate commerce, the Congress has enacted two statutes that have the greatest effect on advertising. These are the Federal Trade Commission (FTC) Act and the Lanham Act.

Employees

Your employees of usually the people who interact the most with your customers. Ask them about products and services that customers are asking for. Ask employees about what the customers complain about.

Comment Cards

Provide brief, half-page comment cards on which they can answer basic questions such as: Were you satisfied with our services? How could we provide the perfect services? Are there any services you'd like to see that don't exist yet?

Competition

What is your competition selling? Ask people who shop there. Many people don't notice sales or major items in stores. Start coaching those around you to notice what's going on with your competition.

Customers

One of the best ways to find out what customers want is to ask them. Talk to them when they visit your facility or you visit theirs.

Documentation and Records

Notice what customers are buying and not buying from you. If you already know what customers are buying, etc., then is this written down somewhere? It should be so that you don't forget, particularly during times of stress or when trying to train personnel to help you out.

Focus Groups

Focus groups are usually 8-10 people that you gather to get their impressions of a product or service or an idea.

Surveys by Mail

Competitive Analysis

Marketing should include competitor analysis. Who are your competitors? What customer needs and preferences are you competing to meet? What are the similarities and differences between their products/services and yours? What are the strengths and weaknesses of each of their products and services?

How do their prices compare to yours? How are they doing overall? How do you plan to compete? Offer better quality services? Lower prices? More support? Easier access to services? How are you uniquely suited to compete with them?

Competitive Intelligence for Business Success

Some businesses think it is best to get on with their own plans and ignore the competition. Others become obsessed with tracking the actions of competitors (often using underhand or illegal methods). Many businesses are happy simply to track the competition, copying their moves and reacting to changes.

Competitor analysis has several important roles in strategic planning:

- To help management understand their competitive advantages/disadvantages relative to competitors
- To generate understanding of competitors' past, present (and most importantly) future strategies
- To provide an informed basis to develop strategies to achieve competitive advantage in the future
- To help forecast the returns that may be made from future investments (e.g. how will competitors respond to a new product or pricing strategy?

Questions to Ask

What questions should be asked when undertaking competitor analysis? The following is a useful list to bear in mind:

- Who are our competitors?
- What threats do they pose?
- What is the profile of our competitors?
- What are the objectives of our competitors?
- What strategies are our competitors pursuing and how successful are these strategies?
- What are the strengths and weaknesses of our competitors?
- How are our competitors likely to respond to any changes to the way we do business?

The table below lists possible sources of competitor data using Davidson's categorisation:

Recorded Data	Observable Data	Opportunistic Data
Annual report and accounts	Pricing / price lists	Meetings with suppliers
Press releases	Advertising campaigns	Trade shows
Newspaper articles	Promotions	Sales force meetings
Analysts reports	Tenders	Seminars / conferences
Regulatory reports	Patent applications	Recruiting ex-employees
Government reports		Discussion with shared distributors
Presentations / speeches		Social contacts with competitors

In his excellent book Even More Offensive Marketing, Davidson likens the process of gathering competitive data to a jigsaw puzzle. Each individual piece of data does not have much value. The important skill is to collect as many of the pieces as possible and to assemble them into an overall picture of the competitor. This enables you to identify any missing pieces and to take the necessary steps to collect them.

What Businesses Need to Know about their Competitors

The tables below lists the kinds of competitor information that would help businesses complete some good quality competitor analysis.

You can probably think of many more pieces of information about a competitor that would be useful. However, an important challenge in competitor analysis is working out how to obtain competitor information that is reliable, up-to-date and available legally.

What businesses probably already know their competitors
Overall sales and profits
Sales and profits by market
Sales by main brand
Cost structure
Market shares (revenues and volumes)
Organisation structure
Distribution system
Identity / profile of senior management
Advertising strategy and spending
Customer / consumer profile and attitudes
Customer retention levels

What businesses would really like to know about competitors
Sales and profits by product
Relative costs
Customer satisfaction and service levels
Customer retention levels
Distribution costs
New product strategies
Size and quality of customer databases
Advertising effectiveness
Future investment strategy
Contractual terms with key suppliers
Terms of strategic partnerships
Competitor array

One common and useful technique is constructing a competitor array. The steps include:

- Define your industry - scope and nature of the industry
- Determine who your competitors are
- Determine who your customers are and what benefits they expect
- Determine what the key success factors are in your industry
- Rank the key success factors by giving each one a weighting - The sum of all the weightings must add up to one.
- Rate each competitor on each of the key success factors - this can best be displayed on a two dimensional matrix - competitors along the top and key success factors down the side.
- Multiply each cell in the matrix by the factor weighting.
- Sum columns for a weighted assessment of the overall strength of each competitor relative to each other.

Based on material presented in "Beat the Competition: How to Use Competitive Intelligence to Develop Winning Business Strategies", Ian Gordon, Basil Blackwell Publishers, Oxford, UK, 1989.

Competitor Profiling

Another common technique is to create detailed profiles on each of your major competitors. These profiles give an in-depth description of the competitor's background, finances, products, markets, facilities, personnel, and strategies. This involves:

- Background
  - Location of offices, plants, and online presences
  - History - key personalities, dates, events, and trends
  - Ownership, corporate governance, and organizational structure

- Financials
  - P-E ratios, dividend policy, and profitability** various financial ratios, liquidity, and cash flow
  - Profit growth profile; method of growth (organic or acquisitive)
- Products
  - Products offered, depth and breadth of product line, and product portfolio balance
  - New products developed, new product success rate, and R&D strengths
  - Brands, strength of brand portfolio, brand loyalty and brand awareness
  - Patents and licenses
  - Quality control conformance
  - Reverse engineering
- Marketing
  - Segments served, market shares, customer base, growth rate, and customer loyalty
  - Promotional mix, promotional budgets, advertising themes, ad agency used, sales force success rate, online promotional strategy
  - Distribution channels used (direct and indirect), exclusivity agreements, alliances, and geographical coverage
  - Pricing, discounts,and allowances
- Facilities
  - Plant capacity, capacity utilization rate, age of plant, plant efficiency, capital investment
  - Location, shipping logistics, and product mix by plant
- Personnel
  - Number of employees, key employees, and skill sets
  - Strength of management, and management style
  - Compensation, benefits, and employee morale and retention rates
- Corporate and marketing strategies

- Objectives, mission statement, growth plans, acquisitions, and divestitures
- Marketing strategies

Media Scanning

We can learn a lot about the competitive environment by scanning our competitors' ads. Changes in a competitor's advertising message can reveal new product offerings, new production processes, a new branding strategy, a new positioning strategy, a new segmentation strategy, line extensions and contractions, problems with previous positions, insights from recent marketing or product research, a new strategic direction, a new source of sustainable competitive advantage, or value migrations within the industry. It might also indicate a new pricing strategy such as penetration, price discrimination, price skimming, product bundling, joint product pricing, discounts, or loss leaders.

It may also indicate a new promotion strategy such as push, pull, balanced, short term sales generation, long term image creation, informational, comparative, affective, reminder, new creative objectives, new unique selling proposition, new creative concepts, appeals, tone, and themes, or a new advertising agency.

It might also indicate a new distribution strategy, new distribution partners, more extensive distribution, more intensive distribution, a change in geographical focus, or exclusive distribution. Little of this intelligence is definitive : additional information is needed before conclusions should be drawn.

New Competitors

In addition to analysing current competitors, it is necessary to estimate future competitive threats. The most common sources of new competitors are:

- Companies competing in a related product/market
- Companies using related technologies
- Companies already targeting your prime market segment but with unrelated products

- Companies from other geographical areas and with similar products
- New start-up companies organised by former employees and/or managers of existing companies

The entrance of new competitors is likely when:

- There are high profit margins in the industry
- There is unmet demand (insufficient supply) in the industry
- There are no major barriers to entry
- There is future growth potential
- Competitive rivalry is not intense
- Gaining a competitive advantage over existing firms is feasible

MARKETING THROUGH ADVERTISING

Marketing is a social and managerial function that attempts to create, expand and maintain a collection of customers. It attempts to deliver demand satisfying output through profitable exchanges.

- Marketing, as suggested by the American Marketing Association, is "an organizational function and a set of processes for creating, communicating and delivering value to customers and for managing customer relationships in ways that benefit the organization and its stakeholders".
- Philip Kotler, in his earlier books, defines marketing as: "human activity directed at satisfying needs and wants through exchange processes". Still another marketing definition, coined by Brian Norris: "The process of repeatedly moving people closer to making a decision to purchase, use, follow, refer, upload, download, obey, reject, conform, become complacent to another person's, society's or organization's value. Simply, if it doesn't facilitate a "sale" then it's not marketing."
- Identifying needs/wants and finding and implimenting solutions that satisfy those needs and wants.

- Add to Kotler's and Norris' definitions, a response from the Chartered Institute of Marketing (CIM). The association's definition claims marketing to be the "management process of anticipating, identifying and satisfying customer requirements profitably". Thus, operative marketing involves the processes of market research, market segmentation, new product development, product life cycle management, pricing, channel management as well as promotion.
- Marketing-"taking actions to define, create, grow, develop, maintain, defend and own markets".
- An approach to business that seeks to identify, anticipate and satisfy customers needs.
- Al Ries and Jack Trout defined marketing as simply "war" between competitors.
- Any activity that connects producers with consumers.
- At a macro level, marketing is the process of raising the standards of living, by identifying the existing problems and unsatisfied needs of people and then satisfying that need with a product/service that delivers value to the customer.

The practice of marketing is almost as old as humanity itself. Whenever a person has an item or is capable of performing a service, and he or she seeks another person who might want that item or service, that person is involved in marketing. A Market was originally simply a gathering place where people with a supply of items or capacity to perform a service could meet with those who might desire the items or services, perhaps at a pre-arranged time.

Such meetings embodied all the aspects of today's marketing methods, although in an informal way. Sellers and buyers sought to understand each other's needs, capacities, and psychology, all with the goal of getting the exchange of items or services to take place. Open air markets throughout the world, with buyers and sellers freely mingling, are today's example of this basic activity. Today's New York Stock Exchange had its humble beginnings as an open air market located at Wall Street in New York City.

The rise of Agriculture undoubtedly influenced markets as the earliest means of 'mass production' of an item, namely foodstuffs. As agriculture allowed one to grow more food than could be eaten by the grower alone, and most food is perishable, there was likely motivation to seek out others who could use the excess food, before it spoiled, in exchange for other items.

Prior to the advent of market research, most companies were product-focused, employing teams of salespeople to push their products into or onto the market, regardless of market desire.

A market-focused, or customer-focused, organization instead first determines what its potential customers desire, and then builds the product or service. Marketing theory and practice is justified on the belief that customers use a product/service because they have a need, or because a product/service has a perceived benefit. Two major factors of marketing are the recruitment of new customers (acquisition) and the retention and expansion of relationships with existing customers (base management).

Once a marketer has converted the prospective buyer, base management marketing takes over. The process for base management shifts the marketer to building a relationship, nurturing the links, enhancing the benefits that sold the buyer in the first place, and improving the product/service continuously to protect her business from competitive encroachments.

Marketing methods are informed by many of the social sciences, particularly psychology, sociology, and economics. Anthropology is also a small, but growing, influence. Market research underpins these activities. Through advertising, it is also related to many of the creative arts.

Corporate Level Marketing

Marketing at the corporate levels asks this question as 'What business should we be in and what opportunities should we pursue?' This is marketing before we even have a business, idea or product. This is what is known as entreprenuership.

This level of marketing strategy is where the Ted Turners, Bill Gates' and Michael Dells of the world make market changing decisions. This level is also where corporate management of existing companies decide to branch off into new uncharted territories and opportunities.

Business Level Marketing

Marketing at the business level asks this question as 'How are we going to compete against the competition?' When Jack Trout says that marketing is 'the war between competitors' and 'the conflict between companies' what he is really doing is defining marketing at the business level. Business level marketing deals with high level strategic marketing concerns. This level deals with long term sustainable advantages and business models.

Functional Level Marketing

Marketing at the functional level (also known as the operating level) ask this question as 'How do we create and keep customers?' This level deals with marketing tactics and the '4ps' of the marketing mix. This level of marketing defines and develops products, prices them, promotes them and then distributes them in a way that helps a company create and sustain demand for their products.

In popular usage, "marketing" is the promotion of products, especially advertising and branding. However, in professional usage the term has a wider meaning which recognizes that marketing is customer centered. Products are often developed to meet the desires of groups of customers or even, in some cases, for specific customers. E. Jerome McCarthy divided marketing into four general sets of activities. His typology has become so universally recognized that his four activity sets, the Four Ps, have passed into the language.

The four Ps are:

- Product: The Product management and Product marketing aspects of marketing deal with the specifications of the actual good or service, and how it relates to the end-user's needs and wants.

- Pricing: This refers to the process of setting a price for a product, including discounts.
- Promotion: This includes advertising, sales promotion, publicity, and personal selling, and refers to the various methods of promoting the product, brand, or company.
- Placement or distribution refers to how the product gets to the customer; for example, point of sale placement or retailing. This fourth P has also sometimes been called Place, referring to the channel by which a product or service is sold (e.g. online vs. retail), which geographic region or industry, to which segment (young adults, families, business people), etc.

These four elements are often referred to as the marketing mix. A marketer can use these variables to craft a marketing plan. The four Ps model is most useful when marketing low value consumer products.

Industrial products, services, high value consumer products require adjustments to this model. Services marketing must account for the unique nature of services. Industrial or B2B marketing must account for the long term contractual agreements that are typical in supply chain transactions. Relationship marketing attempts to do this by looking at marketing from a long term relationship perspective rather than individual transactions.

As well as the standard four Ps (Product, Pricing, Promotion and Place), services marketing calls upon an extra three, totalling seven and known together as the extended marketing mix. These are:

- People: Any person coming into contact with customers can have an impact on overall satisfaction. Whether as part of a supporting service to a product or involved in a total service, people are particularly important because, in the customer's eyes, they are generally inseparable from the total service. As a result of this, they must be appropriately trained, well motivated and the right type of person. Fellow customers are also sometimes referred to under 'people', as they too can affect the customer's service experience, (e.g., at a sporting event).

- Process: This is the process(es) involved in providing a service and the behaviour of people, which can be crucial to customer satisfaction.
- Physical evidence: Unlike a product, a service cannot be experienced before it is delivered, which makes it intangible. This, therefore, means that potential customers could perceive greater risk when deciding whether or not to use a service. To reduce the feeling of risk, thus improving the chance for success, it is often vital to offer potential customers the chance to see what a service would be like. This is done by providing physical evidence, such as case studies, or testimonials.

As well as the other 7 Packaging has been added to this list by some people. The rationale is that it is very important how the product is presented to the customer, and the packaging is often the first contact that a customer has with a product. Although some disagree because packaging is seen as a subfield of promotion.

"Philosophy" is the potential 8th P of marketing. Products (or services) should reflect the underlying philosophy or ethos of the organization. It should also be clear what the philosophy behind the introduction of the particular product is, as well. In his book, "Meeting Need", Ian Bruce explains this concept as it relates to marketing for charities. It also applies to other products and services

Business Models

Marketing in the past focused mainly on basic concepts like the 4 Ps, and primarily on the psychological and sociological aspects of marketing. Competitive advantage was created by directly appealing to the needs, wants and behaviours of customers, better than the competition. Successful marketing was based on who could create the better brand or the lowest price or the most hype.

Marketing in the future will be based on a more strategic

approach to competitive marketing success. Marketers will consciously build and allocate resources, relationships, offerings and business models that other companies find hard to match. Companies with a greater amount of resources than their competitors will have an easier time competing in the marketplace.

Resources include: financial (cash and cash reserves), physical (plant and equipment), human (knowledge and skill), legal (trademarks and patents), organizational (structure, competencies, policies), and informational (knowledge of consumers and competitors). Small companies usually have a harder time competing with larger corporations because of their disadvantage in resource allocation.

Success in business, as in life, is based on the relationships you have with people. Marketers must aggressively build relationships with consumers, customers, distributors, partners and even competitors if they want to have success in today's competitive marketplace.

Customer Focus

Most companies today have a customer orientation (also called customer focus). This implies that the company focuses its activities and products on ever changing consumer demands. Generally there are three ways of doing this: the customer-driven approach, the sense of identifying market changes and the product innovation approach.

In the consumer-driven approach, consumer wants are the drivers of all strategic marketing decisions. No strategy is pursued until it passes the test of consumer research. Every aspect of a market offering, including the nature of the product itself, is driven by the needs of potential consumers. The starting point is always the consumer.

The rationale for this approach is that there is no point spending R&D funds developing products that people will not buy. History attests to many products that were commercial failures in spite of being technological breakthroughs.

The next big thing is a concept in marketing that refers to

a product or idea that will allow for a high amount of sales for that product and related products. Marketers believe that by finding or creating the next big thing they will spark a cultural revolution that results in this sales increase.

Product Focus

In a product innovation approach, the company pursues product innovation, then tries to develop a market for the product. Product innovation drives the process and marketing research is conducted primarily to ensure that a profitable market segment(s) exists for the innovation. The rationale is that customers may not know what options will be available to them in the future so we should not expect them to tell us what they will buy in the future. However, marketers can aggressively over pursue product innovation and try to overcapitalize on a niche. When pursuing a product innovation approach, marketers must ensure that they have a varied and multi-tiered approach to product innovation. It is claimed that if Thomas Edison depended on marketing research he would have produced larger candles rather than inventing light bulbs. Many firms, such as research and development focused companies, successfully focus on product innovation. Many purists doubt whether this is really a form of marketing orientation at all, because of the ex post status of consumer research. Some even question whether it is marketing.

Other Aspects

- An emerging area of study and practice concerns internal marketing, or how employees are trained and managed to deliver the brand in a way that positively impacts the acquisition and retention of customers (employer branding).
- Diffusion of innovations research explores how and why people adopt new products, services and ideas.
- A relatively new form of marketing uses the Internet and is called internet marketing or more generally e-marketing, affiliate marketing or online marketing. It typically tries to perfect the segmentation strategy used in traditional marketing. It targets its audience

more precisely, and is sometimes called personalized marketing or one-to-one marketing.

- With consumers' eroding attention span and willingness to give time to advertising messages, marketers are turning to forms of Permission marketing such as Branded content and Reality marketing.
- The use of herd behaviour in marketing.

Some aspects of marketing, especially promotion, are treated as the subject of criticism. It is especially problematic in classical economic theory, which is based on the assumption that supply and demand are independent. However, product promotion is an attempt coming from the supply side to influence demand. In this way producer market power is attained as measured by profits that would not be realized under a free market. Then the argument follows that non-free markets are imperfect and lead to production and consumption of suboptimal amounts of the product.

Critics acknowledge that marketing has legitimate uses in connecting goods and services to the consumers who want them. Critics also point out that marketing techniques have been used to achieve morally dubious ends by businesses, governments and criminals. Critics see a systemic social evil inherent in marketing. Marketing is accused of creating ruthless exploitation of both consumers and workers by treating people as commodities whose purpose is to consume.

EXPANDING BUSINESS THROUGH ADVERTISING

The need for advertising of the several prospect of the hotel is utmost important for the development of the business in long term. It will create awareness of the people. Advertising is typically paid communication through a non-personal medium in which the sponsor is identified and the message is controlled. However, it can also include variations, such as publicity, public relations, personal selling, product placement, sponsorship, underwriting, and sales promotion. Major advertisers are typically corporations, but may also include schools, the military, political candidates, advocacy groups, churches, and other organizations that pay to have their message delivered to an audience. The media through which the message is delivered are varied: they include network and cable TV, radio, magazines, newspapers, the internet, billboards, handmade signs, sky writing, and bumper stickers; the list is almost endless.

Strictly speaking, word-of-mouth is not advertising because it is not paid, the message is not controlled, and it is delivered by a personal rather than non-personal medium. Ironically, word-of-mouth communications are often far more effective than advertising campaigns that may have cost many millions of dollars. "Buzz advertising" is a recent term used to describe an attempt by advertisers to simulate word-of-mouth communications.

In ancient times, commercial messages and political campaign displays have been found in the ruins of Pompeii. Egyptians used papyrus to create sales messages and wall posters, while lost-and-found advertising on papyrus was common in Greece and Rome. Wall or rock painting for commercial advertising is another manifestation of an ancient media advertising form, which is present to this day in many parts of Asia, Africa, and South America. For instance, the tradition of wall painting can be traced back to Indian rock-art paintings that goes back to 4000 BC. As printing developed in the 15th and 16th century, advertising expanded to include handbills. In the 17th century advertisements started to appear in weekly newspapers in England.

These early print ads were used mainly to promote books,and newspapers which became increasingly affordable thanks to the printing press, and medicines, which were increasingly sought after as disease ravaged Europe. However, false advertising and so-called "quack" ads became a problem, which ushered in regulation of advertising content.

As the economy was expanding during the 19th century, the need for advertising grew at the same pace. In the United States, classified ads became popular, filling pages of newspapers with small print messages promoting all kinds of goods. The success of this advertising format led to the growth of mail-order advertising such as the Sears Catalog, at one time referred to as the "Farmer's Bible". In 1843 the first advertising agency was established by Volney Palmer in Philadelphia. At first the agencies were just brokers for ad space in newspapers, but it wasn't until N.W. Ayer & Son came along, advertising agencies started to take over responsibility for the content as well. N.W. Ayer and Son was the first full service Ad Agency. They were also the first agency to start to charge commission on ads.

When commercial radio stations began broadcasting in the early 1920's, the programmes were aired without advertising. Many radio stations were established by radio equipment manufacturers and retailers. Programming was provided to sell radio transmitters and receivers. The radio station owners soon realized they could earn more money by selling sponsorship rights to other businesses. In those days, each show was usually sponsored by a single business, in exchange for a brief mention of the sponsor at the beginning and end of the show. This practice was carried over to televsion in the late 1940's and early 1950's.

Product Advertising

Certain products use a specific form of advertising known as "Custom publishing". This form of advertising is usually targeted at a specific segment of society, but may also "draw" the attention of others.

The same advertising techniques used to promote commercial goods and services can be used to inform, educate and motivate the public about non-commercial issues, such as AIDS, political ideology, energy conservation, religious recruitment, and deforestation.

Advertising, in its non-commercial guise, is a powerful educational tool capable of reaching and motivating large audiences. "Advertising justifies its existence when used in the public interest - it is much too powerful a tool to use solely for commercial purposes." - Attributed to Howard Gossage by David Ogilvy

Public service advertising, non-commercial advertising,

public interest advertising, cause marketing, and social marketing are different terms for (or aspects of) the use of sophisticated advertising and marketing communications techniques (generally associated with commercial enterprise) on behalf of non-commercial, public interest issues and initiatives.

In the United States, the granting of television and radio licenses by the FCC is contingent upon the station broadcasting a certain amount of public service advertising. To meet these requirements, many broadcast stations in America air the bulk of their required Public Service Announcements during the late night or early morning when the smallest percentage of viewers are watching, leaving more day and prime time commercial slots available for high-paying advertisers.

Public service advertising reached its height during World Wars I and II under the direction of several governments. Commercial advertising media can include wall paintings, billboards, street furniture components, printed flyers, radio, cinema and television ads, web banners, web popups, skywriting, bus stop benches, magazines, newspapers, town criers, sides of buses, taxicab doors and roof mounts, musical stage shows, subway platforms and trains, elastic bands on disposable diapers, stickers on apples in supermarkets, the opening section of streaming audio and video, posters, chicken niblets, and the backs of event tickets and supermarket receipts. Any place an "identified" sponsor pays to deliver their message through a medium is advertising.

Covert advertising embedded in other entertainment media is known as product placement. A more recent version of this is advertising in film, by having a main character use an item or other of a definite brand - an example is in the movie Minority Report, where Tom Cruise's character Tom Anderton owns a computer with the Nokia logo clearly written in the top corner, or his watch engraved with the Bulgari logo. Another example of advertising in film is in I, Robot, where main character played by Will Smith mentions his Converse shoes several times, calling them "classics," because the film is set far in the future. Cadillac chose to advertise in the movie

The Matrix Reloaded, which as a result contained many scenes in which Cadillac cars were used. Similarly, product placement for Omega Watches, BMW and Aston-Martin cars are featured in recent James Bond films, most notably, Casino Royale.

The TV commercial is generally considered the most effective mass-market advertising format and this is reflected by the high prices TV networks charge for commercial airtime during popular TV events. The annual Super Bowl football game in the United States is known as much for its commercial advertisements as for the game itself, and the average cost of a single thirty-second TV spot during this game has reached $2.5 million (as of 2006).

Advertisement Impact

The impact of advertising has been a matter of considerable debate and many different claims have been made in different contexts. During debates about the banning of cigarette advertising, a common claim from cigarette manufacturers was that cigarette advertising does not encourage people to smoke who would not otherwise. The (eventually successful) opponents of advertising, on the other hand, claim that advertising does in fact increase consumption.

According to many media sources, the past experience and state of mind of the person subjected to advertising may determine the impact that advertising has. Children under the age of four may be unable to distinguish advertising from other television programmes, whilst the ability to determine the truthfulness of the message may not be developed until the age of 8.

As advertising and marketing efforts become increasingly ubiquitous in modern Western societies, the industry has come under criticism of groups such as AdBusters via culture jamming which criticizes the media and consumerism using advertising's own techniques. The industry is accused of being one of the engines powering a convoluted economic mass production system which promotes consumption. Recognizing the social impact of advertising, Mediawatch-uk, a British special interest group, works to educate consumers about how they can register their concerns with advertisers and regulators. It has developed educational materials for use in schools. The award-winning book, Made You Look How Advertising Works and Why You Should Know, by former Mediawatch (a feminist organisation founded by Ann Simonton not linked to mediawatch-uk) president Shari Graydon, provides context for these issues for young readers.

Advertising Campaign

An advertising campaign is a series of advertisement messages that share a single idea and theme which make up an integrated marketing communication (IMC). Advertising campaigns appear in different media across a specific time frame.

The critical part of making an advertising campaign is determining a campaign theme, as it sets the tone for the individual advertisements and other forms of marketing communications that will be used. The campaign theme is the central message that will be communicated in the promotional activities. The campaign themes are usually developed with the intention of being used for a substantial period but many of them are short lived due to factors such as being ineffective or market conditions and/or competition in the marketplace.

Communication Design

Communication design is a sub-discipline of design which is concerned with how media intermission such as printed, crafted, electronic media or presentations communicate with people. A communication design approach is more concerned with messages communicated than aesthetics in media. The distinction between communication design and other applied arts is in the motivation: while the communication design process does involve a certain amount of self-expression and creativity, the goals are often those of the commissioning body rather than the artist's, and the parameters set by the commissioning body are often more constraining.

The term communication design is often used interchangeably with visual communication and more specifically graphic design, but has an alternate broader meaning that includes auditory communications as well as visual. Examples of Communication Design include information architecture, editing, typography, illustration and professional writing skills applied to creative industries.

Environmental Scanning

For a company to gain or maintain a sustainable competitive advantage, it must be ever vigilant, watching for changes in the business environment. It must also be agile enough to alter its strategies and plans when the need arises.

There are three ways of scanning the business environment:

- Ad-hoc scanning - Short term, infrequent examinations usually initiated by a crisis
- Regular scanning - Studies done on a regular schedule (say, once a year)
- Continuous scanning - (also called continuous learning) - continuous structured data collection and processing on a broad range of environmental factors

Most commentators feel that in today's turbulent business environment the best scanning method available is continuous scanning. This allows the firm to act quickly, take advantage of opportunities before competitors do, and respond to environmental threats before significant damage is done.

Environmental scanning usually refers just to the macroenvironment, but it can also include industry and competitor analysis, consumer analysis, product innovations, and the company's internal environment. Macroenvironmental scanning involves analysing:

- The Economy
  - GNP or GDP per capital
  - GNP or GDP growth
  - Unemployment rate
  - Inflation rate
  - Consumer and investor confidence
  - Inventory levels
  - Currency exchange rates
  - Merchandise trade balance

  - Financial and political health of trading partners
  - Balance of payments
  - Future trends
- Government
  - Political climate - amount of government activity
  - Political stability and risk
  - Government debt
  - Budget deficit or surplus
  - Corporate and personal tax rates
  - Payroll taxes
  - Import tariffs and quotas
  - Export restrictions
  - Restrictions on international financial flows
- Legal
  - Minimum wage laws
  - Environmental protection laws
  - Worker safety laws
  - Union laws
  - Copyright and patent laws
  - Anti- monopoly laws
  - Sunday closing laws
  - Municipal licences
  - Laws that favour business investment
- Technology
  - Efficiency of infrastructure, including: roads, ports, airports, rolling stock, hospitals, education, healthcare, communication, etc.
  - Industrial productivity
  - New manufacturing processes
  - New products and services of competitors
  - New products and services of supply chain partners
  - Any new technology that could impact the company
  - Cost and accessibility of electrical power
- Ecology
  - Ecological concerns that affect the firms production processes

- Ecological concerns that affect customers' buying habits
- Ecological concerns that affect customers' perception of the company or product

- Socio-Cultural
  - Demographic factors such as:
    - Population size and distribution
    - Age distribution
    - Education levels
    - Income levels
    - Ethnic origins
    - Religious affiliations
  - Attitudes towards:
    - Materialism, capitalism, free enterprise
    - Individualism, role of family, role of government, collectivism
    - Role of church and religion
    - Consumerism
    - Environmentalism
    - Importance of work, pride of accomplishment
  - Cultural structures including:
    - Diet and nutrition
    - Housing conditions
- Potential Suppliers
  - Labour supply
    - Quantity of labour available
    - Quality of labour available
    - Stability of labour supply
    - Wage expectations
    - Employee turn-over rate
    - Strikes and labour relations
    - Educational facilities
  - Material suppliers
    - Quality, quantity, price, and stability of material inputs
    - Delivery delays
    - Proximity of bulky or heavy material inputs
    - Level of competition among suppliers

- Service Providers
  - Quantity, quality, price, and stability of service facilitators
  - Special requirements

Scanning these macroenvironmental variables for threats and opportunities requires that each issue be rated on two dimensions. It must be rated on its potential impact on the company, and rated on its likeliness of occurrence. Multiplying the potential impact parameter by the likeliness of occurrence parameter gives us a good indication of its importance to the firm.

Sustainable Competitive Advantage

Competitive advantage (CA) is a position that a firm occupies in its competitive landscape. Michael Porter posits that a competitive advantage, sustainable or not, exists when a company makes economic rents, that is, their earnings exceed their costs, especially including cost of capital. That means that normal competitive pressures are not able to drive down the firm's earnings to the point where they cover all costs and just provide minimum sufficient additional return to keep capital invested. Most forms of competitive advantage cannot be sustained for any length of time because the promise of economic rents drives competitiors to duplicate the competitive advantage held by any one firm.

A firm possesses a Sustainable Competitive Advantage when it has value-creating processes and positions that cannot be duplicated or imitated by other firms that lead to the production of above normal rents. An SCA is different from a competitive advantage (CA) in that it provides a long-term advantage that is not easily replicated. But these above-normal rents can attract new entrants who drive down economic rents. A CA is a position a firm attains that lead to above-normal rents or a superior financial performance. The processes and positions that engender such a position is not necessarily non-duplicable or inimitable. It is possible for some companies to make profits for a time above the cost of capital without sustainable competitive advantage.

In marketing and strategic management, sustainable

competitive advantage is an advantage that one firm has relative to competing firms.

The source of the advantage can be something the company does that is distinctive and difficult to replicate, also known as a core competency – for example Procter & Gamble's ability to derive superior consumer insights and implement them in managing its brand portfolio. It can also be an asset such as a brand (e.g. Coca Cola) or a patent, such as Viagra. It can also simply be a result of the industry's cost structure – for example, the large fixed costs that tend to create natural monopolies in utility industries. To be sustainable, the advantage must be:

- Distinctive, and
- Proprietary

Building Sustainable Competitive Advantage

There are basically three types of assets that help build an SCA. These categories are exhaustive and include all of the company's SCAs:

- Organization and managerial process
  - Coordination and integration: Coordination among teams in organization is key to organizational success. Interdepartmental coordination and resource sharing to reach a common goal is fundamental to creating "value". Integrating resources is key to the success of firms. Firms that are able to integrate resources see synergistic effects of resources coming together.
  - Learning: Organizational learning is key to the success of a firm. It determines how a firm collects, distributes, interprets and responds to market based information collection and changes in the environment. These changes in the environment could be customer based changes, technological developments, legal and government restrictions. Firms have to develop robust market sensing and spanning capabilities to effectively collect information. Once they

collect info they have embed this knowledge in the products they produce.

- Reconfiguring and transformation: The environment for firms is constantly changing and constant reconfiguring and transformation is key to forming SCA. A double loop learning and transformation is key to producing innovative products. Innovative capacity of a firm determines how it reacts and learns from market information.

- Positions: market positions are the assets of a company. Most of them are self-explanatory:
  - Technological assets
  - Financial assets
  - Reputational assets
  - Structural assets: The structure of a company can determine how it performs. The hierarchy of a company can influence its culture, procedure and routines.
- Paths:
  - Path dependencies: At the birth of a company usually accompanied with certain orientations. The progenitor brings certain orientations and attributes that stay with the company for a long time. The path the company takes then determines the development of its competencies.
  - Technological opportunities: technology development at a time can determine how a firm can exploit opportunities to form SCA. Very often we see the advent of several technological factors converging into a capability that forms a SCA. An example would be the rise of companies such as Genentech at the turn of the previous century with the advent of gene mapping, significant developments in target selection and databases of previous studies and gene pools.

Strategic Management of hotel

Strategic management is that set of managerial decisions

and actions that determines the long-run performance of a corporation. It includes environmental scanning, strategy formulation, strategy implementation and evaluation and control.

An organization's strategy must be appropriate for its resources, environmental circumstances, and core objectives. The process involves matching the company's [internal resources (eg IT) and capabilities (eg quality management)] to the external business environment the organization faces. Strategy formulation involves:

- Doing a situation analysis: both internal and external; both micro-environmental and macro-environmental.
- Concurrent with this assessment, objectives are set. This involves crafting vision statements (long term view of a possible future), mission statements (the role that the organization gives itself in society), overall corporate objectives (both financial and strategic), strategic business unit objectives (both financial and strategic), and tactical objectives.
- These objectives should, in the light of the situation analysis, sugsgest a strategic plan. The plan provides the details of how to achieve these objectives.

This three-step strategy formulation process is sometimes referred to as determining where you are now, determining where you want to go, and then determining how to get there. These three questions are the essence of strategic planning. SWOT Analysis: I/O Economics for the external factors and RBV for the internal factors.

Strategy Implementation involves:

- Allocation of sufficient resources (financial, personnel, time, technology support)
- Establishing a chain of command or some alternative structure (such as cross functional teams)
- Assigning responsibility of specific tasks or processes to specific individuals or groups
- It also involves managing the process. This includes monitoring results, comparing to benchmarks and best practices, evaluating the efficacy and efficiency

of the process, controlling for variances, and making adjustments to the process as necessary.

- When implementing specific programmes, this involves acquiring the requisite resources, developing the process, training, process testing, documentation, and integration with (and/or conversion from) legacy processes.

Time Scales

Strategic management operates on several time scales. Short term strategies involve planning and managing for the present. Long term strategies involve preparing for and preempting the future. Marketing strategist Derek Abell (1993), has suggested that understanding this dual nature of strategic management is the least understood part of the process. He claims that balancing the temporal aspects of strategic planning requires the use of dual strategies simultaneously.

Strategic Management is actually a solid foundation or a framework within which all the functionning managerial operations are bundled together. This is the highest level corporate activity that sets the terms and goals for a company that it should follow for prosperity.

In general terms, there are two main approaches to strategic management which are opposite but complement each other in some ways:

- 'The Industrial Organization Approach'
  - Based on economic theory – deals with issues like competitive rivalry, resource allocation, economies of scale
  - Assumptions – rationality, self discipline behaviour, profit maximization
- The Sociological Approach
  - Deals primarily with human interactions
  - Assumptions – bounded rationality, satisficing behaviour, profit sub-optimality. An example of a company that currently operates this way is Google

Strategic management techniques can be viewed as

bottom-up, top-down, or collaborative processes. In the bottom-up approach, employees submit proposals to their managers who, in turn, funnel the best ideas further up the organization. This is often accomplished by a capital budgeting process. Proposals are assessed using financial criteria such as return on investment or cost-benefit analysis. The proposals that are approved form the substance of a new strategy, all of which is done without a grand strategic design or a strategic architect. The top-down approach is the most common by far. In it, the CEO, possibly with the assistance of a strategic planning team, decides on the overall direction the company should take. Some organizations are starting to experiment with collaborative strategic planning techniques that recognize the emergent nature of strategic decisions.

In most (large) corporations there are several levels of strategy. Strategic management is the highest in the sense that it is the broadest, applying to all parts of the firm. It gives direction to corporate values, corporate culture, corporate goals, and corporate missions. Under this broad corporate strategy there are often functional or business unit strategies.

Why Strategic Plans Fails

There are many reasons why strategic plans fail, especially:

- Failure to understand the customer
  - Why do they buy
  - Is there a real need for the product
  - Inadequate or incorrect marketing research
- Inability to predict environmental reaction
  - What will competitors do
    - Fighting brands
    - Price wars
  - Will government intervene
- Over-estimation of resource competence
  - Can the staff, equipment, and processes handle the new strategy
  - Failure to develop new employee and management skills

- Failure to coordinate
  - Reporting and control relationships not adequate
  - Organizational structure not flexible enough
- Failure to obtain senior management commitment
  - Failure to get management involved right from the start
  - Failure to obtain sufficient company resources to accomplish task
- Failure to obtain employee commitment
  - New strategy not well explained to employees
  - No incentives given to workers to embrace the new strategy
- Under-estimation of time requirements
  - No critical path analysis done
- Failure to follow the plan
  - No follow through after initial planning
  - No tracking of progress against plan
  - No consequences for above
- Failure to manage change
  - Inadequate understanding of the internal resistance to change
  - Lack of vision on the relationships between processes, technology and organization
- Poor communications
  - Insufficient information sharing among stakeholders
  - Exclusion of stakeholders and delegates
- Failure to focus
  - Inability or unwillingness to make choices which are true to the strategic mission (i.e. to do fewer things, better), leads to mediocrity, inability to compete

Although a sense of direction is important, it can also stifle creativity, especially if it is rigidly enforced. In an uncertain and ambiguous world, fluidity can be more important than a finely tuned strategic compass. When a strategy becomes internalized into a corporate culture, it can lead to group think. It can also cause an organization to define itself too narrowly.

An example of this is marketing myopia. Most theories of strategic management seem to have a lifespan less than that of the popularity of the latest teen music idol.

Many critics claim that this is because most of them generally do not work. Keep in mind that this article describes only the 50 or so most successful theories, thus exhibiting survivorship bias (ironically, itself an area of research in strategic management).

For every theory that gets incorporated into strategic management textbooks there are many that are quickly forgotten. Many theories tend either to be too narrow in focus to build a complete corporate strategy on, or too general and abstract to be applicable to specific situations.

The low success rate is further fueled by the management lecture circuit in which hundreds of self-appointed gurus, many without serious academic credentials or substantial expertise, attempt to sell books and explain their "revolutionary" and "groundbreaking" theories to audiences of business executives for a sizable fee. While there are undoubtedly inspirational ideas contained in these seminars, the theories expounded therein have not, for the most part, been subjected to serious study.

Chapter 4

Basic Concepts of Housekeeping

An uncluttered workplace is fundamental to any plant's safety programme. In addition to cleanliness, industrial housekeeping must include other factors, such as orderliness and proper arrangement of materials. It is important to know the benefits of good industrial housekeeping. Let's review the importance and meaning of order in achieving good housekeeping, and discuss some guides for checking your own work area. Sloppy working conditions can lead to a lack of pride in your work. We should not overlook slippery floors, obstacles in aisles, tools on the floors, floors and platforms that are not in proper condition, or other housekeeping hazards.

In addition to encouraging poor attitudes, bad industrial housekeeping can lead to:

- Slips from slick or wet floors, platforms, and other walking and working surfaces.
- Trips from objects or materials that are left in walkways and work areas.
- Falls from holes in walking and working surfaces, uneven flooring, uncovered pits or drains, and boxes and pallets that are used instead of adequate platforms.
- Collisions caused by poorly stored materials, overhanging or protruding objects, haphazard spotting of pallets, and use of aisles for storing materials and equipment.

Poor industrial housekeeping creates hazards for all employees in the immediate area.

Good industrial housekeeping:

- Eliminates accident and fire causes
- Saves energy by eliminating the need to work "around" congested areas and "deadwood" stored in the work area.
- Provides the best use of space
- Keeps inventory of materials to a minimum
- Helps control property damage
- Guarantees a good workplace appearance
- Encourages better working habits
- Reflects an image of a well-run operation
- Reduces the amount of cleanup and janitorial work

Housekeeping is more than just sweeping the floor and wiping dust off machines and equipment. Cleanliness is only a part of housekeeping. The most critical and most overlooked part of housekeeping is order. A work area is in order when there are no unnecessary objects in the area and when all necessary items are in their proper places.No in this definition means none—not any—not even one! A workplace is not considered to be in order simply because "there is a place for everything and everything is in its place." Do you use your production area for storage? Do you keep supplies in the area because "they'll be needed one of these days?" If there is one item in an area that is unnecessary or not in its proper place, then you do not have order.

Order is maintained, not achieved. You cannot put an area in order and then forget about it. A daily conscious effort by everyone working in the area is necessary to maintain order. Order also must be obtained throughout the day. If you wait until the end of the day and then place everything in order, what good did it do you during the day? Disorder wastes time, energy and materials.

HOUSEKEEPING RULES

- Walking and working surfaces should be clean, dry and unobstructed.
- Aisleways and exits should be clearly marked and unobstructed.

- Approved trash receptacles should be provided to assure proper waste disposal.
- Splash guards and oil pans should be available for machinery as needed.
- Work area floors should be kept free of pallets, parts, equipment, extension cords and hoses.
- Floors, platforms and stairways should be kept in good repair.
- Adequate platforms should be provided; never use additional platforms or boxes and pallets as substitutes.
- Walls and ceilings should be free of hangings and temporary wiring.
- Materials should be stacked in a stable manner; limit height as necessary to maintain stability.
- Overhanging or protruding storage should be eliminated.
- Storage areas in and around buildings should be free of refuse and debris.
- Stock should be stored in a manner that will not obstruct sprinklers (18-inch clearance for ordinary combustibles, 36-inch clearance for flammable liquids).

Combustible materials should never be stored on radiators, steam coils, ovens or other heat sources; in transformer vaults; or around electrical switch gear.

- Production equipment should be arranged to prevent overcrowding.
- Storage areas should be placed in a convenient location to encourage their use.
- Adequate lighting, both natural and artificial, should be provided to assure good visibility for work activities and to reveal dirt, obstructions and poor housekeeping conditions.
- Leaks from hoses, pipelines and valves should be repaired immediately.
- Racks, shelves and lockers should be maintained for tools, personal protective equipment and personal items.

- Lunch facilities, locker rooms and toilet areas should be clean, orderly and sanitary.
- Order results in greater and safer production of better products at lower costs. Improved production and costs mean increased business and prosperity for our company and you, its employees.

HOTEL HOUSEKEEPING

What Can Happen

Cuts, bruises, sprains, strains, electrocution, Chemical-related injuries, infections etc.

What we Can Do

Watch for things that may cause accidents and report them immediately to your supervisor. Place mops, buckets and other equipment where no one can fall over them.

Practise safe lifting techniques, lift with your legs, not your back. Be careful with cleaning solutions or chemicals read product labels. Store cigarette butts and sharp objects in a separate, metal container. Roll up all linen, rugs and spreads before putting them in the soiled laundry bundle. Wear rubber gloves when using strong cleaning solutions. Push tall or heavy pieces of furniture get help if necessary.

Do not touch light switches or handle electrical equipment when your hands are wet or you are standing on a damp floor Do not stand on the edge of bathroom tubs

Do not mix ammonia and chlorine-based cleaners together, poisonous gas is produced. Do not run up or down stairs, always walk and use the handrail. Do not try to repair machines or equipment, report problems to your supervisor. Do not run your hands along or inside objects unless you have checked first for razor blades, needles, broken glass, etc.

Do not use your hands to compress garbage in a bag, use a stick or plunger. Do not unplug the vacuum cleaner by pulling on the cord, pull on the plug.

Housekeeping in a hotel is a very physically demanding job that includes many, varied tasks. Typically, in this case study, housekeepers were responsible for cleaning 16 rooms per shift. The actual amount of work depends on the size of the room and the number of beds. A housekeeper needs between fifteen and thirty minutes to do one room.

A housekeeper carries out the following tasks:

- Making beds
- Tidying rooms
- Cleaning and polishing toilets, taps, sinks, bathtubs and mirrors
- Washing floors,
- Removing stains, and
- Vacuuming

Housekeeping in a hotel is a very physically demanding job that includes many, varied tasks. Typically, in this case study, housekeepers were responsible for cleaning 16 rooms per shift. The actual amount of work depends on the size of the room and the number of beds. A housekeeper needs between fifteen and thirty minutes to do one room.

The main risk factors for repetitive motion injuries (RMIs) in housekeeping are:

Heavy physical workload and excessive bodily motions which are a high risk for back injuries and forceful upper limb motions in awkward positions which are a high risk for neck or shoulder and arm injuries. Space limitations require workers to use many uncomfortable postures.

These are:

- Standing or walking,
- Stooping,
- Squatting,
- Kneeling,
- Stretching,
- Reaching,
- Bending,
- Twisting, and
- Crouching.

A housekeeper changes body position every three seconds while cleaning a room. If we assume that the average cleaning time for each room is twenty-five minutes, we can estimate that a housekeeper assumes 8,000 different body postures every shift. In addition, forceful movements while using awkward body positions include lifting mattresses, cleaning tiles, and vacuuming every shift. Housekeeping is a physically demanding and very tiring job. It can be classified as "moderately heavy" to "heavy" work because the energy required is approximately 4 kilocalories per minute (4 kcal/ min.)

New approaches, other than strictly ergonomic ones, need to be investigated. For example, action can be taken from the administrative level.

Options for improvement include:

- Job rotation,
- Job enrichment and job enlargement,
- Team work, and
- Education and training on work practices.

Job rotation is one possible approach. It requires workers to move between different tasks, at fixed or irregular periods. However, it must be a rotation where workers do something completely different. Different tasks must use different muscle groups to allow muscles already stressed to recover.

Another approach is job enlargement. This increases the variety of tasks built into the job. It breaks the monotony of the job and avoids overloading one part of the body. Job enrichment involves more autonomy and control for the worker.

HOSPITALITY SERVICE

The concept of Hospitality Services, also known as "accommodation sharing", "hospitality exchange", and "home stay networks", refers to centrally organized social networks of individuals who trade accommodation without monetary exchange. While this concept could also include house swapping or even time share plans, it has come to be associated mostly with travellers and tourists staying with one another free of charge. Since the 1990s, these services have increasingly moved away from using printed catalogs and phone trees to connect users towards Internet websites. These have grown exponentially since 2000 and today it is estimated that well over 100,000 people are registered users of these networks. These vary in operational structure, place different emphasis on graphical vs. textual formatting, and cater disproportionately to specific geographic regions.

In 1949, Bob Luitweiler founded the first hospitality service called Servas Open Doors as a cross national, non-profit, volunteer run organization advocating interracial and international peace. The next earliest began in 1965 when John Wilcock set up the Traveller's Directory, originally as a listing of his mutual friends willing to host each other when traveling. This later became the Hospitality Exchange in 1988 when Joy Lily rescued the organization from imminent demise. Hospitality Club is the direct successor Hospex, the first Internet-based service, operating out of Poland since 1992. It is currently the largest hospitality exchange network, growing rapidly. CouchSurfing is a newer but also rapidly growing hospitality exchange organization founded in 2004. Just as all the individual services have their own individual creation stories and organizational histories (often including demise and resurrection), many also have specific niche markets that they cater to including students, activists, religious pilgrims, and even occupational groups like police officers. However, the trend in recent years points to a greater consolidation of users in networks without a specific group, value, or lifestyle affiliation.

Chapter 5

Dealing with the Customer in Hotel Management System

Every company must be able to satisfy and retain customers. That is the key to its business performance. Your job—as an executive in charge of improving quality, customer satisfaction, or loyalty—may be to enable others to act through training and support. Alternatively, if you're in the quality, customer assessment, or development areas of your company, your job may be to do the work directly—to collect, analyse, or use customer data to improve quality, satisfaction, and retention. Whether you are an enabler or a doer, customer satisfaction and retention are your responsibility. Providing high-quality products and services builds strong relationships with customers and ensures future revenue streams.

Even though you may agree about the importance of customers in driving performance, an important question remains. Does your company align its activities to satisfy and retain customers? Too often the answer is either "no" or "not so well." To help understand the problem, consider how a customer focus has evolved in recent decades.

A systems approach to customer measurement and management also requires that you tailor the system to your unique purpose, customers, and contexts. As an illustration, Volvo's model incorporates the positive effects of improving internal quality on both productivity and customer perceptions of quality, satisfaction, and loyalty. In contrast, a major retailer such as Sears incorporates the central role that satisfied employees play in delivering quality and value to customers. These measurement systems and models are not substitutes for decision making. Rather, they provide the information you need to make resource allocation decisions and manage the process. The system provides information on how the company and its competitors are performing in different areas and how important the areas are to customers.

When combined with cost and strategy considerations, the system allows both enablers and doers to create organizational value through a continuous focus on customers. To maximize the value generated by the system, make sure your company's own staff perform the bulk of the work of collecting and interpreting customer data, so that you get the full benefit of the insights generated by the effort.

Before you dive in and start conducting customer interviews or surveys, you must know how your measurement system will be used. This chapter focuses on the strategy and planning for such a system. Since a customer orientation builds on internal quality, we'll start with a brief overview of quality management and its role in driving company strategy and customer measures. We'll then discuss two related approaches to translating strategy into action: policy deployment and balanced performance measures. Then we'll focus on the process of getting started on developing a customer measurement and management system—or improving an existing one—which involves taking a look at the breadth and depth of the proposed system and the role of market segmentation in it.

In our customer satisfaction framework, internal quality is the first in the chain of events that drives financial performance. It's important not to underestimate the role of *total quality management* (or TQM, also known as *company-wide quality management*, CWQM, and as *total quality control*, TQC)—nor to exaggerate it. For longterm survival, businesses have been forced to improve their abilities to change and innovate. But internal quality management is not in itself sufficient to assure success. Internal quality improvements must be linked to improvements in external quality, satisfaction, loyalty, and financial performance. And the links must be established in an environment of constantly evolving customer preferences, markets, competitors, and technologies.

The broad principles and methods of quality management apply directly to the development of a customer measurement system. The concept of quality should unify all of a company's activities. After all, only your customers can ultimately define quality for you! In the end, it doesn't matter how well the production system works, how well marketing functions are performed, or how good the company's strategy is. If no one buys, there will be no revenues.

Quality experts emphasize three basic strategies for successful quality management: use reference models or benchmarks, set priorities for quality improvement, and focus your resources.

Do not try to do things completely on your own. Instead, make use of reference models or benchmarks when they're available. Benchmarking is particularly important in developing a customer measurement and management system.

For *output* or *performance benchmarking,* you will measure your product or service against direct or indirect competitors on various dimensions such as internal or technical quality, external or perceived quality and value, and overall customer satisfaction, loyalty, and retention. External benchmarks will help you interpret your findings regarding your own customers and decide just where to devote your resources to get the most mileage from your improvement efforts.

SET PRIORITIES FOR QUALITY IMPROVEMENT

The second basic strategy of quality management is the universal law of priorities. In a quality context, it is often said that 20 percent of parts, processes, or people account for 80 percent of quality problems (often called the *Pareto principle*). Each customer and each market will react differently to the various drivers of satisfaction and loyalty, so one of your primary goals in customer measurement is to identify the drivers that are most important to improve. As described in earlier, you need to find out where the impact on customers is high and your current performance is poor. Your goal should be to set priorities and *optimize* rather than *maximize* your quality and satisfaction improvement efforts.

FOCUS YOUR RESOURCES

Once you have chosen the area or areas to change, the third basic strategy of quality management is to concentrate your resources to maximal effect. The goal is to create a company-wide focus on the things that matter most for performance and survival.

This is one of the most important yet also most often neglected aspects of quality management. Increasingly, managers face a common problem in that their customer measurement systems point out specific needs for improvement, but their organizations don't respond. The manager knows what area or areas to attack, but has difficulty getting anyone to do anything about it. This is where the lens of the customer shows its usefulness. Once the concept spreads through an organization the independent actions of each individual and department are much more likely to fit into the overall improvement effort.

TWO WAYS TO TRANSLATE STRATEGY INTO ACTION

Since no amount of information will do you any good if no one will act on it, creating an environment where resources get focused on quality management is in many ways the key element of the process. One basic approach to this problem, called *policy deployment,* has proven very effective where a company has a clear priority regarding what policy to deploy. A variation known as *balanced performance measures* allows a company to determine and deploy a balanced mix of quality improvements.

Policy deployment, or hoshin planning *(hoshin kanri)* as it is sometimes called, is a powerful quality management process that converts a company's strategy into operational change and effectively moves different units within the company in the same direction. Customer policy deployment, in particular, aims to move the entire organization to focus more on customers in order to increase their satisfaction and loyalty.

Policy deployment includes four major steps:

- *Mission and Vision:* Clearly state the organization's philosophy, mission, and vision (also called the *president's diagnosis*).
- *Goals:* Understand exactly where the organization is today and where it wants to be in the short, medium, and long term with regard to specific criteria or goals.
- *Communication Strategy:* Communicate the mission, vision, and goals throughout the organization.
- *Priority Setting and Implementation:* Set priorities, align the incentives, and implement quality improvement projects accordingly (using project management).

Making customers a priority became a strategy for Volvo's survival in the intensely competitive global automotive industry. Back in 1991, the question was how to create a customer orientation in a traditionally engineering-driven company. Volvo quickly realized that policy deployment was a natural means of building on its quality management foundations to move the company from an engineering focus to a customer focus. Here is a summary of how Volvo implemented the four major phases of policy deployment:

- *Volvo's Mission and Vision:* "To be the world's most desired and successful premium car brand."
- *Volvo's Goals:* "To be number 5 in customer satisfaction (according to the J. D. Power IQS study) in 1995 and number 3 in 1997."
- *Volvo's Communication Strategy:* Stop keeping secrets about customer complaints; give employees an open information system and a broad view of the customer value-added process that encompasses the vehicle sales and service experience throughout the life of the vehicle.
- *Volvo's Priority Setting and Implementation:* Use quality teams to focus on the two hundred highest-priority areas (out of two thousand possibilities identified in an initial review), and reward team members based

on the degree to which Volvo met its corporate goals as well as on the degree to which the team met its own goals.

At each level in the customer chain, the market segmentation scheme is the key element in your strategic market plan to build a customer measurement system. Market segmentation is the process of identifying and targeting unique populations or *segments* of customers and developing tailored marketing strategies to meet the individual segment needs. To identify and target segments, take the following steps:

- Group customers into segments based on customer needs, benefits sought, or personal values served.
- Identify or describe the segments according to their behaviours, lifestyles, or demographics.
- Evaluate the attractiveness of each segment in terms of, for example, profit potential, risk, capacity utilization, and core competencies required to serve the segment.
- Determine strategically which segments to target and pursue and, as a result, which segments to measure, analyse, and manage separately.

These steps bring you to a framework for just which customers to measure, analyse, and monitor. Because the drivers of satisfaction and loyalty may be very different from segment to segment, be wary of averaging across segments. Averages can be deceiving. If customer data are aggregated too highly, they provide a profile of an average customer who simply does not exist. If the segments are different enough, they will require separate survey development and analysis. Even when the same survey is applicable to more than one group of customers, be sure to analyse importance and performance levels separately for each group.

SEGMENTATION IN A HOTEL CHAIN

Consider, for example, the needs of business customers and vacation customers at "Wolverine Inns" a fictitious name for a major mid-priced hotel chain we worked with recently.

The chain recently segmented its franchisees according to which segment of customers they are most likely to serve, based on the idea that downtown properties cater more to the business customer segment and leisure-area properties cater more to the vacation customer segment.

The matrices are used to set priorities for quality improvement. The company's satisfaction and loyalty survey covers eight general quality areas or customer benefits (reservation process, staff, facilities, grounds, bathroom, room, breakfast, and perceived value) and each area is rated on a variety of attributes. For the moment, just look at the impact and performance aspects of the eight types of benefit. Later we will take up the issue of setting priorities among the attributes that provide each benefit, such as the friendliness, helpfulness, efficiency, and grooming and appearance of the hotel staff.

The vertical axes show how each type of property performs on each of the eight benefits using a weighted average of customers' attribute ratings (on a scale where 1 is poor and 5 is excellent). Both downtown and leisure-area properties, for example, perform very well on the quality of the reservations process. The horizontal axes show the relative importance of each benefit as revealed by its statistical impact on overall satisfaction.

For example, the impact score of.75 for quality of the room for the downtown properties shows that as room quality increases by 10 percent, satisfaction increases by 7.5 percent (10 percent ×.75). (This example is based on standardized scale values.)

The results reveal vast differences in the drivers of satisfaction across the two property types. Business customers who frequent downtown Wolverine Inn locations look for the hotel to simply provide a clean and comfortable room. They use the hotel for a place to get a good night's sleep and have little interest in its other services. In contrast, a much wider variety of factors drive satisfaction for the vacation customers who frequent the chain's leisure-area properties. The quality of the room is secondary to the quality of service and advice that the staff provides. The quality of the grounds, bathroom, and breakfast are also more important for the vacation customer.

QUALITY-SATISFACTION

You'll usually need several sources of data to establish all the links from quality through to profits. Consider the experience at Sears and Volvo. Sears uses one survey to measure internal quality in the form of employee perceptions and attitudes and a second survey to measure external quality and satisfaction from the customers' perspective. Information from both sources is then combined with financial performance information for individual stores to trace the links in the employee-customer-profit chain. Volvo tracks internal quality with engineering-based measures of vehicle performance, and uses customer surveys to track external quality.

Now we focus on ways to develop and administer the survey that measures customer perceptions of quality, satisfaction, and loyalty. The lens of the customer – built from the qualitative research – will serve as a blueprint for your survey, identifying the attributes to include and the order they should appear. To make the survey results useful, however, you will also need to specify and include measures of satisfaction and loyalty so as to be able to combine the individual customer responses into a meaningful pattern of causes and effects.

Step 1: The Preliminaries

As in any other activity, if you don't know what you want to get out of customer measurement, it's going to be hard to tell if you've found it. So before you develop the survey itself, you need to figure out what information is required – which is a function of what you're planning to do with it – as well as how to segment your customer base, what survey method or methods to use, and how to sample the population.

What Information Is Required?

Start by restating in simple terms what you want your

customer survey to tell you, and what you plan to do about it. This might be as generic as "We want to know what our customers want so we can give them more of it—and what they don't want, so we can avoid including it, " or it might be tailored to your particular business. Then look back at the lens of the customer and list the attributes and benefits it identifies as having the potential to drive customer satisfaction and loyalty. Then list some direct questions about customer satisfaction and loyalty. From a statistical standpoint, these are the primary dependent variables that the model is to explain based on customer perceptions of attribute and benefit performance.

Make sure that the things you're asking about are at least partially under your control, so the results will be meaningful and useful. There is no point in finding out that your customers are uniformly unhappy that every day they get a day older, unless you're in the business of providing some way to preserve youth and prolong life. So consider just how the results will affect areas and individuals in your organization and what actions you may need to take based on the results.

How to Segment Survey Respondents?

The next step is to figure out which market segments to include in the survey—and just how to classify respondents into those segments. The choice of segments should be based on their importance in your strategic market plans. Beyond the choice of key segments (such as "daily" and "weekly" convenience store customers), another important question related to segmentation and sampling is whether to include current, past, or potential customers in the research. Companies are often content to focus only on current customers. Unfortunately, if current customers are systematically different from those you've lost or those you would like to pursue in the future, your results from a currentcustomer survey could be misleading or incomplete.

THE INDIRECT APPROACH

Using the indirect approach, you might include

descriptive items in the survey such as demographic variables (age, sex, income level, education level, ethnic background), geographic variables (city, country, or geographic area), and experience-related variables (frequency of purchase or consumption of the product or service, confidence in evaluating the product or service, and so on).

These measures would then be analyzed *after* the surveys are administered to develop distinct clusters or groups of customers that differ on the variables of interest (such as male versus female or frequent versus infrequent convenience store customers).

This approach is indirect in the sense that the descriptive measures are only proxies for identifying more needs-based segments. A disadvantage of this approach is that it can lead to the inclusion of so many descriptive variables that the survey becomes long and cumbersome. An advantage of the approach is that it provides a database that can be used to develop and identify new segments. This allows you to *cut,* or sort the data, in various anticipated and unanticipated ways. Descriptive variables are typically collected near the end of the survey. If a customer feels sensitive about answering particular questions (such as age, income, or education level), encountering such questions up front may bias the responses to the whole questionnaire or lead the customer to give up on it entirely.

THE DIRECT APPROACH

Using the direct approach, you provide an existing segmentation within which customers place themselves in a needs-based segment. Often companies have some existing knowledge of the major segments or populations in their customer base. If simple descriptions of each of the different segments can be included in the survey, customers can indicate directly which segment they most identify with. For the convenience store survey, for example, independent research conducted prior to the survey helped us define five major segment profiles. We then used the profiles to develop descriptive statements for each segment:

Segment 1: I tend to visit a convenience store several times a day for snacks as well as meals.

Segment 2: I am a parent who occasionally goes to a convenience store mainly to buy fill-in items, emergency items, or things for the kids.

Segment 3: I visit a convenience store daily to buy one or two items such as a soda, coffee, cigarettes, or candy.

Segment 4: I go to a convenience store once or twice a week to buy a snack, soda, or coffee.

Segment 5: I shop at a convenience store less than once a week, mainly to buy snacks and party items or items for a trip.

In the resulting convenience store survey (presented in Appendix B at the end of the book), we asked survey respondents to indicate which of these statements best described their behaviour. The primary advantage of this approach is that it is based directly on an existing segmentation scheme. This greatly simplifies the analysis of the survey data. The responses are simply sorted according to their segment identification and analyzed. The disadvantage of using existing segment profiles is that it assumes that the profiles provide an accurate description of the underlying segments. If the nature of the segments changes between the segmentation study and the quality-satisfaction-loyalty survey, the results of the latter will be skewed in unpredictable ways.

Chapter 6

Customer Information Managing

CUSTOMER INFORMATION

Firms cannot claim a customer focus or attempt to satisfy customers unless they have customer knowledge—that is, a deep understanding of the needs of the customer. With all the brouhaha regarding the growing importance of customer relationship management (CRM), too many hotel companies are still vexed when it comes down to delivering on a service promise. For hotel companies looking to differentiate themselves from the competition, exceeding guest expectations is paramount since it leads to building loyalty. In this complex era, it is crucial to truly understand and anticipate guest desires in order to fulfill that service promise.

But just how to do it effectively has been an elusive and vague notion not fully grasped by many hoteliers. Customer-focused firms really understand their customers by proactively acquiring information on the entire consumption process, especially the consumption activities of the customer. Such information must be processed and used to guide each and every interaction with that customer. This information can be used not only to make changes and improvements in the value-creation and delivery processes of a firm but also in managing relationships with the right customers.

Managerial decisions and actions cannot be customer oriented when customer data is lacking. Do we know enough about the customer's consumption activities to enable us to create and deliver customer-focused value and manage relationships with the customer? Hotel companies need to be in the customer intimacy business. They have to focus on delivering what the customer wants. You have to have some product leadership to deliver on customer intimacy but you have to focus on the relationship above all else. All goals should be focused on customers rather than the product or operations. And getting those loyal relationships are paramount to the property or brand's success. 10 percent of all hotel guests account for 44 percent of all hotel nights.

To get those loyal customers, it's crucial a hotel employ a culture of managing the "total customer experience" and also embrace a culture of managing "moments of truth" when that experience is on the line. Also, property leadership should demand a culture that puts the customer at the "centre of your world."

While a hotelier doesn't have direct control over what someone says after they walk out, it's very possible to control the guest experience in such a way that they leave with only positive thoughts. Customer intimacy is essential for success in today's world. "If people don't feel welcome and have an emotional connection, their loyalty will be in question."

It's also a matter of creating emotional loyalty rather than functional loyalty. Whereas functional loyalty comes into play if a hotel is conveniently located near an airport, for example, emotional loyalty transcends pure need and promotes frequent stays because the experience moves beyond the brand attributes to an attachment to the guest's psyche.

The Total Customer Experience. Customers want:

- A positive, enjoyable and unique experience from the beginning until the end of their experience
- They desire an emotional connection that, once made, often ensures long-term loyalty
- They must be valued for a lifelong contribution versus a one-time contribution to revenues
- Customers desire the perception that they are in control - ensure your customer-facing processes are engineered for how customers buy, when they buy and what they buy

- Customers want choice
- And they want this across all channels

The convergence of numerous information technologies in the gathering, storing, processing, disseminating, accessing, and using data has revolutionized the most generic of all business tasks—making informed business decisions. Communication, storage, and computational technologies have made this possible. Firms have found ways to deploy these technologies toward of increasing productivity. When the promise of technology is not delivered, as in many CRM and ERP projects, the focus has turned to how and why this data is useful for a business to support the investment in information technology.

NEED OF CUSTOMER INFORMATION

The customer's desire to be known, confidence in service consistency, convenience, a feeling of welcoming and belonging and a comfort level where they know if there is a problem it will get handled right away. Of course, true loyalty goes beyond the physical hotel. These days loyalty is built with every single customer communication as well.

One way hotel companies communicate to customers is via emails. However, many companies are not communicating to their guests based on established preferences. For example, hotel brands will still offer ski vacations to die hard sun worshippers. At the hotel, many hotels are at the point where they are collecting information but are simply not tapping into that information to improve a guest stay. This can actually disenfranchise the guest since they have gone tot her trouble of providing their desires which are not being executed.

It's better to not gather the information, or say when it will actually be used. "It is more harmful to ask for that information and then not use it,In earlier, we saw that delivering superior customer value is a prerequisite for sustainable competitive advantage and that to be able to deliver superior customer value, a firm requires a good understanding of what customers value.

A good understanding of customer value presupposes

good customer information. You cannot claim a customer focus, or seriously attempt to satisfy your customers, unless you understand their needs. An effective customer information system ensures that the appropriate knowledge of the customer is available for customer-focused decisions and actions. Without customer information, for example, it would be impossible to customize customer experiences, let alone manage customer relationships.

Customization, as a term, is used broadly here to denote making changes in value creation and delivery such that the customer value is adjusted to each customer when and where appropriate. To know when and where customization is appropriate, you need to know your customer. Customer-focused firms pay attention to their customers. They listen to their customers. They really know their customers. The more knowledge the firm has about its customers, the more poised and able the firm is to deliver superior customer value.

Ritz-Carlton is known for its ability to personalize its service encounters with its frequent guests by maintaining a detailed preference profile at the individual customer level. With smart customer information systems, Ritz-Carlton's frontline employees are empowered to address guests by their first names and with knowledge of the guest's specific preferences. CLASS (Customer Loyalty Anticipation and Satisfaction) is an example of the information technology backbone to the Ritz-Carlton's guest relationships management programme.

Nadia Kyzer knows that having a database system is not enough, saying: "If our employees didn't put the information to real concrete use, the system would be worthless." Many firms use their knowledge of the customer to tailor their products and messages, or to promote new services to their customers.

For example, on the Internet, firms use knowledge gained from cookies to model patterns of customer behaviour on their Web sites so as to target promotions deemed appropriate for that customer. But good customer information management goes beyond targeting messages and promotions. QVC, the television-based retailer, uses a "daily activity report" to capture, monitor, and respond to customer perceptions of quality. Indeed, customer information should drive all business processes of the firm, including anticipating and meeting customer needs, creating and delivering services, and anticipating and recovering from service failure. Customer-focused firms must have good customer information to support the decisions and activities of the firm.

Customer-focused decisions affecting customer value require information on customers' needs, their product preference criteria leading to brand choice or loyalty and their perceptions and behaviour with regard to the product. This is true not only in the acquisition and use, but also in the disposition of products. Since service firms interact with the customer during consumption of the product there is ample opportunity to obtain and respond to customer information.

For example, New England's largest bank, FleetBoston, recently instituted the "customer experience crusade." The firm hired new staff to be stationed in the lobbies of its large-volume banks to serve as "meeter-greeters" assisting customers with their banking problems. Ostensibly, the attempt was to reverse the lousy service reputation FleetBoston had acquired due to its preoccupation with challenges following its merger with BankBoston.

With the knowledge gained from the activities of these customer service agents, the bank could be learning a lot about customer experiences and about how its customers actually use a number of the bank's services. This knowledge could then be used to drive all decisions about structuring and delivering the bank's services.

Good customer information is an asset of the firm. Logically, anything that contributes to sustainable competitive advantage is an asset to the firm. Since information on customers is useful in better matching a firm's products as solutions to customer needs, customer information is an asset that contributes to sustainable competitive advantage. For example, retailing has become so fiercely competitive that customer information assets are now seen as a competitive advantage. Customer loyalty programmes in retailing are an attempt to link customer information to transaction data. Customer databases with purchase histories showing shopping preferences can be used in customercentric business decisions. Customer information is so valuable that firms who share customer information have to be careful about ownership of the database. At the end of a joint project, for example, Wells Fargo bank and Microsoft went to court to determine who owned a customer database that was created as part of that joint venture.

Kinds of Customer Information

Customer-focused decisions and actions require customer information at two levels. At the aggregate level, customer information is about the market—or more specifically, about the typical customer in the segment(s)—and at the individual level, it is about a specific customer. When the number of customers for a firm is large and there is no opportunity to directly interact with the customer, it does not make economic sense to get down to the level of individual customer-specific profiles.

For example, Procter & Gamble may not be able to interact with each and every Crest toothpaste user. In such a situation, the customer profile is aggregated and constructed at the market segment level. On the other hand, for firms that directly interact with the customer, it makes sense to profile specific individual customers. For example, General Electric interacts with individual customers of kitchen appliances who contract customer service agreements. GE can use their knowledge of each individual customer to target service contract renewal offers or offers for replacement products when the normal life of the appliance has passed.

In general, it should become apparent that the more the aggregation, the less specific and accurate the information on individual customers. The level of aggregation of the information will also determine whether that information is useful for individualized or segment-level decisions, processes, and activities. As the level of aggregation of customer information increases, the level of aggregation of the customer solution increases and the firm is working at the segment level. With lower levels of aggregation, the firm is working at the individual customer level.

Defining Customer Identity

The background profile helps to identify the customer and to understand the customer's product-related behaviour. Firms have been diligent about gathering demographic and psychographic data to establish the background profiles of customers in the B2C market. Customer-focused firms use this background profile to understand product-related consumption behaviour. Such information is managed on an ongoing basis. In the B2C context, "who the customer is" can be profiled along the dimensions of demographic, psychographic, and consumption behaviour.

Of these three dimensions, the demographic and psychographic dimensions provide the background profile. Similarly, the background profile of the B2B customer needs to be in terms of their size, type of industry, their corporate culture, and other characteristics used to identify the firm.

In the B2C context, customers purchase and consume solutions for individual or household use. Consumers' consumption of products are determined to a great deal by their backgrounds. Their personality, family, economic, social, ethnic, and cultural profile influence the way they think, feel, and behave at home, with their friends and social circles and in society in general.

This background profile helps us understand their consumption profile and the customer value they seek in specific product solutions for their needs in the context of their activities. Similarly, in the B2B context, the background profile of customers helps us understand their consumption profile and the customer value they seek in product solutions in the context of their value chain activities.

The Consumption Profile

Whereas the background profile serves to identify the

customer, to truly understand customer value one needs systematic information on the purchase and use of the product by the customer. This information is crucial to get a complete picture of benefits and costs to the customer. A consumption profile comprises information that provides a comprehensive view of the customer's knowledge, attitude, and behaviour with respect to a specific need and associated solutions. The consumption profile containing information on product-related behaviour helps profile a customer in terms of the how the product is acquired, consumed, and disposed. Such a framework allows the provider of the solution to get into the "customer activity cycle, " as Sandra Vandermerwe calls it.

Consumer behaviour models frequently divide a customer's consumption experience or customer activity cycle into the three stages of preconsumption, consumption, and postconsumption. In essence, when the customer recognizes a need to be filled, the customer

- Processes the options and selects a solution to meet that need,
- Engages in procuring and utilizing that solution, and
- Evaluates the effectiveness of that solution.

The valence of the evaluation of the experience with the solution provider then determines the predisposition of the customer toward that solution provider for subsequent consumption cycles. A positive predisposition may materialize in the form of repurchase, brand loyalty, and favourable word-of-mouth behaviour. All of the customer activities in each of the three stages of consumption should be the focus of the firm's attention.

CUSTOMER KNOWLEDGE MANAGEMENT

Among other reasons firms have a low return on their information technology investments is that they only poorly understand what the technology makes possible. The objectives and role of information in customer-focused management must be understood. Customer-intelligent firms use their customer knowledge to drive all of the firm's activities and decisions. When firms have so much opportunity to interact with their customers, why is it that they treat their customers like strangers? The reason is not lack of information on their customers, but a lack in a firm's managing of that information. Firms may have the ability to capture that information, but may not process and utilize the knowledge to manage relationships with their customers. Information technology has only placed this realization in sharp focus.

On the other hand, the power of information technology has also raised the ugly specter of abuse of privacy when firms have access to a vast amount of customer information. Network Solutions, the first company that registered addresses on the .com, .org, and .net domains for the Internet, now a unit of VeriSign, raised eyebrows when it planned to sell names, street addresses, and other information gathered from businesses and individuals who signed up for an Internet address. There are several examples of Internet companies that have been reined in for their use of customer information. DoubleClick Inc., decided against combining Web-tracking data with offline databases. Toysmart was not allowed to sell its customer database when it shut down.

Knowledge gained on the customer from each and every customer interaction when recorded and made available can be valuable in improving the customer focus of any of the firm's decisions or actions. The major sources for customer knowledge are discussed below.

Customer Information Files are typically transaction-related and purchase-related individual-level customer data found in sales records, customer interaction records, and customer service incident records. What is perhaps not in these files, which needs to be considered as a necessary component of individual customer profiles where available, is information related to the activities of preconsumption, consumption, and postconsumption.

Research Reports have segment-level aggregate data that are found in product development reports, advertising research reports, sales and marketing reports, and customer service reports. What needs to be seen is whether research on market segments is an ongoing pursuit of the firm—to indicate that the firm is proactively assessing customer value being delivered by the firm.

Knowledge held by employees and managers—Tacit knowledge of the customers—is by definition not completely identified and its utility not realized. If there is no formal process to regularly capture and utilize this information, a wealth of knowledge resident in the firm is being ignored.

Upstream and downstream sources: When suppliers and intermediaries are regularly included in discussions of value-creation and delivery decisions, there is an opportunity to discover information on market trends, technology, ideas for product improvement, and so on that are useful at the aggregate level. At the individual level, where there are (downstream) intermediaries, if it is possible, it would be highly valuable to obtain individual customer level information.

Now let us look at opportunities that may be missed by firms that are not proactive in looking for customer information. For example, how many firms capture and utilize data on referrals? If it is appropriately captured and analyzed, firms can use this information to proactively stimulate referrals. Firms can identify customers who could be bringing in new customers. Firms can determine what incentives would be effective in stimulating referrals. From the referring and referred customers, firms can learn what messages are being conveyed about the firm and which messages are most effective in stimulating product trial from new customers.

Firms can learn what types of customers are most liable to switch from their current patronage based on word of mouth. Firms can track and follow the patronage behaviour of these new customers and nurture their loyalty and referral behaviour. Firms can also find out from these new customers valuable information on the competition as well. Similarly, what about prospective customer queries? How well is this information captured and utilized? What would such information contain?

They are a good source of what customers look for in a

product, a reflection of their choice criteria. How many firms systematically record information on complaints and praises? This type of information would be very helpful in understanding how the firm is faring on creating and delivering customer value. It could highlight failpoints in the value-creating processes and provide input into frontline evaluation and motivation activities.

Many firms have loyalty programmes to reward the frequent user. What sort of frequent-user data do these firms maintain? How many firms really use the frequent-purchase data? Some firms who know their customers well recognize the importance of sorting out the most profitable customers from their customer base and treating them differently. Some customers are indeed more equal than others! Most firms use frequent-purchaser data for targeting specials and promotions. However, this data can also provide invaluable information on customer value and customer profile information to align the firm's value-creation and delivery processes.

Traditionally, firms have gathered routine customer information only at purchase and when a customer returns a product for a refund or invokes a guarantee. Firms have also attempted to obtain customer reactions through customer feedback mechanisms. Feedback forms and customer surveys are administered on a regular basis in some firms. However, most often the information gathered from these efforts is worthless because of faulty designs and worse, sometimes even result in misdirected decisions because of flawed survey methodology. More often than not, the surveys are neither reliable nor valid.

The Research Process

When the information is not available from the day-to-day activities of the firm, then research needs to be conducted on the customer on a project-by-project basis. There are a number of choices and decisions to be made regarding the methods available in researching the customer. For example, to determine what changes are needed to improve customer satisfaction, there are formal and informal customer satisfaction measures. There are qualitative and quantitative methods to obtain the information.

For unique project-based decisions, there are several datacollection methods. Among the quantitative methods typically used are paper and pencil surveys administered over the telephone or by mail. On the other hand, qualitative methods typically utilize structured and unstructured interviews, focus groups, or observation methods. A number of innovative qualitative approaches are being introduced.

For example, Kimberly Clark for its diaper market, Intuit with its personal finance software, and Patagonia for its outdoor gear have used the method of "story-telling" by getting customers to tell real-life stories expressing how they use the product and feel about it. Customer case research is another method that conducts chronological case studies of actual purchases to discover previously unknown purchase drivers by systematically capturing all events leading up to the purchase decision. These approaches can uncover customer experiences and thought processes that may not be accessible through a pencil-and-paper survey approach.

Any research project should take a systematic approach for maximum benefit and to reduce errors (such as measurement and sampling errors) and biases. As depicted, in general, the steps are:

- *Framing the research*—Management needs for the decision or objective.
- *Examining existing and available information*—for hypotheses, specific research questions and to guide research design.
- Specifying the research questions.
- *Determining the research design*—Questionnaire construction, sampling frame, data collection method, and plan of analysis.
- Administering the research and collecting and analyzing the data.
- Reporting the results and findings.

First, the research objective frames the management decision to be made. Information already available is used to guide the research design. The research is then designed by making decisions on what information is needed and how and where to collect the information. The research design includes determining the questions to solicit the information, the method for administering these questions, the sample of subjects, and a plan of analysis. Qualitative research designs are appropriate when there is a need to generate ideas on what to focus on, or to get in-depth information on specific issues. Qualitative research, such as focus-group methods, can complement quantitative research, such as surveys.

Quantitative research designs are useful when a broader cross-section of the customers needs to be polled about a broad range of issues. Sampling techniques are used when it is not possible or necessary to contact all the sources of information. Statistical techniques allow for generalizing inferences and conclusions on the entire population of interest based on data from a representative sample of that population. The research instrument or questions and response format are constructed and pretested on a small subset of the population for validity and reliability before obtaining responses from the final sample.

Interpretation, and Utilization

Especially in service firms and in the service component of manufacturing firms, where there is a significant opportunity to interact with the customer and to customize value, firms have used customer information in a number of ways. Observe any service encounter and you will see tacit or explicit customer knowledge being used. When the data from these interactions are systematically documented and analyzed, patterns in customer data can detect the dynamics in consumption behaviour. When aggregated, customer data provides an opportunity to analyse customer segments for anything from price sensitivity to demand patterns to why, when, and how customers behave in the various activities within each of the consumption stages.

Firms can divide their customer base into segments based on profitability. When customer purchase information is mapped onto capacity utilization data, for example, a deeper analysis of the firm's value-creation and delivery processes can help determine which of the firm's marketing and operations practices contribute to its profitability. Which frequent customer promotion programmes are most/least effective? Where are the low and peak demand periods? A yield analysis of the utilization levels at the various price levels would help determine the most effective pricing decisions.

Each customer has a value to the firm, and that information is also valuable to the firm to determine the right customer. The lifetime value of the customer to the firm is a function of what they bring to the firm as revenues over the lifetime of the customer. By the same token, it is also important to know what it costs the firm to serve that customer. Loyal customers with a favourable disposition toward the service provider are also likely to engage in favourable word-of-mouth behaviour. They are valuable in trying new products being offered by the firm.

They are also less costly to serve because they are familiar with the firm and are socialized into the procedures of the firm that they encounter in their consumption. As customers' loyalty with the firm grows over time, the firm also has a better knowledge of the customer and is more efficient and effective in serving that customer.

Firms that have the data on their customers are able to engage their best resources for their best customers. For example, firms have used information on a customer's profitability to the firm to determine the level of service appropriate for each customer. A *Business Week* (October 23, 2000) special report titled "Why Service Stinks" cites several examples of firms pampering their premium customers. Charles Schwab's premium customer waits no longer than 15 seconds for a phone call to be answered, while others could wait as long as 10 minutes.

Centura Bank's most profitable customers—rated 5 on a scale of 1 to 5—get an annual call from the CEO; customer retention in this group improved by 50 percent in five years. Even utility companies, believed to be less sophisticated in their marketing than the consumer packaged goods firms, have a higher proportion of service representatives per customer for their higher-revenue customer groups. In each example, unless the firm knew what each customer was worth to the firm, it would not be able to proportionally allocate its resources to the "right" customers.

A grid guided by the three consumption stages can be a useful framework for determining what decisions need to be based on what customer information. All the functions and processes that affect the creation and delivery of customer value in each of the stages need to be aligned with customer information.

TECHNOLOGY-ENABLED CUSTOMER INFORMATION MANAGEMENT

Technology has revolutionized customer information management. Information technologies allow firms to gather, store, and interpret demographic and behavioural data so that each subsequent interaction with the customer is customized, based on historical data gathered from each customer interaction. Digitized purchase transactions in commerce have enabled numerous opportunities to track customer interactions. Chip technology has progressed so rapidly that soon there could be a computer chip in just about any product that would enable mindboggling links to improve customer value and the customer-firm relationship.

For example, take the Internet and e-commerce. Most Web sites will ask simple unobtrusive questions of customers when they browse the site. This information identifies the customer and tracks the customer's activities or "clickstreams" on the Web site. Subsequently, software can use this information to personalize the Web site and the experience for the customer.

A number of firms have emerged that provide customer information management software. Such software can customize Web pages for each customer depending on the customer's profile, which is created based on the customer's previous interactions with the firm and the Web site. Vignette's software allows Web sites to dynamically generate pages that are custom-made for each customer. Silknet's virtual sales assistant guides customers through a series of questions about their need situations and then makes product recommendations.

Marriott has an enterprise-wide software that integrates information on customers from different departments so that its sales reps can anticipate and respond more quickly to customer needs. Similarly, H&R Block uses software from Clarify to combine and coordinate customer records from its tax offices, discount brokerages, its customer service centre, and its Web site so that customer interaction personnel in each department have access to all of the information on the customer.

Creating and Delivering Superior Customer Value

Firms create and deliver customer value as a bundle of benefits contained in a core and supplementary product. Since the core of any product is a commodity, the competitive advantage comes from the supplementary product. Designing and delivering superior customer value is all about adding value to the customer's value chain and doing it better than the competition. Paying careful attention to the details in each and every encounter with the customer ensures a customer-focused delivery of the value created by the firm.

Since the customer-focused firm competes on service, it also faces the classic challenge of any service firm—matching demand and supply. In order to maximize the profitability from its value-creating assets, firms have to determine the most profitable mix of segments for its customer portfolio.

Designing and Developing Superior Customer Value

How do you design customer-focused solutions that compete on service? Let customer information drive the decision on how best to leverage the productive assets of the firm. Market-based as well as asset-based assessments are necessary to configure value-creating assets into core and supplementary product benefits that provide a sustainable competitive advantage.

How does a small startup bank beat the big boys of the banking industry in their own backyard? Commerce Bancorp in New Jersey is not your standard bank. You will find their branches open at 8:00 AM and at 8:00 PM, and for most of the day on weekends. Vernon Hill, founding CEO of the bank, who also owns Burger King franchises, has embraced retailing practices in successful firms such as Walmart, Home Depot, and Starbuck's. The core product at Commerce Bancorp is the business of banking, of course. But the total solution includes access and convenience benefits for the customer that most definitely distinguish it from other banks.

There are even bathrooms for patrons in each branch at Commerce Bancorp. The total solution for any product includes a core product with supplementary features that in combination present a resultant value to the customer. Product differentiation and superior customer value is not in its core product, but in that total solution. The total solution for Commerce Bancorp is not just banking delivered by human or automated tellers in physical branches, it is banking at the customer's convenience when, where, and how the customer wants it.

Indeed, the difference in a customer-oriented firm is very evident at any Commerce Bancorp branch. Commerce bank has found powerful ways of differentiating itself by being customer focused and then it has been able to execute its customer-focused value creation and delivery.

TRANSLATING CUSTOMER NEEDS TO PRODUCT CONCEPT

The assessment must be done both at the aggregate, segment level and at the individual, customer level, where appropriate. The aggregate, segment-level assessment orients the firm's thinking about overall product strategy. When a firm directly interacts with its customer, the individual, customer-level assessment helps the firm configure the product within that strategy to the individual customer.

In keeping with the view that a product is really a bundle of benefits, the core value in any product for any firm is the primary benefit that the firm provides. The supplementary product includes as parts of the solution additional benefits that augment the core product.

Typically, a large part of the supplementary product is comprised of services. For the most part, the core product is a commodity, as in the example of Commerce Bancorp. All banks offer deposits, withdrawals, and investments and banking products such as checking and savings accounts, and fixed and variable income securities, and today most banks offer mutual funds. These products comprise the core product for banks.

The Supplementary Product

If product differentiation is derived from the enhancement that the supplementary product provides the core benefit, what constitutes supplementary product? Starting with the familiar customer service is a common supplementary product (sometimes mistaken as the only element in the supplementary product).

A firm can add to the customer value when its billing and payment process is customer focused or can detract from customer value if it is unpleasant in the customer's experience. Thus, there are some supplementary features that are found in all products that may not necessarily be recognized as such. Services marketing scholar Christopher Lovelock visualized this concept as a flower with petals. Think of the supplementary product as composed of elements of the total value bundle that facilitate and enhance (or detract from) the primary benefit sought in a product. Visualize these elements in three broad categories: facilitating services, quality of customer experience, and brand image.

Facilitating Services

Facilitating services are all those features of the product and activities of the firm that serve to facilitate the consumption of the core product. All firms have to provide some of these services at some level. Large retailers such as Sears, Walmart, and Lowe's will provide assembly and installation services for a fee and sometimes for no charge. The four broad categories of facilitating services—complementary services, customer education, customer access, and customer service. Customer-focused firms differentiate themselves by excelling in these facilitating services.

Complementary services are those related to the consumption of the core product. Some are almost necessary, like the waiting area in a physician's clinic or parking facilities at a hotel. Passengers on long international flights enjoy a wide range of inflight entertainment activities such as films, TV channels, and even casino-style gambling or electronic shopping and services such as being able to rent a car or book hotel rooms from the technology at their seats. Some complementary services are product differentiators.

For example, recognizing that some of its customers were coming in to the bank to conduct their business bringing little children with them, some Wells Fargo branches have a play area with television cartoons, Nintendo, and the like—and even sells toys to children. Washington Mutual offers calculators, pens, and piggy banks for a small fee.

Ultimately, these complementary products ought to be consistent with the positioning strategy for the product. When a complementary feature is offered by all competitors in a particular product category, it becomes a commodity and part of the core product for that category and ceases to be a product differentiator.

Customer education is a form of facilitating service in that it provides information to the customer about the firm or the product in such a way that it facilitates the acquisition and consumption of the product. Instruction manuals and product support via telephone, fax, or the Internet are examples of customer education. Consider what some banks are doing to be more accessible for customers looking for assistance.

Tellers and managers are dressed in khakis and casual shirts to appear approachable and friendly. Bank of America has tested concierges in their lobby to help direct customer questions. Home Depot provides free classes on home improvement projects. Once again, the service feature might be a necessary component of the total product, but how it is designed and delivered may be a source of product differentiation.

Customer access has to do with everything that the firm does to make its products available to the customer and to facilitate the acquisition and consumption of the product. The hours of operation and location are a simple example of customer access for a service. The various touch points that are available to the customer to access the services of the firm or to reach someone within the firm would be a measure of the customer access. The methods of billing and payment for the product would relate to access to the product and can be a product differentiator.

For example, the convenience of payment by credit card was once a source of competitive advantage. Convenience and ease of use is a critical component of customer value for any product. Services such as financing options are also related to this idea of customer access. If these are not customer-focused, they will fail the customer and the firm.

Customer service is a key facilitating service and includes the commonly understood activity of businesses related to product complaints or failures, product returns, refunds, and such. The accommodation of special requests or adapting to unusual or irregular customer situations would be an example of customer service as well. Poor customer service reduces customer value and risks losing the customer.

Quality of Customer Experience

When the total product provided by all firms contains the same set of facilitating services, the product is not necessarily a commodity. The quality of the service offered remains a source of differentiation and therefore a supplementary feature of the product. Perceived quality enhances, and lack thereof reduces, the value of the core product. For example, even when Internet service is offered by all hotels, the quality of the customer experience with the Internet service is still a differentiator.

One hotel may require you to get into a closet, fish out

the cables and force you to shape yourself into a yoga pose to hook up those cables to your laptop, while another hotel may offer wireless Internet access from anywhere on the property. All airlines provide seating and, depending on distance and class, also provide meals and entertainment while transporting you from point A to point B. Differentiation in seating can come in legroom and comfort. First-class services can offer six and a half feet of seat length, single seats, pajamas, and privacy partitions between seats. The quality of the entire customer experience is most definitely a source of differentiation.

Brand Image

Brand image is a supplementary feature of the product in that it adds to customer value. Brand image is the sum total of all the perceptions and attitudes about a brand. The image of the firm in the general media as well as for each individual customer provides a measure of the perceived quality of the product. The reputation of a firm is usually a result of the firm's product and actions.

Where there is very little tangible evidence of the product, as in the case of Web-based services, an entire industry of so-called "reputation managers" has emerged. These reputation managers are Web sites that rate the reputation of others! A firm's image is an implicit source of differentiation in the market. Brand image is the ultimate differentiator. When all else can be seen as equal, the brand image captures the essence of the difference in customer value among the alternatives available to the customer.

Firms have to determine what their total product offering is and what it should be. The value bundle of core and supplementary product needs to be designed based on what the customers expect as standard from all providers of a solution in a product category. The supplementary product might also contain features that are sources of differentiation among solution providers reflecting the positioning strategy of the firm. Firms must constantly watch the various solutions that are being offered. Sometimes the threat of competition comes from newer business models.

For example, online broker ETrade surprised the banking business when it began to open ATMs with new services. A deep and broad analysis of customer needs could reveal value-creating opportunities.

Matching Product to Customer Value Chain

To determine how best to match the total product as the superior solution to fit customer need, the firm must understand the customer's value chain. This is an integral part of the product concept development of the customer-focused firm. A thorough understanding of the customer needs and the customer value chain will help the firm conceive its product from the customer's point of view. Firms that best relate their own value chain to the buyer's value chain, said Michael Porter, will enjoy a sustainable differentiation strategy.

The value chain is essentially a chain of value-creating and value-consuming activities, where the value created as output from one activity becomes the input to another value-creating activity that in turn creates value as input for another activity, and so on. Thus, any activity can be assessed by the value it creates versus the value it consumes. This is why activity-based costing practices make a lot of sense. As, the value creating activities *within a firm* are those that contribute to the creation of either the core product or the supplementary product.

The value created by these activities is derived by the processing of the productive factors of the firm—its people, facilities, and equipment. There may be assets or value components sourced from external suppliers or intermediaries that contribute toward producing either the core or the supplementary product. Some outsourced services may even be delivered directly to the customer.

When any value component of the total product is outsourced, as in the case of a retailer offering customers outsourced financing options for purchases, or airlines outsourcing catering services, there is the obvious issue of quality assurance in the value creation that is outside the control of the firm. Externally (to the firm) when you relate other firms' value-creation activities into a value chain, you see that the value created by one entity contributes to the value created by the next entity in the value chain.

The same idea is referred to by economists, in the context of forecasting, as "derived demand." The demand for a product is dependent on the market for another product, such as aluminum and aircraft sales for example. A homeowner who gets a home improvement job done receives (customer) value from the home contractor who in turn is receiving value from the retailer who in turn receives value in the form of products and services from the supplier or manufacturer.

CUSTOMER VALUE OPPORTUNITIES

An understanding of the role that the firm's product plays in the customer's value chain could open up value-creating opportunities. A customer-focused firm has a detailed picture of the customer's consumption domain. When a firm views value consumption activities, it can see if there are other value creating opportunities that it can leverage from its assets. The watchmaker Swatch, for example, offers wrist watches with the technology that allows them to function as electronic passes at ski resorts in Switzerland or for public transportation in Finland.

Wrist gadgets can now serve not only the function of telling time, but also making phone calls, playing music and videos, browsing the Internet, or sending email. This example defies categorization of product. What is the product? It is a wallet or a pocketbook, as well as a telephone, a personal stereo, a personal VCR, and an Internet communications device! The exercise of determining what revenue opportunities Swatch's value-creating assets would offer forces a complete redefinition of the product.

The (product) solution is conceived to take advantage of opportunities to meet the needs in the customer's life with the assets that the firm has. Swatch has found a way to provide value to a recreational activity—skiing—and a functional activity—public transportation. It is contributing to the "customer access" components of the ski resort's and public transportation's product. By enabling customer access, information technology provides a whole range of supplementary benefits to a variety of products.

Conceiving and Designing

All decisions about the product and, therefore, the value-creating activities of the firm are based on an understanding of the value-consumption activities of its customers. What are the decisions and what are the issues to be considered in determining the total product by a firm? The three major decisions constituting the product strategy are: the product concept, the operations design, and the value creation and delivery process. The *product concept* defines the customer to be served and what value is to be provided. The *operations design* defines the productive assets of the firm required to create and deliver that value for that customer.

Together, the product concept and the operations design define the scope and configuration of the productive assets that can be leveraged to produce the specific customer value that maximizes profits to the firm. The *value creation and delivery process* executes the product concept with the operations design. In developing the product strategy, the firm makes a fundamental decision in answering the question of how the product will be positioned among all potential solutions to the customer's need.

This positioning question poses an asset- and market-based decision that comprises two perspectives.

- The *market-based perspective* looks outward at the market and asks what customer needs can be most profitably served by the firm.
- The *asset-based perspective* looks inward, at the firm's assets, and asks what assets of the firm can be most profitably leveraged by the firm.

The Market-Based Perspective

A market analysis to determine what would be the most profitable segment mix for a configuration of the productive assets of the firm is the foundation for product strategy. First you need to identify the segments and the solutions that are currently available to the segments. The target market selection or the selected market segments to be served can be based on the profitability and size of each segment that the firm's assets are best positioned to serve.

Here, a formal comparison of all the current solutions from the customer's perspective is necessary. Based on this analysis, the firm is able to determine what it can provide better than the alternative available to the appropriate target market, thus framing the firm's competitive advantage. Only after such customer needs analysis is it possible to specify what would be the desired customer value in the product offering.

The Asset-Based Perspective

The operations design decision rests on how best the assets of the firm can be most profitably leveraged and follows a sequence of questions that pertain to the productive assets and capabilities of the firm and how they should be deployed: What people, facilities, equipment assets are needed to create and deliver the product? Which employees' skills and knowledge would be needed? When and where would specific human capital be needed and for how much time? Similar questions are asked about the facilities and equipment of the firm. Of course, when the asset or resource is not available within the firm, it seeks suppliers or outsources that part of the value creation. Ultimately, the question is what competitive advantage the firm is capable of and how the assets needed should be configured.

Value Creation and Delivery Process

The process decisions are about determining the specific activities of the value creation and delivery. The process of making the product and delivering it to the customer must be detailed. The value creation and delivery activities required are set in a specific sequence. The firm must deliberate on the structure, content, and process of creating and delivering the product to the customer.

No product differentiation from supplementary product can be seen in isolation. If the total benefits from the product are not worth the costs that the customer incurs in acquiring and using the product, the product is likely to fail. The more carefully the firm designs the process with the customer in mind, the more likely the process ensures ease, convenience and quality for the customer. Thus, the customer-focused firm designs the creation and delivery process with the customer's perception of benefits and costs in the value consumption process.

Ensuring Customer-focused Value Creation

Firms must also recognize that since customer value is dynamic, they need to continually monitor and improve this customer value. Ignorance of the need to innovate to sustain competitive advantage is a common mistake committed by the complacent firm. The argument is sometimes made that the firm's priority of customer focus minimizes the attention to innovation. Customer focus and innovation are not contradictory, an either/or strategic decision. Indeed, to be customer-focused would mean that the firm is continually looking for new ways and solutions to meet customer needs—and to be aware that customer needs evolve as well.

Visualize what the firm needs to do to ensure that it is creating and delivering customer-focused value that can be sustained. To sustain superiority in customer value the firm must ensure that management continually assess its market and its assets to ensure that the choice of customer and the value being created and delivered by the firm maximizes the profit goals of the firm.

How well is the customer value in the product concept translated to the operations design and the value creation and delivery process? Is the superiority in customer value being executed. The answer lies in the customer's judgment. Customer-focused firms will let the customer decide whether the firm's value creation and delivery is customer-focused.

Continual customer satisfaction assessment information needs to be available for the customer-focused firm to improve by changing the product concept, the operations design, and the value creation and delivery process, or to continually reassess whether its assets and capabilities are being leveraged to realize the maximum profit potential. To ensure customer-focused value creation and delivery, firms must assess customers' perceptions of the benefits they receive as well as the costs incurred by them.

Managing Customer Interactions

The process of delivering value is a tricky and detail-rich exercise; it requires careful planning, using techniques such as blueprinting to visualize the entire customer experience. From the customer perspective, some service encounters are critical incidents requiring more attention than others. All service encounters must be staged for a customer-focused experience just as in the production of theater.

Why does Kimberly-Clark manage the discount retailer Costco's inventory of its diapers? The firm has a salesperson live near the Costco headquarters, and a data analyst responsible for overseeing stock at 155 Costco stores in the western United States. Similarly, Procter & Gamble stations 250 people near Wal-mart's headquarters in Bentonville, Arkansas. Large retailers are asking suppliers to more actively manage the movement of products from factory to retail store shelves. P&G estimates that stock-outs amount to 11 percent of an average retailer's annual sales.

When firms like Kimberly-Clark pay more attention to how its immediate customers—the retailers—create value to their customers, they demonstrate that they are being customer focused. In fact, the Kimberly-Clark salesperson passed on information on how customers place packages in their shopping cart that played into package design for diapers. Wayne Sanders, chairman and CEO of Kimberly-Clark, attributes this change to the information age.

Prior to the industrial revolution, a service orientation and the individual-to-individual interaction was the predominant mode of competitiveness. Assembly-line production distanced the firm from the customer due to the sheer number of customers and the physical distance between the customers and the firm brought about by the wonders of modern transportation. Manufacturing goods became the engine of individual and collective (national) economic growth.

Mechanization far outpaced services and replaced producer-customer interaction, relying instead on intermediary institutions to provide a specialized set of competencies that the producing firm lacked. Businesses lost sight of the customer. Now, information technology has brought this full circle, back to the customer.

We call it the information age because what has changed in our time is that new technology has revolutionized the way information is handled. Another equally significant revolution is the change in the customer's domain. Customers not only have access to more information on products and service offerings, they also have the ability to interact with the providers of products and services in ways not previously possible. Providers can also present enhancements to customer experiences from the functionalities presented by technology. Service providers must, however, also manage customer participation when they utilize technology.

When firms take advantage of online marketplaces, it might be necessary to make changes in organizational structure so that value creation and delivery processes are adjusted to the addition of the online delivery. Two key technologies underlie this information age technology phenomenon: the Internet and wireless communications. What customer access to these technologies has done is to bring customer interactions to a new level and to the front and centre in how a firm deals with the customer. These interactions are essentially service encounters with the customer.

The Ingredients of Customer Interactions

Analyzing customer interactions can be very rewarding. Amazon constantly tracks the reasons for every customer contact. It has made numerous changes to its value creation and delivery process based on customer input. The customer service function at Amazon is considered a research lab for ways to improve the Amazon customer experience. We can turn to the unique characteristics of services to obtain a clear understanding of what is involved in a customer interaction. Something intangible is always exchanged in the interaction (intangibility). Without a customer, there is no interaction and the separation of production and consumption is irrelevant (inseparability).

To conduct the interaction, the firm has the resources and infrastructure in place that "perish" when not utilized (perishability). Each interaction is unique (variability). From these characteristics, emerge situations that are challenges and opportunities typical to the service firm. We need to keep these in mind as we design the process of creating and delivering customer value. At the most general level, all customer interactions occur in a certain place (or space), at a certain time, for a certain duration, between certain entities, in a certain manner for a certain purpose.

Consider these as ingredients in a customer interaction and categorize them into elements of structure, content, and process. When the customer interaction is mapped onto the consumption activity cycle, the objective of the interaction becomes the driving force behind the design of the interaction in terms of its structure, content, and process.

- *Structure* relates to who or what entities are involved in the interaction.
- *Content* relates to the subject, the task, and its significance in the interaction.
- *Process* relates to the sequence of steps in the interaction.

The primary decisions that would configure the structure of the interaction involve the nature of the interaction—what entity should represent the firm, should the interaction be face-to-face or not, what technology can be utilized, where should it occur, and so forth. As a complementary question about the customer: What entities from the customer's domain are involved in the interaction? Similarly, decisions determining the content of the interaction should centre around the task and include what information should be required in the interaction, what should transpire between the parties, and what value should be created and consumed in the interaction.

THE VALUE CREATION AND DELIVERY PROCESS

As, the execution of the product concept as the delivery of the product involves a process, a sequence of activities. Therefore, designing the product must necessarily include a design of the delivery process. Lynn Shostack proposed a technique called "blueprinting" to detail the process design in the delivery of services. The service blueprint is a map or flowchart as a visual representation of the process of service delivery.

Essentially, the blueprint design is diagramed in three steps. In the first step, all types of customer interactions with the firm are listed. Next, these interactions are arranged in sequence of occurrence. In the final step, processes within the firm that are required to create and provide each customer interaction are mapped. How and what information, materials, facilities and equipment, and people are processed must be included in the service blueprint.

The customer-focused blueprint is one that is designed with the customer in mind. With the activities in the customer's consumption cycle in mind, processes within the firm need to be designed in such a way that the desired value added in the solution is reflected at each and every encounter with the customer. Commerce Bancorp, for example, encourages its employees to make suggestions in streamlining the service delivery process. Commerce Bancorp employees receive a fifty-dollar reward for finding something about a process that does not contribute to customer value and instead is an impediment to serving the customer; the bank immediately adjusts its operations.

Even as a simple representation of the value creation and delivery process, the service blueprint has a variety of important strategic, analytical, and diagnostic uses. In designing the delivery of the product, it can be used to determine the uniqueness of the service process. When compared with competitive blueprints, where and at which points in the process the firm derives its competitive advantage and superiority in customer value become evident.

Thus, the service blueprint can be used in a strategic

analysis of the differentiating features and benefits of the service delivered by the firm. Only with such comparative analysis of the service blueprint is it possible to ensure that the value creation and delivery processes are commensurate with the superior customer value planned in the product concept and operations design.

The Problem of Waiting Time

All the service components in the total product, being susceptible to the inherent characteristic of being produced and consumed in real time, force customers to the experience of "wait." As, demand and supply need to be matched as closely as possible. To avoid idle capacity, services adopt the queuing (and scheduling) approach to processing customers, resulting in a certain amount of wait before the process begins. In multi-stage processes, which many services are, in-process waits are common as well. The problem of course is that no one wants to wait.

Customers will wait for a certain amount of time that is reasonable to them as per their expectations. What is reasonable is a very subjective judgment, of course—one that requires analysis of the factors that determine the perception of waits.

Maister's work on the psychological cause and effects of wait suggests a way to reduce the negative consequences where wait is a given.

- Preprocess waits feel longer than in-process waits. Allow the customer to begin the process by completing the first step in the value delivery process.
- Unoccupied waits feel longer. Keep the customer in wait occupied with activities, preferably related to the product or service.
- Uncertain waits feel longer. Keep the customer informed about how long the expected wait is to likely to be.
- Unexplained waits feel longer. Keep the customer informed about why they are having to wait.

- Inequitable waits feel longer. Serve customer based on priority, determined by what is considered just in the ambient society.
- Value of the service. Ensure that the customer value you are providing is clearly superior to any alternative.

The most important common thread through all of these suggestions is that they all have to do with managing the customer perceptions. The firm is better placed if the customer perceptions can be influenced favourably by managing customer role and expectations in the value creation and delivery.

The Customer-focused Firm

To varying degrees, customers play a role in the production of products and not just in the consumption. Firms that realize this have paid serious attention to how the customer fits in the organization. In services, the role of the customer is abundantly evident. Customers engage in a coproduction role. In services or in the service component of the product, customers are coproducers in self-service configurations.

All services as we saw earlier involve some kind of customer participation, as in the case of providing required information to the tax preparer, for example. Even when placing the order with the provider, the customer is essentially contributing to the production of the product by providing input into product specifications.

When the customer is interacting with the firm and this interaction has some relevance to the production of the product, by definition we have the customer engaging in coproducing the product. Service firms instinctively manage the role of the customers in their participation in the service.

Staging the Customer Interaction

The essence of customer-focused design of the value delivery process is in the design of the customer interactions that make up the blueprint. Customer interactions have gone by various names in research on services—service encounters and moments of truth, for example. Designing the customer interaction requires analysis and decisions regarding three of the structural dimensions of the value delivery process: the process itself, the participants, and the physical facilities and equipment. Customer roles have to be defined so that customer participation can be designed into the delivery process as appropriate.

One useful framework that has utility in managing customer interactions is to view service encounters metaphorically as "drama." When firms and customers interact, firms try to put on the best performance—like theater. The firm's *actors* perform their roles for the *audience*, the customer. In any service, there are actors and audiences involved in producing *performances* in a *setting*.

For example, restaurant customers are audiences with hosts and waitstaff as actors in the physical setting of the restaurant. Just as in theatrical production, there is a stage (the dining area) and a backstage (the kitchen); there are acts (welcome and seating, appetizers, main course, and dessert), scripts (menu and specials), props (menu card and table setting), and costumes.

Each element is carefully choreographed to produce the intended impression on the audience. Any service provider can examine each of these elements and determine the exact impression that would be appropriate for each customer segment. The "drive-thru" or take-out type of fast-food restaurant confronts different impression management challenges compared to the sit-down type of restaurant.

	such as free parking that facilitate the consumption of the core product

Supplementary Feature	*Description and Examples*
b. Customer education Information	and assistance to the customer, for example, on the use of the product or about customer role in the service interaction
c. Customer access	Convenient locations and hours of the service such as, for example, a wide variety of customer touch points and 24/7 access to customer service
d. Customer service customer	Problem resolution that requires personal attention as in product failures, refunds or special situations
2. Quality	Quality of the product (core and supplementary) as well as the quality of customer interactions—including such things as professionalism, courtesy, understanding and general empathy shown to the customer during all interactions
3. Brand image	The image of the firm or the brand contributes to the value of the product such as the reputation and status of the firm, as well as any customer relationship benefits that might be accrued as a source of customer value

Only with an intimate understanding of the customer's value chain consumption (and creation) activities can firms begin to see what opportunities there might be to facilitate the consumption of the core product. Sometimes complementary products are outsourced and provided directly to the customer by the supplier, as Wells Fargo did when it invited Starbuck's to open locations at some of its branches. Ultimately, these complementary products ought to be consistent with the positioning strategy for the product. When a complementary feature is offered by all competitors in a particular product category, it becomes a commodity and part of the core product for that category and ceases to be a product differentiator.

LOOKING FOR CUSTOMER VALUE OPPORTUNITIES

An understanding of the role that the firm's product plays in the customer's value chain could open up value-creating opportunities. A customer-focused firm has a detailed picture of the customer's consumption domain. When a firm views value consumption activities, it can see if there are other value creating opportunities that it can leverage from its assets. The watchmaker Swatch, for example, offers wrist watches with the technology that allows them to function as electronic passes at ski resorts in Switzerland or for public transportation in Finland. Wrist gadgets can now serve not only the function of telling time, but also making phone calls, playing music and videos, browsing the Internet, or sending email.

This example defies categorization of product. What is the product? It is a wallet or a pocketbook, as well as a telephone, a personal stereo, a personal VCR, and an Internet communications device! The exercise of determining what revenue opportunities Swatch's value-creating assets would offer forces a complete redefinition of the product. As we saw the (product) solution is conceived to take advantage of opportunities to meet the needs in the customer's life with the assets that the firm has. Swatch has found a way to provide value to a recreational activity—skiing—and a functional activity—public transportation. It is contributing to the "customer access" components of the ski resort's and public transportation's product. By enabling customer access, information technology provides a whole range of supplementary benefits to a variety of products.

Contrast this with the example of a firm that does not understand the value of complementary product components and the customer's value chain. A customer came out of a movie theater in Kendall Square, Cambridge, and experienced a 40-minute ordeal trying to leave the theater's parking lot. She spent 30 minutes standing in line in frigid weather to pay the $2.50 parking fee and a further 15 minutes to exit the parking lot. When complaining to the management of the movie theater, she asked if she could pay the parking fee as she bought the movie ticket. She was told that the parking lot was owned by a different company and the theater would not take responsibility for the customer's bad experience at the parking lot. In contrast, the airline SAS has been known to provide an annual dinner to taxicab drivers in Stockholm because the SAS management wants the drivers to treat passengers on the way to and from the airport with professional courtesy and respect. Clearly, firms that are customer-focused conceive their product differently from other firms, because of their intimate knowledge of the customer's consumption activities.

MANAGING CUSTOMER INTERACTIONS

The process of delivering value is a tricky and detail-rich exercise; it requires careful planning, using techniques such as blueprinting to visualize the entire customer experience. From the customer perspective, some service encounters are critical incidents requiring more attention than others. All service encounters must be staged for a customer-focused experience just as in the production of theater.

Why does Kimberly-Clark manage the discount retailer Costco's inventory of its diapers? The firm has a salesperson live near the Costco headquarters, and a data analyst responsible for overseeing stock at 155 Costco stores in the western United States. Similarly, Procter & Gamble stations

250 people near Wal-mart's headquarters in Bentonville, Arkansas. Large retailers are asking suppliers to more actively manage the movement of products from factory to retail store shelves. P&G estimates that stock-outs amount to 11 percent of an average retailer's annual sales. When firms like Kimberly-Clark pay more attention to how its immediate customers—the retailers—create value to their customers, they demonstrate that they are being customer focused. In fact, the Kimberly-Clark salesperson passed on information on how customers place packages in their shopping cart that played into package design for diapers. Wayne Sanders, chairman and CEO of Kimberly-Clark, attributes this change to the information age.

Prior to the industrial revolution, a service orientation and the individual-to-individual interaction was the predominant mode of competitiveness. Assembly-line production distanced the firm from the customer due to the sheer number of customers and the physical distance between the customers and the firm brought about by the wonders of modern transportation. Manufacturing goods became the engine of individual and collective (national) economic growth. Mechanization far outpaced services and replaced producer-customer interaction, relying instead on intermediary institutions to provide a specialized set of competencies that the producing firm lacked. Businesses lost sight of the customer. Now, information technology has brought this full circle, back to the customer.

We call it the information age because what has changed in our time is that new technology has revolutionized the way information is handled. Another equally significant revolution is the change in the customer's domain. Customers not only have access to more information on products and service offerings, they also have the ability to interact with the providers of products and services in ways not previously possible. Providers can also present enhancements to customer experiences from the functionalities presented by technology. Service providers must, however, also manage customer participation when they utilize technology. When firms take advantage of online marketplaces, it might be necessary to make changes in organizational structure so that value creation and delivery processes are adjusted to the addition of the online delivery. Two key technologies underlie this information age technology phenomenon: the Internet and wireless communications. What customer access to these technologies has done is to bring customer interactions to a new level and to the front and centre in how a firm deals with the customer. These interactions are essentially service encounters with the customer.

Maister's work on the psychological cause and effects of wait suggests a way to reduce the negative consequences where wait is a given.

- Preprocess waits feel longer than in-process waits. Allow the customer to begin the process by completing the first step in the value delivery process.
- Unoccupied waits feel longer. Keep the customer in wait occupied with activities, preferably related to the product or service.
- Uncertain waits feel longer. Keep the customer informed about how long the expected wait is to likely to be.
- Unexplained waits feel longer. Keep the customer informed about why they are having to wait.
- Inequitable waits feel longer. Serve customer based on priority, determined by what is considered just in the ambient society.
- Value of the service. Ensure that the customer value you are providing is clearly superior to any alternative.

The most important common thread through all of these suggestions is that they all have to do with managing the customer perceptions. The firm is better placed if the customer perceptions can be influenced favourably by managing customer role and expectations in the value creation and delivery.

CUSTOMER INTERACTION

The essence of customer-focused design of the value

delivery process is in the design of the customer interactions that make up the blueprint.

Customer interactions have gone by various names in research on services—service encounters and moments of truth, for example. Designing the customer interaction requires analysis and decisions regarding three of the structural dimensions of the value delivery process: the process itself, the participants, and the physical facilities and equipment. Customer roles have to be defined so that customer participation can be designed into the delivery process as appropriate.

DEMAND ANALYSIS

Demand analysis is a critical review of the profitability of customers being served at any given time so that demand management methods. Creative financing skills and practices by the firm can provide cost efficiencies in raising capital and purchase conveniences.

Demand analysis begins with detecting and identifying the demand patterns. Are there discernible nonrandom fluctuations in demand? Firms must first establish the cycles of demand in terms of the time frame across which demand fluctuations occur. Take the example of customer call centres. Utilization patterns may reveal that there are peaks and valleys during the day as well as across the days of the week, weeks of the month, and months of the year. By mapping customer interactions over a demand period, firms can identify all of these peaks and valleys in customer demand patterns. Since each time frame has a different pattern of fluctuation, firms must identify when they occur in each time frame. What is the extent of the fluctuation—how high are the peaks and how low are the valleys? Firms might want to focus on those peaks and valleys that display the highest variance from the desired levels of capacity utilization.

As the timing and patterns of the fluctuations are determined, it is also important to establish at which points in the firm customers interact and to identify the utilization patterns at each point of customer interaction. Managers must look at their blueprints and determine the demand patterns, particularly at the failpoints, for all of the appropriate time frames. The variation in significance of the failpoints makes it imperative to prioritize capacity allocation decisions according to their significance in affecting customer value.

It is necessary to identify the customers or the segments that interact at the different times and to determine their prospects for profitability. Different segment-mixes are likely to patronize the services at different times. Further, the proportion of each segment within the total number of customers served at any given time could be different. To enable prioritizing capacity allocation, the size and profitability of each segment need to be examined. The size relates to the volume of revenues received from the customer, whereas profitability includes the revenues as well as the costs associated with serving that customer.

MODIFYING CUSTOMER BEHAVIOUR

Why do customers perform those interactions when they do? What will it take to change their behaviour to perform those interactions during other times? In other words, what is their behaviour sensitive to? Essentially, this analysis is reflected in a change in customer value. Segments differ in price sensitivity; different segments will switch their interaction times at different price levels. Insofar as customer value is affected by price, pricing is a powerful tool to modify customer behaviour.

Firms can do this with adjustments to the value bundle, by manipulating elements in the supplementary product. Adjustments to benefits and costs as reflected in customer value can be analyzed for its effect on customer behaviour. In how it affects customer value, the amount of customer participation sometimes allows flexible pricing. Automation versus personalized service can be used to provide varying degrees of levels of service to the customer. Customers may choose the technology during peak periods such as in the case of the self-service checkout counters in many stores. Standardized versus tailored versions can be used to shift demand. Different versions of the product with different combinations of features using product bundling are effective demandshifting mechanisms. Firms in some industries do this instinctively without much sophistication while others such as airlines and hotels use very sophisticated methods. Firms that have a good customer understanding are better equipped to adjust customer value without losing superiority among its competitors.

Price promotions are powerful demand-shifting tactics. There are numerous examples of price promotions, from early bird specials to discounts during low periods. The problem with most price promotions is that they are not aligned with demand fluctuations, so that the effect on the customer is random—where the firm is simply hoping to build demand without a sense of timing and how it would affect demand fluctuation patterns. Unless the firm's assets always operate at the same level of capacity, every firm should be offering price promotions to bring in customers during periods when the assets are idle. Anything from customer convenience in payment such as interest-free deferred payment schedules to outright price bargains are common uses of pricing for this purpose.

MANAGING CUSTOMER RELATIONSHIPS

The task of creating and delivering superior customer value must be complemented with the selection of the appropriate customers and the effective management of relationships with those customers. Managing customer relationships should be guided by an understanding of what the customer's equity is to the firm. Customer equity, the value of customer to the firm, improves as superiority in customer value improves. Since customer equity is perhaps the firm's most valuable asset, the firm must continually seek to improve customer value for it best customers. A firm's potential return on customer equity should determine the investment it makes in customers. For its most valuable customers, the firm must guarantee superior service quality and customer service, with special attention to recovering from inevitable product failures when they occur. Maximizing long-term profitability comes from maximizing customer equity—firms must maximize the lifetime value of the customer, including revenues, referrals as well as costs of serving the customer. Customer acquisition and retention efforts must be guided by the worth of the customer to the firm.

Maytag provides premium service to its premium customers—those who purchase the Neptune line of laundry machines. Neptune customers get a dedicated staff, a separate toll-free number and fast response on service calls. This is an example of the common business practice where firms allocate resources by the profitability and value of the customer. They utilize the opportunity in directly interacting with individual customers to determine customer profitability and allocate assets accordingly. And what are the benefits of the practice of differentiating among your customers?

SELECTING THE RIGHT CUSTOMER

Markets consist of customers with diverse needs and differences in customer profitability. When serving multiple groups of customers, the goal must be to maximize the profitability of the combination of segments. When different segments are targeted, the firm essentially has a portfolio of customer segments—just as investors have an investment portfolio that maximizes returns at a certain level of risk, firms manage customer portfolios for maximum profits. In other words, this is the selection of customers at any point in time, compared to other segments, from which the firm can generate maximum profits. Firms must attract these most profitable customers and then must establish systems and procedures to retain them.

Most firms serve different segments depending on how the definition of segment is aggregated. The "segment-of-one" used in common business parlance to refer to customization at the individual level is really a maximum disaggregation of a market segment. As we saw in the preceding chapter, most firms facing fluctuating demand and experiencing peak, shoulder and low periods of demand find it inevitable that, at different times, different segments must be served. Of course, each of these segments must have a compatible fit with the overall corporate image as well as a compatible fit with the products, services, employees and other customers. The question is, are they selected based on their combined long term value to the firm?

A FIRM'S MOST PRECIOUS ASSET – CUSTOMER EQUITY

Ask a manager, "What is your firm's most valuable asset?" Chances are that you will not get the response, "my customers." You will find even fewer firms that actually make an assessment of this value in any real sense. The valuation of the customer is implicit in sales figures – essentially, the revenues generated by customers of the firm. What is the flaw in using sales as a proxy in valuing a firm's customers? Consider this. Two customers with the same cash value of purchases may not be of the same value to the firm. There may be differences in the cost of serving these two customers. The true value of the customer to the firm, or the equity that the firm has in that customer, must include all revenues and also all costs related to that customer, as in financial investments.

A recent framework by a team of researchers defines customer equity as the "total of the discounted lifetime value of all the firm's customers." They articulate three drivers of customer equity: value equity, brand equity, and relationship equity. They define value equity as the objective assessment of the utility of the brand, and value equity is driven by quality, price, and convenience; brand equity as the subjective assessment of the brand above and beyond the perceived value, and brand equity is driven by brand awareness, attitude toward the brand, and corporate ethics; and relationship equity as the tendency of the customer to stick with the brand, and relationship equity is driven by loyalty programs, special recognition and treatment, affinity programs, community-building programs, and knowledge-building programs. Their framework – the customer equity diagnostic – is offered as a way to determine which customers to acquire as well as what will enable their retention.

If we define customer value as the value of the firm or a product as perceived by the customer, customer equity is the converse and refers to the value of the customer to the firm. If the objective is to maximize the returns from your investments—the customer portfolio—you must maximize customer equity. This makes sense because you can maximize sustainable return on assets by maximizing customer equity for the long term. To maximize customer equity, we must be able to measure it. If customer equity is simply the value of a customer to the firm, we can articulate that value in the same way that customers articulate our value to them. Just as customer value is the difference between benefits and costs to the customer, conversely, customer equity is the difference between the benefits and costs to the firm in serving a customer. One team of researchers describes their method of measuring customer equity as follows: "[we] first measure each customer's expected contributions toward offsetting the company's fixed costs over the expected life of that customer. Then we discount the expected contributions to a net present value at the company's target rate of return for marketing investments. Finally, we add together the discounted expected contributions of all current customers." Evident in their metric are the following important points about customer equity:

- It is the sum of the equity of all of a firm's customers.
- It summates the gross contribution of each customer, taking into account benefits as well as costs of serving a customer.
- It includes consideration of future revenues and variable costs from each customer.
- It is a time-discounted present value of future benefits to the firm.

It becomes evident that the customer equity concept when disaggregated to the individual customer level allows us to look at the revenues and costs of serving an individual customer. It helps answer the question, which customer should we serve? The ideal customer to the firm is the one that gives it the maximum long-term customer equity, which theoretically you want as a brand-loyal customer. However, as we will see in the next section, the converse is not true, because not all brandloyal customers provide maximum customer equity.

LIFETIME COSTS

An activity-based costing approach allows a firm to account for direct costs that the firm incurs in the relationship with a specific customer. Once again, with information technology it is possible, where it makes sense, to attribute marketing and operating costs to individual customers. To obtain the full benefit from CRM investments, it is important to track costs at the individual customer level as well. Costs include acquiring and remarketing to the customer over the lifetime of the customer. Costs also include value creation and delivery costs of serving the customer. Thus, the costs after acquisition include not only the costs of serving the customer, but also relationship maintenance and development costs such as the costs of cross-selling or upselling, called remarketing costs. Once again, as in Equation B, the costs related to the first purchase are separated from that of lifetime purchases so that the probability of repeat purchase is taken into account when calculating lifetime costs.

The indirect revenue of referrals from a loyal customer is an often overlooked aspect of customer equity. The typical CRM solution and database marketing approaches ignore the referral power of a customer in calculating the lifetime value of a customer. Most firms do not even capture this data, partly because it is difficult to obtain information when knowledge systems in a firm are not configured to obtain it. The other reason may be that firms are not proactively looking for referrals from their loyal customers in any systematic way.

How is the value of referrals from a customer calculated? To answer this question requires looking at the process and mechanics of how referrals work. Who provides a referral? Customers who are satisfied and who have a certain degree of loyalty are the ones who are likely to convey favourable messages about a firm and its products and services. A key piece of information needed here is what level of satisfaction a brand-loyal customer needs to have before being likely to refer a customer. The next obvious question is, who receives the referral? Customers are likely to convey this information to family, friends, and colleagues. However, not all who receive the referrals are appropriate customers for the firm. What proportion of the customers who received the referral are good candidates for the firm? Out of the ones that are appropriate for the firm, not all are likely to be suitably influenced by the referral to make the first purchase. Finally, if a purchase is actually made, what proportion of referred customers makes repeat purchases? Those that are moved to try the product may not all turn into loyal customers, but if they do, then their lifetime purchases add to the value of the customer making the initial referral. Equation C reflects these fractional outcomes in the mechanics of calculating referral value.

Maximizing the collective lifetime value of its customers should be the goal in managing customer relations. By increasing the number of customers *and* by increasing the lifetime value of each customer, firms can maximize their long-term profitability. From earlier study it becomes clear that to maximize the lifetime value of customers, you need to:

- Maximize lifetime revenues
- Maximize lifetime referrals
- Minimize lifetime costs

Potential customers in a target market are by definition not yet customers. They may or may not be aware of or inclined to purchase from the firm. Firms have to nurture customers' dispositions to the firm through a number of stages before they can benefit from the loyalty of those customers. The acquisition process of customers could begin at any of the different stages on the road to loyalty. Customers may or not be aware or have an understanding of the features and benefits of the product. If the knowledge of the product is favourable, customers may have a liking or preference for the product. Some customers may even have purchased the product but may not be repeat purchasers, may not be loyal to the product, or may have switched to a competitor. The right customers from any stage need to be moved toward a state of loyalty to the firm and its products. Can CRM technology be configured to capture information about the customer's stage in this process?

ATTRACTING CUSTOMERS

To maximize the total lifetime value of their customers, firms must proactively manage customer relationships. As seen proactive customer relationship management should seek customer appreciation from the heavy user and attract more interest from light users with better value bundles if they can contribute more in their lifetime value to the firm. This is in contrast to the firm that may have good customer service, for example, but in its reactive mode will leave the light user relatively indifferent to the firm and the heavy user susceptible to a competitor.

Most loyalty programs involve some kind of reward for the continued patronage of their customers. Referred to as frequency marketing, continuity programs, awards or points programs, or simply loyalty programs, the goal of these programs is to market and manage relationships with customers. First instituted by American Airlines in the 1970s to get around government regulation that prevented price competition, now many firms' programs attempt to solidify their relationships with its customers. The rewards or awards, as they are called, may come in the form of free products and services at the firm, or sometimes even free products from other firms. The smart firms impose restrictions on the use of these rewards, so that they are used to increase demand when and where needed. For example, the hospitality industry blocks out certain dates so that the promotions are targeted at different segments to entice customer utilization at low demand periods. The problem is that many of these programs are misguided in design and implementation. One obvious omission is evident when the lifetime calculus is compared to the criteria for the rewards.

The rewards focus on revenues for the most part. That

costs are taken into account is not clear at all. A recent *Harvard Business Review* article offers data that would be a surprise for managers who have not considered costs of serving the customer. Brand-loyal customers are not necessarily profitable customers. In their knowledge of their own value and indispensability to the firm, the brand-loyal customer could make costly demands of the firm. The firm, in doling out the goodies along with the product and other business favours, may actually be spending more than it recognizes as costs of serving that customer. The only criterion for these (brand) loyalty programs should be that they should maximize the customer equity for each customer, based on the calculus of lifetime value that we have discussed. To be meaningful and powerful in managing relationships with the right customers, these customer acquisition and loyalty programs must specify the following:

- Objectives of the programme
- Market and customer scope of the programme
- Value for customer scope of the programme
- Impact scope (costs, timing, impact on people, process, physical assets, other customers, publicity opportunities, etc.)

Chapter 8

Sociability in Catering Business

MULTI-LAYERED MORALS

Picnicking is eating in the open, and thus being seen by others. In interpreting the behaviour of people eating in the open, it is crucial to consider frames of interpretation and connotation, grounds for moral and legal judgements. Places where alcohol was being served, especially, proved prone to moralizing and comments.

Results of new research on everyday and festive eating and drinking yield an interesting variation on the debate, launched by Peter Burke in the 1970s, about the growing divergence between elite and popular cultures.

Differentiation is a key concept here, next to appropriation and demarcation.

In this book Christoph Guggenbiihl makes use of emic interpretations of elite groups in Switzerland.

He emphasizes that from the end of the eighteenth century a differentiation of catering businesses established itself. Guggenbiihl discusses the many functions of inns and shows how they were decanted into moral issues.

The moralizing gaze was also present in middle-class observations of the (eating) habits of French labourers in the nineteenth century, as Anne Lhuissier demonstrates. Oliver Haid adds to this debate the case of Meran, where the introduction of a beer culture in a wine region did not pass unnoticed.

Beat Kumin discusses gastronomic culture in early

modern inns. He questions the sharp cut-off before and after the 'modern' restaurant, with enhanced consumer choice, flexible dining times and menus with different dishes. Sources for early-modern Central Europe, in particular the Swiss republic of Bern and the principality of Bavaria, reveal variety, both in dining options and catering quality, a la carte selection options and table d'hote menus.

The major towns provided exquisite dining contexts. Kumin launches the thesis that what was crucial was not the invention of individualized service, but the creation of establishments exclusively dedicated to customer choice. Restaurants built on earlier practices but wrapped the eating experience in a special context, promoted an environment of leisurely and quality time consuming indulgence and bourgeois ostentation.

In contrast to inns, they gradually moved away from the table d'hote system and the offer of accommodation facilities.

BENEATH THE PAYING CUSTOMERS, THE CUSTOMS

There is a relation between eating out and having a home. Soup kitchens or charity meals in the open air, in city streets or squares, are not addressed here. People invited to a feast usually do not pay (but bring gifts and invite their hosts on another occasion). This is often embedded in what Pierre Bourdieu called an economy of symbolic goods.

Eszter Kisban emphasizes that in nineteenth- and early twentiethcentury Hungary wedding meals were the opposite of everyday meals, having their own rules and norms. Alexander Fenton describes how, in mid-twentieth-century Scotland, employers had to provide meals free of charge to children granted exemption from school attendance for helping in the harvest. In a number of chapters of this book, 'cash' is suspended. Food can be carried to the field but it is not paid for there; it is distributed. Paying at the picnic is also not customary, although, as noted above, pooling was organized or people brought their own food. Nevertheless, the carrying has its price: a time investment at home, an effort to keep and store food on the way (and money is more economical, it takes up less space, volume and weight).

We may discover a number of occasions of eating and drinking out where the food or drinks are not paid for by the diners themselves. Marc Jacobs explores a tip of the iceberg of eating food for free (but, on a closer look, with social strings attached). Reciprocity and unwritten rules are important topics in the history of semi-public wining and dining. Eating in public is also a way to communicate with other groups or individuals. The concept of the tournee generale, when someone pays for all the clientele at an inn, is not usual in a restaurant. It is possible to invite a whole group to a restaurant, on the occasion of a wedding or a funeral, but at the time a number of the normal rules change (no menu, no open access for outsiders).

Rituals involving eating out, or in front of other households, remind us of alternative needs, codes and expectations and bring to mind a broad range of possibilities and repertoires. Symbolic violence often accompanied rites of passage or forms of collective action, resulting in free meals or in conspicuous food consumption.

Cookery Writing and Culinary Zeniths

The perception, denotation, classification and representation of semi-public eating places may be explained by three intimately related phenomena, namely food, eaters and writers. 'Culinary zeniths', or places in certain periods that are generally viewed as successful with regard to food (in terms of gastronomy and sales), necessitate innovative supply, high demand and extensive discourse. An example of a successful culinary epoch would be the surrounding of the Parisian Jardin du Palais Royal in the 1800s, with great chefs, affluent eaters and culinary commentators.

Another example, suggesting that the gourmet connotation is not required, would be the global burger-culture in the 1990s, with the setting up of thousands of similar restaurants, a desirous public and extensive, albeit often hostile, writing (and action). The role of writing cultivating culinary zeniths has already been assessed, but it has primarily been limited to the culinary criticism of professionals like Grimod, Curnonsky or Gault and Millau.

'Culinary discourse' is understood here as the bundle of all written accounts dealing with food. The discourse actually contributed to the shaping of a new culture, for which it was a requirement. Such is a central point made by Karin Becker and Alan Warde in this book, and by Stephen Mennell, who attributes to gastronomic writing a cardinal place in the forming of 'public opinion'. All three authors stress the importance of writing with regard to the construction of gastronomy, gourmets and taste, and they explore further the information provided by culinary discourse.

Restaurants in All Forms, Dishes of All Tastes

Luxury food was, of course, not only prepared in fancy restaurants. Long before and after 1800, the rich and famous used professional cooks. Also, domestic caterers brought and served fine food at home. Against Kiimin's assertion, several authors suggest here and elsewhere that the emergence of the modern restaurant around 1800 marked an important qualitative leap in many respects.

First, restaurants were open luxurious places, in principle accessible to everyone (but totally different from the openness of a picnic!). Surely, the salle (or dining room) was a restricted area, only accessible to an elite. Their privacy was brought into the public: the ambiguity between private and public is nicely illustrated by the placing of individual ('own') tables in one room (opposed to the 'collective' table d'hote). Hence, our classification of 'semi-public' (or 'semi-private'). In this, Hans-Jiirgen Teuteberg stresses the emergence of the 'private' table, while Stephen Mennell addresses the issue of the 'bourgeois public sphere' of eating. Adel den Hartog, in turn, addresses a crucial condition of the restaurant's selective accessibility, namely technology. Among other things, he demonstrates the importance of subsequent types of lighting to create special effects, new gimmicks and prolonged opening hours.

Second, this 'private eating in public' entailed new rules

and prescriptions. The eater could be recognized as a gourmet or a connoisseur by other eaters, the staff and - when talked and written about - the wider public, only if certain (invisible, subtle, discrete) rules had been met. Such rules did change over time (again, here was a crucial role for writers in judging and creating 'good' and 'bad' taste, places and manners). Social codes in restaurants were used to exclude and include, but they could also be acquired, interpreted and applied for transgression. In a way, the temperance movement (restriction and self-control) may be seen, mutatis mutandis, as an example of severe but clear rules and prescriptions.

Third, a restaurant offered a choice of dishes, thus leaving the decision of what to eat to the individual - a theme addressed by Teuteberg and Warde. The change of the menu card reflected this innovation: before the breakthrough of the restaurant (and still today at weddings or private parties) a menu was mostly a card that informed the eater what he or she would eat, but with the restaurant a menu became a card that informed the eater about the choice and the price. It was a key element that allowed the marking of boundaries, the stressing of preferences, the construction of good taste, and distinguished the connoisseur from the parvenu.

Fourth, restaurants were enterprises, confronted with market rules of price setting, production cost, sale figures, workforce turnover, productivity and competitiveness. Equally, wage demands, unions, strikes, apprenticeship, working conditions and schooling were part of a restaurant's daily life. Such matters have hardly been studied, except perhaps for businesses and businessmen if they had names like Escoffier, Bocuse and other stars. Alain Drouard explores the covert world of (French) cooks, stressing their search for status, recognition and professionalism.

Fifth, individual and collective pleasures were also of great importance, with fine food being one element among many to enjoy alongside conversation, flirting, joking, laughing, etcetera. Hans-Jiirgen Teuteberg and Virginie Amilien stress this element of pleasure. The combination of these five features resulted in a semi-public place that soon became the locus of nineteenth-century bourgeois culture in the entire world. The plot between chefs, eaters and writers consisted of a non-stop search for distinction, innovation, novelties, surprise and amazement with new tastes, new dishes, new drinks, new tastes, new experiences, new forms, new chefs, new everything... Amilien demonstrates that this plot is still very active nowadays.

Fast, Faster and Fastest Food

Accessibility, choice, expanding supply and pleasure are characteristics of fancy and tourist restaurants; it may be argued that the same goes for fast-food restaurants. The accessibility of such restaurants is general, though, in 1970s Europe, for various reasons (such as relatively high prices and a type of eating experience and an image that were culturally unfamiliar) there was some reluctance to enter a Burger King. Today, these places are wide open to a diverse clientele, with particular focus on youngsters.

This kind of eating out provoked the most sturdy reactions related to pureness, authenticity, identity, taste, gourmandise, and so on, brought together in the slow-food movement and erupting sometimes in assaults on burger restaurants. The intensity of this movement may be linked to globalization processes that conflict with national agriculture, the local restaurant industry and 'authentic' taste. Here, globalization andregionalization come together.

Yet fast-food businesses have long existed and can hardly be viewed as a pure US import. John Burnett shows that fish-and-chip shops, charcutiers, tea-shops?, coffee and sandwich bars and food stalls of various sorts were set up in cities and places with crowds long before the coming of the US-style hamburger restaurant. Two chapters address the history of the snack restaurant. Derek Oddy surveys the British fastfood industry since the 1880s, linking its development to work, shopping and leisure, and thus underlining once more the mixture between coercion and pleasure.

He surveys the development of various forms of eating out in the fast way, seeing a period of transition in the 1970s, and ends up trying to define the fast-food eater in the UK in the 1990s. Anneke van Otterloo and Adri Albert de la Bruheze discuss the Dutch variant of the snack restaurant, with special emphasis on 'eating out of the wall'.

They detect a clear break around 1960, when the snacking started to reshape the traditional meal pattern. Van Otterloo and Albert de la Bruheze link these developments to broad social and economic changes, like the increase of purchasing power and leisure time, individualization and technological breakthroughs. They stress the implication of the food system, meaning that consumption of snacks cannot be studied without looking at production and distribution.

Diffusing Public Places of Discipline

It would be wrong to conceive the modern history of eating out solely from the angle of fancy and popular restaurants, taverns, snack bars or inns. If it is accepted that 'innovation' is an important feature of the modern eating-out industry, then innovative places were also to be found elsewhere.

Evidently, the luxury Parisian Cafe Riche had a totally different aura than a school canteen of the neighbouring arrondissement, but such canteens were also places of innovation with enormous influence. This opens up the wide field of eating (out) in schools, factories, army and police barracks (and indeed aeroplanes).

It is a mistake to think of these public-eating places wholly in terms of coercion, control and the sphere of grimy barracks. In many such communities, eating was a cherished moment to which special meaning was attributed.

It could be a source of joy when a particular dish was served, a special desert was put on the table, or an extra bottle of beer was allowed. However, discipline was more at stake. In this book Anne Lhuissier uses the investigation of the Le Play group into eating habits of workers in nineteenth-century France, which was conducted with a sheer moralizing end. The workers' lunch was frugal, prodigal or totally excessive (each time with a plausible reason). Control, however, was complete when workers (or students, policemen ...) were fed by the institution.

Up the Cost of a Meal

Of little-known origin, the term, unheard of in the sixteenth century, seems to have been used for the first time in the seventeenth century, more precisely by LaBruyere in Les Caracteres written between 1687 and 1688 and continued until 1694: If he has a picnic at home, he puts aside part of what was brought to him. This date is confirmed by Bloch and von Wartburg, who note the first appearance of the term in 1694 without giving a precise reference.

If we refer to the dictionaries of the period, the term appears neither in the Dictionnaire Universel by Furetiere (1690), although it is true that it precedes the first usage of the term by four years, nor in the Richelet (1719). The first time the word is mentioned is in the third edition of the Dictionnaire de I'Academie, which appeared in 1740. Therefore it was only officially introduced into the French language in the middle of the eighteenth century, when it is defined as an adverbial way of speaking that is only used in phrases such as a 'picnic supper', 'to have a picnic meal'. It is used to say, 'to have a meal where each person pays his or her share'.

That form fell out of use, pushed aside by its noun form, 'a picnic', which was used in the elliptical form of a meal in the picnic style, which later led to the simplified use of 'picnic'. How did this term come into being? Who invented it and what was the intention that could not be expressed in the existing vocabulary? None of these questions have any reliable answers. According to Bloch and von Wartburg, the expression comes from the wordpiquer (pick or to pinch/ swipe) but with the meaning of picorer (peck at or pinch food) (as in piquer les tables for someone who lives as a parasite) and from nique with the meaning moquerie ou chose sans valeur (mockery or something without value). According to them, the term, of French origin, was adopted throughout the rest of Europe, ending with 'picnic' in English in 1748 and picknick in German in 1753. That etymology is not universally accepted.

The Littre of 1869 and La Grande Encyclopedic of 1885 consider it of English origin, coming from 'to pick' (grasp) and 'nick' (an instant), and proposes the spelling pikenike, piquenique or picnic. One of the hypotheses proposed and later rejected by the Larousse universel of the nineteenth century (1866–79) shows the extent of the confusion: 'Pique-nique', says Larousse, 'aurait pu s'etre dit originairement d'un repas fait dans un village nomme "Pique-nique"' (Picnic could have come originally from a meal eaten in a village named 'Picnic'). He suggests another hypothesis, just as eccentric, according to which the term comes from a deformation of es beicktet nicht (sic), a phrase which a German traveller might have said after a satisfying meal eaten at a Parisian caterer's.

According to another hypothesis proposed by Larousse, it comes from the expression you offend me, I mock you this expression itself coming from the German nicken (to wink at someone in mockery) - an expression close in meaning to 'get back at someone'. The dominant idea here is both of revenge and a balancing out where 'each person will get his or her own'.

The term could then be used in all sorts of situations: one could love or hate 'in picnic', an expression used by Alphonse Karr, for example. Applied to a meal, the expression would therefore justify the definition 'repas ou chacun paye son ecot' (have a meal where each person pays his or her share), 'ou apporte son plat' (or brings their own dish), or a meal where no one owes anything to anyone else because participants all pay their share, paying in kind or with money. Payment could be of diverse nature: by paying money, by bringing one's own meal or by providing dishes for the group. In this way the term originated to express a practice that was not covered by any other term.

Necessity and an Exceptional Pleasure

First, it must be remembered that in spite of the importance and the prominence of the representations of which it is the object, starting from the last third of the nineteenth century, a meal eaten in the open air was a common practice during the pre-industrial era. There is frequent evidence of this practice ranging from an everyday necessity to an exceptional pleasure.

For field labourers, a meal eaten outdoors was a practice linked to their working conditions and to their meal break. According to the period, countries or regions, it goes by different names, but until the middle of the twentieth century nothing was written and no pictorial representation termed this meal eaten in a field a 'picnic'. These practices, born of necessity, were often seen in paintings or engravings of the seventeenth and eighteenth centuries, showing pastoral or romantic practices. Here, these images must be considered in the light of their depiction of a rural scene close to charitable Mother Nature. They would have the connotation of disgrace if they were situated in an urban setting where the act of 'eating outside', in the open air, was associated for a long time with a practice of the destitute and homeless.

However, both in town and in the countryside since the Renaissance, probably following Italian fashion, and later, when verdure and gardens were customary, dinners and light meals eaten out doors became part of the aristocratic way of life. Put aside hunting meals, which are a particular type of meal, and look at pictorial representations of outdoors meals in gardens of Eden where paradisiacal happiness reigns, such as in the works of Lancret or Vernet. Written evidence is abundant too. For example, we can read about the distinct taste of Catherine de Medici for improvised meals in the Tuileries Gardens. During the seventeenth century, elite Parisians liked to 'manger du jambon le matin aux Tuileries' (eat some ham in the morning in the Tuileries Gardens), where Anne of Austria herself 'joue la collation' (enjoys a light meal). Finally, what can be said about the revolutionary banquets organized in the streets, where everyone brought the food that was to be placed on the common table, and which led to the commemoration ceremony in France in the year 2000, with I'incroyablepique-nique (the unbelievable picnic) as a meal of fraternity?

Travelling was also a pretext for outdoor meals. During

King Charles IX 's tour of France (1564–6), ambassadors tell of the taste of Catherine de Medici for meals in the countryside: as she travelled, she was followed by two beasts of burden carrying 'fruits et confitures' (fruit and jam) and a horse laden with 'la malette ou Ton meet la collation de ladite dame allant par pays' (the chest that contained the meal of the lady going through the country). Other sovereigns too appreciated these improvised meals during their travels: Saint-Simon reports that for his journeys, Louis XIV required that his carriage be supplied with meat, pastries and fruit and that he would often stop on his way to 'diner sans sortir de son carrosse' (dine without getting out of his carriage).

Country Parties and Rustic Meals

During the nineteenth century several factors contributed to the practice of rustic meals: urbanization and industrialization, and at the same time the development of the hygienist trend, progress in the means of transportation, and new legislation on the duration of the working week. Some brief reminders. While the hygienist trend was gaining momentum in the name of public health, and leading to improvement in medicalization and sanitation in the country, representations of urban pathologies, previously based on demographic pressure, anarchical urbanization, deadly epidemics, pollution and physical and moral disorders (alcoholism and debauchery), were supplemented by a new imagery linked to the confusion caused by new technology and to an acceleration of the tempo of modern life. Surrounded by the pathologies of the modern world, including nervous fatigue, exhaustion and anemia, the hygienist trend favoured representations, extensively depicted since the seventeenth century, of nature as a healthy haven and a source of physical and moral rest.

At the same time the extension of the railway system and the rapid improvement of the speed of traveling, leading to a decrease in the price of railway tickets, prompted the growth of the social and geographical counter-urban phenomenon, the recreational day trip to the country called partie de campagne?

A lot of evidence shows an increasing trend of Sunday invasions in the summer of the outskirts of a city like Paris to a distance that varied between 4 and 50 km. In 1878, Zola mentioned 500,000 Parisians, almost a quarter of the population of the city, who 'par certains dimanches de soleil [...] prennent d'assaut les voitures et les wagons pour se rendre a la campagne' (on certain sunny Sundays [...] storm the carriages and trains to get out to the countryside). Finally, the progressive and concomitant compression of work time brought about the 'profanation' of the values of Sunday free time.

This day was traditionally dedicated to religion, but from then on it was (also) used for rest, recreation and family sociability, especially during days spent outside of the cities in a natural setting that became a place of regenerating leisure. In spite of the increase in these recreational day trips and the generalization of rustic meals, the term 'picnic' to describe these countryside meals remains absent from our sources. For example, it never appears in the guidebooks of the outskirts of Paris printed in the eighteenth and nineteenth centuries.

An outdoor Social Occasion or an Inexpensive Meal

Unlike its use in France, the term seems to have become a customary part of English as early as the beginning of the nineteenth century, used to designate a 'rustic meal' and not a way to share the expenses of a meal. In her Journal dated 1803, Dorothy Wordsworth uses the word to designate the custom of certain upper-class young people to eat on the grass on the banks of the Thames.

In his 1806 issue of L'Almanack des Gourmands, Grimod de la Reyniere subscribes to that definition of the term. Presenting the way to organize 'Parties de campagne erotiques et gourmandes' (erotic and gourmet countryside parties), he explains: 'Nous voulons trailer aujourd'hui de ces pique-niques a la campagne que Ton fait parfois entre amis pour tromper le temps, amuser son loisir' (Today we want to deal with picnics in the country that are sometimes organized among friends to pass the time, for entertainment in their leisure hours). The following model differs from the Anglo-Saxon: On forme une societe d'hommes et de femmes bien apparies, mais qui ne doivent pas exceder douze personnes. On nomme un pourvoyeur qui doit etre choisi connaisseur, intelligent, probe, sachant bien acheter [...]; on lui remet les fonds pour lesquels chacun s' est cotise par egale portion, selon les depenses qu'on a voulu faire, et on le charge de tous les details nutritifs (A group of wellmatched men and women is formed, but not more than twelve people. A purveyor is nominated who must be chosen because he is a connoisseur, intelligent, honest, knowing how to buy. [...] He is given the funds to which everyone has contributed in equal shares, according to the purchases desired, and he is charged with all the culinary details.)

A gastronomic meal follows, carried in large baskets: fattened chicken fricassee served in bread, galantine of beef tongue, galantine of rabbit, cold roast turkey, ham from Mayence or Bayonne, boned pullet pate surrounded by some quail or larks, timbale of partridge, frangipane tart, Savoy cake, salad, seasonal fruit, petit fours, biscuits, macaroons, jams, without forgetting, for the men, Swiss or Roquefort cheese, all of which is served with table wine, wine from Juranfon, wine from Champagne, from Malaga, from Frontingnan, liqueurs and coffee. After having specified the order of the dishes, because Grimod's picnic is not an informal meal, he concludes:

Success of Outings and Recognition of the Picnic as a Country Meal

By the end of the nineteenth century the spectacular growth of various means of transportation and the henceforth-recognized success of tourism enabled 'picnic' to gain social recognition and become a standard term used to designate the practice of eating a meal in the outdoors.

From now on, the term 'picnic' was to be associated with a meal eaten during a trip and just as often with one eaten during an outing or a country party. It was now considered a pleasurable meal and could even be a recreational objective.

In effect, the arrival, then the slow popularization, of the bicycle, which, a little later, was followed by the automobile, considerably reinforced the geographical displacement and transposition already induced by the railways, allowing a growing number of people to participate in various outings. At the end of the century, the new series of portable guidebooks that were printed reveal the substantial extension of the road network and the future of new transportation techniques. The Cyclo-guide Miran, the Guide Baroncelli or the Guide Michelin, written for cyclists 1/or motorists, indicate for the outskirts of Paris, for example, itineraries for day trips or longer, organized around natural or monumental, picturesque or imposing sites. At the same time, excursion company publications were becoming more numerous.

With the ease and increase in individual transportation, a pause for refreshment in the open air became for the 'sportsman' an indispensable part of the experience of a site. It added eating pleasure to the sensual and intellectual pleasures that came with the perception of a landscape from the point of view of its sounds, smells and sights. Integrated into the travelling experience, the word 'picnic' gradually took over as the generic term designating 'a packed lunch', formerly a necessity carried along during a trip but which has become a meal that is deliberately eaten in the outdoors, in order to savour the site visited, relish the pleasure of change that comes with travelling, nourish the physical activity enjoyed in nature, and reward the effort.

Chapter 9

The Hospitality and Tourism Industry

For people who think this is the industry for them, strongly suggest that they really think about their personality and be sure they can thrive (and survive) in the atmosphere. It truly is different from anything else.

It is critical that they work for a hotel while they are still in school, preferably in a few different hotels, and departments, so they can get a feel for it and know where they would be the happiest and most successful. The growth in the services sector of the worldwide economy has been phenomenal in the last 25 years. In the United States, services currently account for more than 75 percent of the gross domestic product (GDP), which is a popular measure of an economy's productivity. Similarly, on an international scale, services continue to account for an ever-increasing percentage of economic activity. Most new jobs are created in the service sector, and the growth in the hospitality and tourism industry is a major contributor. Until the mid-1980s, the emphasis within the marketing community was on products. Now services have surpassed products and have taken on a more important role in marketing.

Services Defined

Unlike products, which are tangible, services are usually intangible. A service is not a physical good; rather, it is the performance of an act or a deed. This performance often requires consumers to be present during the production or delivery of the service. Service industries, including hospitality and tourism, are actually selling consumers an experience. Services have been defined to "include all economic activities whose output is not a physical product or construction, is generally consumed at the time it is produced, and provides added value in forms (such as convenience, amusement, timeliness, comfort or health) that are essentially intangible concerns of its first purchaser."

THE NATURE OF SERVICES

Along with the growth in services, an appreciation for the ways in which services are different from products has developed. The traditional ways of marketing tangible products are not equally effective in services marketing. In many industries, marketing involves tangible manufactured products, such as automobiles, washing machines, and clothing, whereas service industries focus on intangible products such as travel and foodservice. However, before we can explore how services get successfully marketed, we need to examine the ways services differ from products. Lovelock and Wright have identified nine key differences.

No ownership by customers: A customer does not take ownership when purchasing a service. There is no transfer of assets.

Service products as intangible performers: The value of owning a high performance car or the latest computer lies in the physical characteristics of the product and to some extent the brand image it conveys. The value of purchasing services lies in the nature of the performance. For example, if you decide to celebrate a birthday or anniversary by dining at an expensive restaurant, the value lies in the way in which the service actors perform. When servers come to the table and present all the entrees simultaneously, the choreographed presentation appears in the same manner as a choreographed play or performance.

RELATIONSHIP MARKETING

All progressive companies devote marketing resources to

attract and retain new customers. Relationship marketing is based on the proposition that it is less expensive to keep the customers you already have than to acquire new customers. It is shortsighted to think that merely attracting new customers will keep the business headed in a successful direction. Rather, an equal amount of attention and resources should be devoted to keeping the customer base that already exists. In times of slow market growth and increasing competition, it will be less expensive to maintain an existing customer base than to seek new customers.

Relationship marketing involves attracting, developing, and retaining customer relationships. This long-term view toward the customer must be seen as being equal in importance to attracting new customers. Many firms make the mistake of focusing on new customers at the expense of existing customers, and the level of service quality diminishes. For example, hotel sales managers are expected to develop new accounts with corporate and association groups.

INTERNAL MARKETING

In addition to focusing efforts on consumers, firms can achieve higher levels of service quality by marketing to their employees. Internal marketing encompasses all activities used by a firm in an effort to improve the marketing effectiveness of its employees.

Efforts should be made to communicate with all employees, especially those in boundary spanning roles who come in contact with customers. The ability to deliver consistent, high-quality service depends on the organization's ability to recruit, train, retain, and motivate dedicated service personnel. First, service firms need to select and hire employees who are willing and able to provide high-quality service. There are many people in the job market, and firms need to create attractive positions that appeal to highly motivated individuals.

A range of potential service exists that an employee can provide from the minimum necessary to retain the position and not be penalized to the maximum possible service. This variability in the level of possible service is referred to as discretionary effort. For example, if an airline passenger leaves a carry-on item on a flight, the airline's personnel have some discretion as to the level of service they will provide. They can take their time and forward the item to the traveller's next destination, or they can try to deliver it to the traveler before he or she boards the next plane or leaves the airport. Second, service firms should provide employees with adequate training so they possess the skills that are required in performing their job tasks.

Improving Customer Service and Customer Satisfaction

Improving customer service should be a top priority of all managers working in the hospitality and tourism industry. Customer satisfaction occurs when a firm's service, as perceived by customers, meets or exceeds expectations. Firms that can consistently meet or exceed customer expectations will develop good reputations and often good quality images. When we travel, we encounter service providers in hotels and restaurants who provide exceptional service. This type and consistency of service does not happen by accident; it begins with a commitment by management to make it that way. Conversely, when the opposite occurs, the finger should be pointed at management as well.

- *Define your standards of quality service with measurable indicators:* Before you can evaluate the level of service provided by employees within your organization, you must establish the standards by which they will be judged.

  These standards, or benchmarks, should be observable and measurable. For example, it might be reasonable to expect front desk agents to answer the telephone within four rings or room service to deliver meals within 30 minutes of when the order was received. Once these standards are developed, they must be communicated to all personnel. It remains crucial that standards be clearly defined before any plans are developed to improve the level of service. Martin suggests two major dimensions to define quality service: the procedural dimension and the convivial dimension. The procedural dimension includes incremental flow of service, timeliness, accommodating consumer needs, anticipating consumer needs before they occur or are requested by the consumer, communicating in a clear and concise manner, customer satisfaction. obtaining consumer feedback, and coordinating through proper supervision. The convivial dimension includes displaying a positive attitude and body language, using the guest's name as a means of delivering personal attention, attending to the guest on a personal basis, providing guidance to guests who are indecisive, and solving problems that arise.

- *Assess your current situation*: As in any continuous improvement programme, before you move forward, you must determine your current position. This can be done by objectively assessing the level of service currently provided within the organization; this involves conducting an audit of the services provided by service personnel within the organization. As a result of the audit, the strengths and weaknesses of the firm can be determined; this will provide a means of building on the aspects of service that are positive and improving the areas that are deficient. Audits can be conducted using mystery shoppers, or corporations may use staff members to audit the performance of units within the company.
- *Develop effective service improvement strategies:* This must be accomplished through well-planned and thorough training of service providers. Attention must be paid to identifying objectives for the training and providing specific instructions and clear descriptions of the expected outcome (s) of the training.
- *Initiate your solutions carefully:* As with any plan, implementation is the most critical stage. You should proceed with caution, taking steps incrementally

rather than all at once. You should build on small successes, rather than trying to accomplish too much too soon.

- *Provide feedback, recognition, and rewards:* Positive feedback must be provided if the change in behaviour continues. A reward structure must be provided that will maintain the level of interest and enthusiasm among the service providers throughout their careers. This represents a major challenge for management, but one that is well worth the effort. Finally, management must continually evaluate the performance of its employees and make the appropriate changes. Over time, customers' expectations of service firms change, and competitive firms may increase the level of service that is considered the standard in an industry. Therefore, firms must constantly reassess their strategies and redefine their service standards. Service performance and customer satisfaction should be measured and evaluated using benchmarks established during previous periods. Also, direct comparisons with the performance of firms considered industry leaders are an excellent way to establish goals for future improvement.

SERVICE FAILURES

The timeliness and form of response by service providers to service failures will have a direct impact on customer satisfaction and quality perceptions.

Service failures are assigned to one of three major categories:

- Responses to service delivery system failures,
- Responses to customer needs and requests, and
- Unprompted and unsolicited employee actions.

Recovery Strategies

When customers complain, firms are presented with the opportunity to recover from service failures. Recovery strategies, and actions occur when a firm's reaction to a service failure results in customer satisfaction and goodwill. In fact, customers who are involved in successful service recoveries often demonstrate higher levels of satisfaction than customers who do not report service failures or complain. The following list describes popular service recovery strategies:

Cost/benefit analysis: Service firms should compare the costs of losing customers and obtaining new customers with the benefits of keeping existing customers. Most firms place a high value on retaining customers. However, some guests take advantage of satisfaction guarantees and complain on every occasion. Many hotel chains, such as Doubletree, maintain a database on complaints and will flag chronic complainers.

Actively encourage complaints: It is better to know when customers are not satisfied so that action can be taken to rectify the situation. It is important to note that while unhappy customers may not complain to service firms, they will often complain to their family and friends. Hospitality and tourism firms use comment cards and toll-free numbers to encourage customers to provide feedback. Also, service personnel are trained to ask customers whether everything was satisfactory.

Anticipate the need for recovery: Service firms should "blueprint" the service delivery process and determine the moments of truth, or critical incidents, where customers interact with employees. The process can be designed to avoid failures, but recovery plans should be established for use in the event that a failure occurs.

Respond quickly: The timelier the response in the event of a service failure, the more likely that recovery efforts will be successful. Once a customer leaves a service establishment, the likelihood of a successful recovery falls dramatically. Based on this principle, firms such as Marriott International provide service hotlines at each hotel to help resolve problems quickly. Managers and associates know that the speed with which they respond is often as critical as what the final resolution becomes.

Train employees: Employees should be informed of the critical incidents and provided with potential strategies for recovery. For example, some hotel training programmes use videotaped scenarios of service failures to show employees potential problems and the appropriate solutions. *Empower the front line:* In many cases, a successful recovery will hinge on a frontline employee's ability to take timely action and make a decision. Firms should empower employees to handle service failures at the time they occur, within certain limits.

For example, Ritz-Carlton allows its employees to spend up to $1,000 to take care of dissatisfied customers. One of the classic examples of a service failure involved Northwest Airlines during a major winter storm at the Detroit airport. Unfortunately, due to the heavy snow, many outbound flights were canceled, and no gates were available for unloading passengers from the inbound flights. This traffic jam left many passengers stranded as the airplanes sat on the taxiways for as long as eight hours. Northwest's inability to provide the passengers with information or a solution resulted in hundreds of unhappy passengers and a class action lawsuit. Having delayed flights and a shortage of gates is not a new phenomenon at airports in climates such as Detroit's, and Northwest Airlines should have had a viable service recovery programme in place that could have lessened the severity of the problem.

Techniques to Assess Customer Satisfaction

One of the critical components of a firm's commitment to customer satisfaction is feedback that provides an assessment of the firm's performance. Then benchmarks can be established and future progress can be evaluated. Also, these measures can be used to reward service personnel in a way that stays consistent with a firm's customer satisfaction goals. The following section describes the most common techniques used by firms to assess customer satisfaction.

Spoken Comments And Complaints

Listening to consumer comments and complaints remains the most straightforward way to evaluate customer satisfaction. Service firms should set up formal systems that encourage customer and employee feedback regarding service experiences. Management should not overlook the value of the information obtained by boundary-spanning personnel through their normal contact with customers. One of the most recent approaches is providing toll-free numbers so that customers can call to voice complaints.

Surveys and Comment Cards

Many hospitality and tourism firms leave comment cards in guest rooms, on tables in restaurants, and at other points of contact so that they can obtain feedback. One of the problems associated with this method is the lack of representation. The response rate is small, and it tends to be biased toward those who are most upset and chronic complainers. Larger operations will conduct surveys through the corporate offices by either telephone or mail. Surveys will normally be more representative than comment cards and provide more detailed information. These types of surveys also provide for a more representative sample of customers.

Number of Repeat Customers

Service firms can gauge customer satisfaction by keeping track of repeat business. Higher levels of satisfaction would be associated with higher percentages of repeat customers. This models an unobtrusive method of assessing customer satisfaction, but it does not provide much detail.

Trends in Sales and Market Share

Another way to evaluate customer satisfaction without direct contact with customers is to examine the firm's internal sales records. Comparisons can be made on a month-to-month basis and with the same period of the previous year. Higher levels of satisfaction would be associated with increases in sales. However, firms should be careful with this method because there are many possible explanations for increases in sales. For example, the firm may have launched a new advertising campaign, a competitor may be renovating or going out of business, or the firm may have decreased its prices. In addition to examining sales records, firms should also look at market share. This measure considers sales in relation to the competition, which is a more accurate assessment of improved market performance. However, there could also be other explanations for changes in market share besides customer satisfaction.

SERVICE TRENDS AFFECTING THE HOSPITALITY AND TOURISM INDUSTRY

Identifying trends within any business is one of the keys to success. Being in a position to identify what is occurring and what is likely to occur in the future remains very important. As discussed earlier, when studying trends in a broad sense, one should examine five major areas: the competitive environment, the economic environment, the political and legal environment, the social environment, and the technological environment. Several issues and trends are critical to understanding hospitality and tourism marketing. They help put into proper perspective what occurs within the competitive marketplace. Three trends that are having an impact on the hospitality industry and will continue to do so are shrinking customer loyalty, increasing customer sophistication, and increasing emphasis on the needs of individual customers.

SHRINKING CUSTOMER LOYALTY

Advertising and promotion for the hospitality and tourism industry's product-service mix have traditionally focused on the product, the services service trends affecting the hospitality and tourism industry provided, and the physical plant or atmosphere in which the customer enjoys the product-service mix. Today, many hospitality and tourism firms focus their promotions on price; that is, heavy price competition exists along with a good deal of discounting. Unfortunately, price discounting exists as a short-term strategy that seldom builds brand loyalty. Consumers often shop around for the best deal and are loyal only to organizations that give them a consistently superior one.

Chapter 10

Role of HR Professionals in Hotel Industry

Most Fortune 1000 employees have been affected by the widespread proliferation of work teams. This holds true also for the millions of employees and managers who work outside the Fortune 1000. Recent evidence about the growth in work teams reinforces the notion that they have become a way of life in many organizations. For example, Osterman (1994) found that over 50 percent of the seven hundred firms he studied were using teams and that over 40 percent had more than half of their employees working in teams. As the use of teams continues to grow, human resource (HR) professionals need more knowledge about teams in general and, more specifically, information about the HR practices that enhance team performance. Human resources play a critical role in developing and implementing organizational strategies and structures. Successful HR professionals will be those who can align their organizational HR practices with the unique demands of team-based organizational structures.

What Teams Are, How Teams Contribute, and When to Use Them

In general, a work team can be defined as a group of individuals working interdependently to solve problems or accomplish tasks. However, a single definition is not sufficient to capture the key differences that exist between the various types of teams being used in organizations. A number of key differences between these types of teams will determine the efficacy of HR practices designed to enhance their effectiveness. For example, compensation structures are normally altered for self-managing work teams to include team-based rewards to encourage cooperation between members and motivate them to reach team goals. Because self-managing members are working on permanent teams, the effort and expense involved in changing compensation structures is often justified. However, in more temporary teams, such as cross-functional or problem solving teams, other types of HR policy changes (for example, altering an evaluation system to include team behaviors) may be more appropriate to encourage positive behaviours.

Our point here is not to review all of the appropriate HR policies for each type of team but rather to acknowledge that our use of the term work team includes several different types of teams.

Work Structure

A second domain of assumptions concerns the structure of work. Traditional work groups were generally formed around common technical or functional skills and areas of expertise (for example, accounting, finance, or production). In recent years, it has become apparent that organizing work around a process (for example, new product development) rather than around a specific task or function is more effective. Doing so often requires extending team members' task skills. Multi skilled teamwork involves teams made up of individuals with multiple and overlapping skills that are deployed around the performance of a whole task, which represents a significant part of a larger work flow. Members are multi skilled so that work can be flexibly allocated among them.

In organizing work around processes, organizational boundaries must often be renegotiated. Increasingly, work teams include external customers and suppliers. For example, General Electric Medical Systems invites representatives from leading health maintenance organizations (HMOs) to serve on its sales and service teams. The American Red Cross has members of communities serving on key committees that set organizational objectives. Eastman Kodak allies itself with key competitors to form market segment task forces. These types of work structures require a whole new notion of collaboration—collaboration with external constituencies. Those who were previously viewed as "them" are now viewed as "us."

Recruitment and Selection

Working effectively in a team requires a particular set of knowledge, skills, and abilities (KSAs) that were not as critical in traditional organizations. Proficiency is needed in at least five areas: conflict resolution, collaborative problem solving, communication, goal setting and performance management, and planning and task coordination. During recruitment, organizations aspiring to create a workforce of effective team members should clearly communicate the importance of these proficiencies. Doing so provides a realistic job preview and can therefore help to reduce turnover. Recruiting individuals who prefer these activities also makes sense because team members' preferences for teamwork are related to team effectiveness.

Task Design

The second set of practices that must be modified relate to task design. Effective teams are designed around the tasks they perform. Two key considerations are that teams should be relatively self contained and handle many aspects of their own functioning. First, teams should be collectively responsible for an identifiable and substantial part of the work of the organization. To the extent possible, support services should be included in the team so that it has the resources necessary to accomplish its goals. Members should be multi skilled and dedicated to the team so that they do not have to split priorities. Finally, the team should report as a unit so that members do not have conflicting directions from different managers.

Second, the team should be responsible for many aspects

of its own functioning. For example, it should be able to determine how to apply the team's resources, strategies for completion of work, and quality monitoring. It should also be responsible for working with internal and external customers. Finally, part of the team's task should be performance evaluation. Whenever appropriate skill levels and task conditions exist, team members should be involved in reviewing their own performance and determining their own rewards.

LESSONS FROM GLOBAL HUMAN RESOURCE PRACTICES IN HOTELS

Given the substantial issues of diversity that all organizations are confronting today, the successful human resource (HR) practitioner needs a conceptual framework to deal with them in both global and single-country business environments. Diversity should be viewed not as a confounding factor but rather as a source of energy that drives change and growth. We believe that diversity can no longer be discussed only from a single-country perspective. Workforces in all countries are be- coming more diverse, not just in gender, age, and race but also in culture. The workforce of any industrialized or developing nation will increasingly be a mix of domestic and international ethnicities. To deal with this challenge, the HR practitioner of tomorrow will have to understand the impact of cultural or global diversity, as well as of country-specific diversity, on the effectiveness of the organization and the workforce.

HOSPITALITY AND LOADGING

Organizing, the process of structuring human and physical resources in order to accomplish organizational objectives, involves dividing tasks into jobs, specifying the appropriate department for each job, determining the optimum number of jobs in each department, and delegating authority within and among departments. One of the most critical challenges facing lodging managers today is the development of a responsive organizational structure that is committed to quality. The framework of jobs and departments that make up any organization must be directed toward achieving the organization's objectives. In other words, the structure of a lodging business must be consistent with its strategy. Managers give structure to a hotel and lodging through job specialization, organization, and establishment of patterns of authority and span of control.

PATTERNS OF AUTHORITY

The delegation of authority creates a chain of command, the formal channel that defines the lines of authority from the top to the bottom of an organization. The chain of command consists of a series of relationships from the highest position in the organization to the lowest. The chain of command specifies a clear reporting relationship for each person in the organization and should be followed in both downward and upward communication. Following the chain of command enables each new employee, no matter what his or her position, to know exactly for whom and to whom he or she is responsible.

When designing an organizational structure, managers must consider the distribution of authority. Defined simply, authority is the organizationally sanctioned right to make a decision. Authority can be distributed throughout an organization or held in the hands of a few select employees. Decentralization is the process of distributing authority throughout an organization. In a decentralized organization, an organization member has the right to make a decision without obtaining approval from a higher-level manager. Centralization is the retention of decision-making authority by a high-level manager. Traditionally, hotel and lodging management has been very centralized, probably due to its roots in small, owner-operated lodging. In recent years, as the hotel and lodging industry has expanded, decentralization has become a more frequent style of operation.

THE FUTURE ORGANIZATION OF HOTELS

As new business practices are evolving as fast as our

technologies, resistance to change has become a primary cause of business failure. The future success of a hotel will be driven in large part by the ability to foresee and capitalize on change. As we go through global transitions, the successful hotel will examine the key factors that will not only define success but also the ability to survive in coming years. These key organizational trends must be acknowledged by the successful hotel organization: visionary leadership, globalization, diversity, flexibility, flat structure, customer focus, zero defects, network orientation, and being in the information fast lane.

The organization must be able to respond to increasingly globalized sales, the movement to maintaining sales offices in many countries and hotel properties across the globe, and an increasingly globalized labor market. Intercontinental Hotels Group recently introduced a new organization structure to more efficiently use regional and global resources to drive higher levels of innovation, customer focus, and revenues.

The Hotel Staffing System

Staffing, which is one of a hotel's most important management functions, is an ongoing challenge because of the high rate of employee and manager turnover. Full-service hotels can experience annual turnover rates in excess of 100 percent in certain employee classifications. Some managers consider an annual employee turnover rate of 33 percent low.

Career Paths and Opportunities

If you complete your course of study and graduate with a bachelor of science degree in hotel management, most likely you will enter the business at the managerial level. Along the way you will have learned that a successful manager provides clear direction, encourages open communication, coaches and supports people, provides objective recognition, establishes ongoing controls, follows up and gives subordinates feedback, selects the right people to staff the organization, understands the financial implications of decisions, encourages innovation and new ideas, gives subordinates clear-cut decisions when needed, and consistently demonstrates a high level of integrity. There are three levels of management careers in the hotel or lodging business: first-line, middle, and top. First-line refers to those who have day-to-day contact with the guests and clients of a lodging business.

The first-line manager oversees the work of the supervisors and line employees. In a hotel or lodging business, first-line positions may include assistant manager of housekeeping, assistant front office manager, and assistant restaurant manager. First-line managers are responsible for a hotel's basic work, such as checking guests in and out, making up the guests' rooms, and preparing and serving the meals. First-line managers are in daily or near-daily contact with line employees. Middle management of most hotel or lodging businesses includes the department manager, general manager, and any position between those levels.

The following is one of the many paths your career might follow:

- Assistant manager of the reservations department
- Reservations department manager
- Rooms department manager
- Resident manager
- General manager
- Regional manager

In a full-service hotel or lodging business, the movement from entry-level position to general manager might encompass 15 years. Career advancement in a limited-service hotel or lodging business can occur more rapidly. A career in a limited-service hotel or lodging establishment might commence at the assistant general manager level, with movement to general manager within three years and to district or regional manager within five to eight years. This accelerated pace is due in large part to the more restricted range of services the manager must master before advancing.

Chapter 11

Managing Working Capital

WORKING CAPITAL CYCLE

Cash flows in a cycle into, around and out of a business. It is the business's life blood and every manager's primary task is to help keep it flowing and to use the cashflow to generate profits. If a business is operating profitably, then it should, in theory, generate cash surpluses.

If it doesn't generate surpluses, the business will eventually run out of cash and expire. The faster a business expands, the more cash it will need for working capital and investment. The cheapest and best sources of cash exist as working capital right within business. Good management of working capital will generate cash will help improve profits and reduce risks. Bear in mind that the cost of providing credit to customers and holding stocks can represent a substantial proportion of a firm's total profits.

There are two elements in the business cycle that absorb cash - Inventory (stocks and work-in-progress) and Receivables (debtors owing you money). The main sources of cash are Payables (your creditors) and Equity and Loans. Each component of working capital (namely inventory, receivables and payables) has two dimensions time and money.

When it comes to managing working capital - time is money. If you can get money to move faster around the cycle (e.g. collect monies due from debtors more quickly) or reduce the amount of money tied up (e.g. reduce inventory levels relative to sales), the business will generate more cash or it will need to borrow less money to fund working capital. As a consequence, you could reduce the cost of bank interest or you'll have additional *free* money available to support additional sales growth or investment. Similarly, if you can negotiate improved terms with suppliers e.g. get longer credit or an increased credit limit, you effectively create *free* finance to help fund future sales.

- Collect receivables (debtors) faster
- You release cash from the cycle
- Collect receivables (debtors) slower
- Your receivables soak up cash
- Get better credit (in terms of duration or amount) from suppliers
- You increase your cash resources
- Shift inventory (stocks) faster
- You free up cash
- Move inventory (stocks) slower
- You consume more cash

It can be tempting to pay cash, if available, for fixed assets e.g. computers, plant, vehicles etc. If you do pay cash, remember that this is now longer available for working capital. Therefore, if cash is tight, consider other ways of financing capital investment - loans, equity, leasing etc. Similarly, if you pay dividends or increase drawings, these are cash outflows and, like water flowing down a plug hole, they remove liquidity from the business. More businesses fail for lack of cash than for want of profit.

Sources of Additional Working Capital

Sources of additional working capital include the following:

- Existing cash reserves
- Profits (when you secure it as cash !)
- Payables (credit from suppliers)
- New equity or loans from shareholders
- Bank overdrafts or lines of credit
- Long-term loans

If you have insufficient working capital and try to increase sales, you can easily over-stretch the financial resources of the business. This is called overtrading.

Early warning signs include:

- Pressure on existing cash
- Exceptional cash generating activities e.g. offering high discounts for early cash payment
- Bank overdraft exceeds authorized limit
- Seeking greater overdrafts or lines of credit
- Part-paying suppliers or other creditors
- Paying bills in cash to secure additional supplies
- Management pre-occupation with *surviving* rather than managing
- Frequent short-term emergency requests to the bank (to help pay wages, pending receipt of a cheque).

HANDLING RECEIVABLES (DEBTORS)

Cashflow can be significantly enhanced if the amounts owing to a business are collected faster. Every business needs to know who owes them money how much is owed how long it is owing for what it is owed.

Late Payments Erode Profits and can Lead to Bad Debts

Slow payment has a crippling effect on business, in particular on small businesses who can least afford it. If you don't manage debtors, they will begin to manage your business as you will gradually lose control due to reduced cashflow and, of course, you could experience an increased incidence of bad debt. The following measures will help manage your debtors:

- Have the right mental attitude to the control of credit and make sure that it gets the priority it deserves.
- Establish clear credit practices as a matter of company policy.
- Make sure that these practices are clearly understood by staff, suppliers and customers.
- Be professional when accepting new accounts, and especially larger ones.
- Check out each customer thoroughly before you offer

credit. Use credit agencies, bank references, industry sources etc.

- Establish credit limits for each customer... and stick to them.
- Continuously review these limits when you suspect tough times are coming or if operating in a volatile sector.
- Keep very close to your larger customers.
- Invoice promptly and clearly.
- Consider charging penalties on overdue accounts.
- Consider accepting credit / debit cards as a payment option.
- Monitor your debtor balances and ageing schedules, and don't let any debts get too large or too old.

MANAGING PAYABLES (CREDITORS)

Creditors are a vital part of effective cash management and should be managed carefully to enhance the cash position. Purchasing initiates cash outflows and an over-zealous purchasing function can create liquidity problems.

Consider the following:

- Who authorizes purchasing in your company - is it tightly managed or spread among a number of (junior) people?
- Are purchase quantities geared to demand forecasts?
- Do you use order quantities which take account of stock-holding and purchasing costs?
- Do you know the cost to the company of carrying stock ?
- Do you have alternative sources of supply ? If not, get quotes from major suppliers and shop around for the best discounts, credit terms, and reduce dependence on a single supplier.
- How many of your suppliers have a returns policy ?
- Are you in a position to pass on cost increases quickly through price increases to your customers ?
- If a supplier of goods or services lets you down can you charge back the cost of the delay ?

- Can you arrange (with confidence !) to have delivery of supplies staggered or on a just-in-time basis ?

INVENTORY MANAGEMENT

Managing inventory is a juggling act. Excessive stocks can place a heavy burden on the cash resources of a business. Insufficient stocks can result in lost sales, delays for customers etc. The key is to know how quickly your overall stock is moving or, put another way, how long each item of stock sit on shelves before being sold. Obviously, average stock-holding periods will be influenced by the nature of the business. For example, a fresh vegetable shop might turn over its entire stock every few days while a motor factor would be much slower as it may carry a wide range of rarely-used spare parts in case somebody needs them.

The key issue for a business is to identify the fast and slow stock movers with the objectives of establishing optimum stock levels for each category and, thereby, minimize the cash tied up in stocks. Factors to be considered when determining optimum stock levels include:

- What are the projected sales of each product?
- How widely available are raw materials, components etc.?
- How long does it take for delivery by suppliers?
- Can you remove slow movers from your product range without compromising best sellers?

Cash and Marketable Securities Management

- Recognize the importance of managing cash and marketable securities.
- Match motives for holding cash with appropriate cash management decisions.
- Determine criteria for selecting marketable securities.
- Choose the proper method of managing cash inflows and outflows, given a scenario.

MANAGING DEBTORS

Many debts in the day today business of hotel that are

left in 'limbo' there is a genuine need to deal with your creditors before the situation gets beyond your control. This is especially so if you have worthwhile assets. In such circumstances, you either need to deal with your creditors yourself, or get someone to do it for you. The 'art' of negotiating with your creditors is one that does not come easy. Debt Management companies deal with many debtor/creditor scenarios every day, and are experienced and knowledgeable to deal with any mixture of debts:

- Credit Cards
- Bank Loans
- Car Finance
- Mortgage/Rent Arrears
- Home Shopping
- Hire Purchase
- And any number of debts where creditors exist

DEBT

Debt is that which is owed; usually referencing assets owed, but the term can cover other obligations. In the case of assets, debt is a means of using future purchasing power in the present before a summation has been earned. Some companies and corporations use debt as a part of their overall corporate finance strategy. A debt is created when a creditor agrees to loan a sum of assets to a debtor. In modern society, debt is usually granted with expected repayment; in many cases, plus interest. Historically, debt was responsible for the creation of indentured servants.

CREDITOR

A creditor is a party (e.g. person, organization, company, or government) that claims that a second party owes the first party some properties or services. The first party, in general, has provided some property or service to the second party under the assumption (usually enforced by contract) that the second party will return an equivalent property or service. The first party is frequently called a lender, and the second party is frequently called a debtor or borrower.

In other words, your creditors are people to whom you owe money. The term creditor is frequently used in the financial world, especially in reference to short term loans, long term bonds, and mortgages. The term creditor derives from the notion of credit. In modern America, credit refers to a rating which indicates the ability of a borrower and likelihood to pay back his or her loan. In earlier times, credit also referred to reputation or trustworthiness.

Credit as a financial term, used in such terms as credit card, refers to the granting of a loan and the creation of debt. Any movement of financial capital is normally quite dependent on credit, which in turn is dependent on the reputation or creditworthiness of the entity which takes responsibility for the funds.

A similar usage is in commercial trade, where *credit* is used to refer to the approval for delayed payments for goods purchased. Sometimes if a person has financial instability or difficulty, credit is not granted. Companies frequently offer credit to their customers as part of the terms of a purchase agreement. Organizations that offer credit to their customers frequently employ a credit manager.

STOCK

In financial markets, stock is the capital raised by a corporation through the issuance and distribution of shares. A person or organisation which holds at least a partial share of stocks is called a shareholder. The aggregate value of a corporation's issued shares is its market capitalization. In the United Kingdom and Australia, the term *share* is used the same way, but *stocks* there refer to either a completely different financial instrument, the bond, or more widely to all kinds of marketable securities.

STOCK DERIVATIVES

A stock derivative is any financial claim which has a value that is dependent on the price of the underlying stock. Futures and options are the main types of derivatives on stocks. The underlying security may be a stock index or an individual firm's stock, e.g. single-stock futures. Stock futures are contracts where the buyer, or long, takes on the obligation to buy on the contract maturity date, and the seller, or short takes on the obligation to sell. Stock index futures are generally not delivered in the usual manner, but by cash settlement.

SHAREHOLDER

A shareholder or *stockholder* is an individual or company (including a corporation) that legally owns one or more shares of stock in a joint stock company. Companies listed at the stock market strive to enhance shareholder value. Stockholders are granted special privileges depending on the class of stock, including the right to vote (usually one vote per share owned) on matters such as elections to the board of directors, the right to share in distributions of the company's income, the right to purchase new shares issued by the company, and the right to a company's assets during a liquidation of the company. However, stockholder's rights to a company's assets are subordinate to the rights of the company's creditors. This means that stockholders typically receive nothing if a company is liquidated after bankruptcy (if the company had had enough to pay its creditors, it would not have entered bankruptcy), although a stock may have value after a bankruptcy if there is the possibility that the debts of the company will be restructured.

Stockholders or shareholders are considered by some to be a partial subset of stakeholders, which may include anyone who has a direct or indirect equity interest in the business entity or someone with even a non-pecuniary interest in a non-profit organization. Thus it might be common to call volunteer contributors to an association stakeholders, even though they are not shareholders.

Although directors and officers of a company are bound by fiduciary duties to act in the best interest of the shareholders, the shareholders themselves normally do not have such duties towards each other. However, in a few unusual cases, some courts have been willing to imply such a duty between shareholders. For example, in California, majority shareholders of closely held corporations have a duty to not destroy the value of the shares held by minority shareholders. The largest shareholders (in terms of percentages of companies owned) are often mutual funds, and especially passively managed exchange-traded funds.

TRADING

A stock exchange is an organization that provides a marketplace (either physical or virtual) for trading shares, where investors (represented by stock brokers) may buy and sell shares in a wide range of companies. A given company will usually list its shares by meeting and maintaining the listing requirements of a particular stock exchange. In the United States, through the inter-market quotation system, stocks listed on one exchange can also be bought or sold on several other exchanges, including relatively new internet-only exchanges. Stocks are broadly grouped into NYSE-listed and NASDAQ-listed stocks. Exchanges where NYSE-listed stocks may be bought are generally not the same group as the exchanges where NASDAQ-listed stocks may be bought. Many large foreign companies choose to list on a U.S. exchange as well as an exchange in their home country in order to broaden their investor base. These shares are called American Depository Receipts (ADRs) – or, in the case of companies such as UBS and Daimler Chrysler – "foreign ordinary shares."

TREASURY STOCK

In the United Kingdom, treasury stocks refer to government bonds or gilts. The British equivalent of *treasury stock* as used in the United States is treasury share. In the United States, a treasury stock or reacquired stock is stock which is bought back by the issuing hotel.

It reduces the number of outstanding stocks on the open market ("open market" including insiders' holdings). On the balance sheet, treasury stock is listed under shareholder equity as a negative number.

Stock repurchases are often used as a tax-efficient method to put cash into shareholders' hands, rather than pay dividends. Sometimes, companies do this when they feel that their stock is undervalued on the open market. Other times, companies do this to provide a "bonus" or incentive compensation plan for employees. Rather than receive cash, recipients receive an asset that might appreciate in value faster than cash saved in a bank account.

Limitations of treasury stock include:

Treasury stock does not pay a dividend

Treasury stock has no voting rights

Total treasury stock can not exceed the maximum proportion of total capitalization specified by law in the relevant country

MANAGING STOCKS

Stock portfolio management is often left to professionals to handle because of the complexities that exist, but for those who want to manage their own investments, there is software available that will help with that task. For those persons who are at ease with numbers and stocks, there are programs that help to evaluate various stocks, educate a person on tracking the history of stocks before investing, and some even make recommendations based on personal information. The investor who wants to take care of his own stock portfolio can do so, but it takes constant monitoring.

Some of the programs available through online merchants even do analysis of stocks for the investor for a monthly fee. There is at least one that can be set to automatically buy and sell certain stocks, according to preset conditions, i.e., they reach certain levels on the stock market. For knowledgeable investors, this could be a time saver in managing stock portfolios. Along with the software for an individual to manage his own stock holdings, there are contacts online for having an expert manage an individual's stock shares.

Chapter 12

Reporting and Responsibilities

MANAGEMENT ACCOUNTING

Management accounting is concerned with the provisions and use of accounting information to managers within organizations, to provide them with the basis in making informed business decisions that would allow them to be better equipped in their management and control functions. Unlike financial accountancy information (which, for the most part, is public information), management accounting information is used within an organization (typically for decision-making) and is usually confidential and access to which is only available to a select few.

According to CIMA, The Chartered Institute of Management Accountants, Management Accounting is "the process of identification, measurement, accumulation, analysis, preparation, interpretation and communication of information used by management to plan, evaluate and control within an entity and to assure appropriate use of and accountability for its resources. Management accounting also comprises the preparation of financial reports for non management groups such as shareholders, creditors, regulatory agencies and tax authorities" (CIMA Official Terminology)

Aims

- Formulating strategies;
- Planning and constructing business activities;
- Making decisions;

- Well use of resources;
- Supporting financial reports preparation; and
- Safeguarding assets.

Traditional vs. Innovative Management Accounting

In the late 1980s, accounting practitioners and educators were heavily criticized on the grounds that management accounting practices (and, even more so, the curriculum taught to accounting students) had changed little over the preceding 60 years, despite radical changes in the business environment. Professional accounting institutes, perhaps fearing that management accountants would increasingly be seen as superfluous in business organizations, subsequently devoted considerable resources to the development of a more innovative skills set for management accountants. The distinction between 'traditional' and 'innovative' management accounting practices can be illustrated by reference to cost control techniques. Traditionally, management accountants' principal technique was variance analysis, which is a systematic approach to the comparison of the actual and budgeted costs of the raw materials and labour used during a production period.

Development of Throughput Accounting

The most significant recent direction in managerial accounting is throughput accounting, which recognizes the interdependencies of modern production processes and provide managers with a tool that will allow them to measure the contribution per unit of constrained resource for any given product, customer or supplier.

FINANCIAL ACCOUNTANCY

Financial accountancy (or financial accounting) is the branch of accountancy concerned with the preparation of financial statements for decision makers, such as stockholders, suppliers, banks, government agencies, owners, and other stakeholders. The fundamental need for financial accounting is to reduce principal-agent problem by measuring and monitoring agents' performance and reporting the results to interested users. Financial Accountancy is used to prepare accounting information for people outside the organisation or not involved in the day to day running of the company. Managerial accounting provides accounting information to help managers make decisions to manage the business. Financial Accountancy is governed by both local and international accounting standards.

FINANCIAL RISK MANAGEMENT

Risk management is the process of measuring risk and then developing and implementing strategies to manage that risk. Financial risk management focuses on risks that can be managed ("hedged") using traded financial instruments (typically changes in commodity prices, interest rates, foreign exchange rates and stock prices). Financial risk management will also play an important role in cash management.

FINANCIAL PLANNER

A Financial Planner or Personal Financial Planner is a practicing professional who helps people deal with various personal financial issues through proper planning, which includes but is not limited to these major areas: tertiary education planning, retirement planning, investment planning, risk management and insurance planning, tax planning, estate planning and business succession planning (for business owners). The work engaged in by this professional is commonly known as *personal financial planning*. In carrying out the planning function, he is guided by a process known as the *financial planning process* which should result in creating a detailed strategy for making their clients as wealthy as possible.

INTERNAL FINANCIAL REPORTING

Management is responsible for establishing and maintaining adequate internal control over financial reporting of the company. Internal control over financial reporting is a process designed to provide reasonable assurance regarding the reliability of financial reporting and the preparation of financial statements for external purposes in accordance with accounting principles generally accepted in the United States of America.

The company's internal control over financial reporting includes those policies and procedures that :

- Pertain to the maintenance of records that, in reasonable detail, accurately and fairly reflect the transactions and dispositions of the assets of the company;
- Provide reasonable assurance that transactions are recorded as necessary to permit preparation of financial statements in accordance with accounting principles generally accepted in the United States of America, and that receipts and expenditures of the company are being made only in accordance with authorizations of management and directors of the company; and
- Provide reasonable assurance regarding prevention or timely detection of unauthorized acquisition, use, or disposition of the company's assets that could have a material effect on the financial statements.

OPERATING THE MANAGEMENT CONTROL SYSTEM

A financial system supports the financial functions required to track financial events, provide financial information significant to the financial management of the agency, and/or required for the preparation of financial statements. A financial system encompasses automated and manual processes, procedures, controls, data, hardware, software, and support personnel dedicated to the operation and maintenance of system functions. A financial system may include multiple applications that are integrated through a common database or are electronically interfaced, as necessary, to meet defined data and processing requirements.

The term "non-financial system" means an information system that supports non-financial functions of the Federal government or components thereof and any financial data included in the system are insignificant to agency financial management and/or not required for the preparation of financial statements. The term "mixed system" means an information system that supports both financial and non-financial functions of the Federal government or components thereof.

MANAGEMENT CONTROL AND STAFFING

Although there is a tendency to want a "bright line" to define businesses as small, medium-size or large, this guidance does not provide such definitions. It uses the term "smaller" rather than "small" business, suggesting there is a wide range of companies to which the guidance is directed. The focus is on businesses that have many of the following characteristics:

- Fewer lines of business and fewer products within lines
- Concentration of marketing focus, by channel or geography
- Leadership by management with significant ownership interest or rights
- Fewer levels of management, with wider spans of control
- Less complex transaction processing systems and protocols
- Fewer personnel, many having a wider range of duties
- Limited ability to maintain deep resources in line as well as support staff positions such as legal, human resources, accounting and internal auditing.

None of these characteristics by themselves is definitive. Certainly, size by whatever measure - revenue, personnel, assets, or other - affects and is affected by these characteristics, and shapes our thinking about what constitutes "smaller."

Costs and Benefits

Management and other stakeholders of public companies, particularly smaller ones, have focused great attention on the cost of complying with Section 404, with less attention given to the associated benefits. Although it may be difficult to measure impacts associated with inaccurate financial reporting, market reactions to corporate misstatements clearly signal that the investment community does not readily tolerate inaccurate reporting, regardless of company size. In that respect and with other benefits described below, effective internal control adds significant value.

Meeting Challenges in Attaining Cost-Effective

Internal Control

The characteristics of smaller companies provide significant challenges for cost-effective internal control. This particularly is the case where managers view control as an administrative burden to be added onto existing business systems, rather than recognizing the business need and benefit for effective internal control that is integrated with core processes.

Among the challenges are:

- Obtaining sufficient resources to achieve adequate segregation of duties
- Management's ability to dominate activities, with significant opportunities for management override of control
- Recruiting individuals with requisite financial reporting and other expertise to serve effectively on the board of directors and audit committee
- Recruiting and retaining personnel with sufficient experience and skill in accounting and financial reporting
- Taking management attention from running the business in order to provide sufficient focus on accounting and financial reporting
- Maintaining appropriate control over computer information systems with limited technical resources.

Wide and Direct Control from the Top

Many smaller businesses are dominated by the company's

founder or other leader who exercises a great deal of discretion and provides personal direction to other personnel. While key to enabling the company to meet its growth and other objectives, this positioning also can contribute significantly to effective internal control over financial reporting.

In-depth knowledge of different facets of the business - its operations, processes, array of contractual commitments and business risks - enables its leader to know what to expect in reports generated by the financial reporting system and to follow up as needed when unanticipated variances surface. A related downside in terms of ability to override established control procedures can be addressed with specified protocols.

Effective Boards of Directors

Smaller hotels typically have relatively straightforward business operations with less complex business structures, enabling directors to gain more in-depth knowledge of business activities. Directors may have been closely involved with the company during its evolution and have a strong historical perspective. Coupled with what often is exposure to and frequent communication with a wide range of managers, this assists the board and its audit committee in performing oversight responsibilities for financial reporting in a highly effective manner.

Compensating for Limited Segregation of Duties

Resource constraints may limit the number of employees, sometimes resulting in concerns regarding segregation of duties. There are, however, actions management can take in order to compensate for potential inadequacy.

These include managers reviewing system reports of detailed transactions; selecting transactions for review of supporting documents; overseeing periodic counts of physical inventory, equipment or other assets and comparing them with accounting records; and reviewing reconciliations of account balances or performing them independently.

In many small companies managers already are performing these and other procedures supporting reliable reporting, and credit should be taken for their contribution to effective internal control.

Information Technology

The reality of limited internal information technology resources often can be dealt with through use of software developed and maintained by others. These packages still require controlled implementation and operation, but many of the risks associated with in-house developed systems are avoided. Typically there is a limited need for Programme change controls, inasmuch as changes are done exclusively by the developer company, and generally a smaller company's personnel lack technical expertise to make unauthorized modifications.

Monitoring Activities

The monitoring component is an important part of the Framework, where a wide range of activities routinely performed by managers in running a business can provide feedback on the functioning of other components of the internal control system. Management of many smaller businesses regularly perform such procedures, but have not always taken sufficient "credit" for their contribution to internal control effectiveness. These activities, usually performed manually and sometimes supported by computer software, should be fully considered in designing and assessing internal control. From a different perspective, there is another way monitoring activities can promote efficiency.

After the first year of assessing and reporting on internal control, many companies repeated the assessment process in year two with little if any cost savings. A different approach, however, can be taken to promote efficiency. By focusing on monitoring activities already in place or that might be added with little additional effort, management can identify significant changes to the financial reporting system since the prior year, thereby gaining insight into where to target more detailed testing. While for effective internal control all five components must be in place and operating effectively and some testing of each component is necessary, highly effective monitoring activities can both offset certain shortcomings in other components and sharpen targeting of assessment work with resulting overall efficiency.

Achieving Further Efficiencies

In addition to considering the above, companies can gain additional efficiencies in designing and implementing or assessing internal control by focusing on only those financial reporting objectives directly applicable to the company's activities and circumstances, taking a risk based approach to internal control, right sizing documentation, viewing internal control as an integrated process, and considering the totality of internal control. The COSO Framework recognizes that an entity must first have in place an appropriate set of financial reporting objectives.

Right-Sizing Documentation

Documentation of business processes and procedures and other elements of internal control systems is developed and maintained by companies for a number of reasons. One is to promote consistency in adhering to desired practices in running the business. Effective documentation assists in communicating what is to be done, and how, and creates expectations of performance. Another purpose of documentation is to assist in training new personnel and as a refresher or reference tool for other employees. Documentation also provides evidence to support reporting on internal control effectiveness. The level and nature of documentation varies widely by company. Certainly, large companies usually have more operations to document, or greater complexity in financial reporting processes, and therefore find it necessary to have more extensive documentation than smaller ones.

Viewing Internal Control as an Integrated Process

It is useful to view the Framework's five internal control components as comprising an integrated process, which indeed internal control is. A process perspective highlights the interrelationship of the components, and recognizes that management has flexibility in choosing controls to achieve its objectives and that an organization can adjust and improve its internal control over time. As noted, the internal control process begins with management setting financial reporting objectives relevant to the company's particular business activities and circumstances.

The Totality of Internal Control

Each of the five components of internal control set forth in the Framework is important to achieving the objective of reliable financial reporting. Determining whether a company's internal control over financial reporting is effective involves a judgment. Internal control has five components that work together to prevent or detect and correct material misstatements of financial reports.

Control over Financial Reporting

This guidance provides a set of twenty basic principles representing the fundamental concepts associated with, and drawn directly from, the five components of the Framework.

Control Environment

- Integrity and Ethical Values - Sound integrity and ethical values, particularly of top management, are developed and understood and set the standard of conduct for financial reporting.
- Board of Directors - The board of directors understands and exercises oversight responsibility related to financial reporting and related internal control.
- Management's Philosophy and Operating Style - Management's philosophy and operating style support achieving effective internal control over financial reporting.
- Organizational Structure - The company's organizational structure supports effective internal control over financial reporting.
- Financial Reporting Competencies - The company

retains individuals competent in financial reporting and related oversight roles.

- Authority and Responsibility - Management and employees are assigned appropriate levels of authority and responsibility to facilitate effective internal control over financial reporting.
- Human Resources - Human resource policies and practices are designed and implemented to facilitate effective internal control over financial reporting.

Risk Assessment

- Financial Reporting Objectives - Management specifies financial reporting objectives with sufficient clarity and criteria to enable the identification of risks to reliable financial reporting.
- Financial Reporting Risks - The company identifies and analyzes risks to the achievement of financial reporting objectives as a basis for determining how the risks should be managed.
- Fraud Risk - The potential for material misstatement due to fraud is explicitly considered in assessing risks to the achievement of financial reporting objectives.

Control Activities

- Integration with Risk Assessment - Actions are taken to address risks to the achievement of financial reporting objectives.
- Selection and Development of Control Activities - Control activities are selected and developed considering their cost and their potential effectiveness in mitigating risks to the achievement of financial reporting objectives.
- Policies and Procedures - Policies related to reliable financial reporting are established and communicated throughout the company, with corresponding procedures resulting in management directives being carried out.
- Information Technology - Information technology

controls, where applicable, are designed and implemented to support the achievement of financial reporting objectives.

Information and Communication

- Financial Reporting Information - Pertinent information is identified, captured, used at all levels of the company, and distributed in a form and timeframe that supports the achievement of financial reporting objectives.
- Internal Control Information - Information used to execute other control components is identified, captured, and distributed in a form and timeframe that enables personnel to carry out their internal control responsibilities.
- Internal Communication - Communications enable and support understanding and execution of internal control objectives, processes, and individual responsibilities at all levels of the organization.
- External Communication - Matters affecting the achievement of financial reporting objectives are communicated with outside parties.

Monitoring

- Ongoing and Separate Evaluations - Ongoing and/ or separate evaluations enable management to determine whether internal control over financial reporting is present and functioning.
- Reporting Deficiencies - Internal control deficiencies are identified and communicated in a timely manner to those parties responsible for taking corrective action, and to management and the board as appropriate.

Chapter 13

Accounting Methods and Revenue Hotel

ACCOUNTING METHODS

Cash Basis

Cash-basis accounting is a method of bookkeeping that records financial events based on cash flows and cash position. Revenue is recognized when cash is received and expense is recognized when cash is paid. In cash-basis accounting, revenues and expenses are also called cash receipts and cash payments. Cash-basis accounting does not recognize promises to pay or expectations to receive money or service in the future, such as payables, receivables, and prepaid expenses.

This is simpler for individuals and organizations that do not have significant amounts of these transactions, or when the time lag between the initiation of the transaction and the cash flow is very short. Two types of cash-basis accounting exist: *strict* and *modified*. Strict cash-basis follows the cash flow exactly. Modified cash-basis includes some elements from accrual-basis accounting such as inventory and property capitalization.

Issues with Cash Basis

Cash-basis accounting fails to meet GAAP requirements because it does not adhere to the following two GAAP principles:

- *Revenue recognition principle*—Revenue should be recognized when it is realized (e.g. a credit sale)
- *Matching principle*—Revenue should be matched to the expense if possible (e.g. sales to COGS)

Additionally, cash-basis accounting is not viable for cost accounting in manufacturing operations because expenses cannot always be correctly associated with product costs.

Example: When you pay your rent, your landlord would record an income event at the time he receives your payment. The landlord would subsequently record an expense event when he pays the rental agent their fee for your apartment. It is the accounting method used by most individuals, and by some businesses, that have limited payables or receivables or whose income and expense cash flows are closely associated with each other in time.

A simplified Income Statement and Balance Sheet for cash basis accounting might look like the following:

Vandalay Industries
Income Statement
For the year ended December 31, 2004

Revenue	$1,000
Expense	$ 800
Net income	$ 200

Vandalay Industries
Balance Sheet
For the year ended December 31, 2004

Assets	
Cash	$5,500
Total assets	$5,500
Liabilities and Stockholders' Equity	
Common stock	$5,500
Total liabilities and Equity	$5,500

Accrual Basis

Accrual-basis accounting records financial events based

on events that change your net worth (the amount owed to you minus the amount you owe others). Standard practice is to record and recognize revenues in the period which they incur and to match them with related expenses in a process known as matching or expense matching. Even though cash is not received or paid in a credit transaction, they are recorded because they are consequential in the future income and cash flow of the hotel. Accrual-basis is GAAP compliant.

Example: Your landlord would record an income event on the day your rent comes due (you owe it to him). He records an expense event when the fee owed to the rental agent comes due for your apartment that month (he owes it to the agent). The details of the actual cash flows and their timing are tracked by bookkeeping.

Comparison

- Using cash-basis accounting, income and expenses are recognized only when cash is received or paid out.
- Using accrual-basis accounting, receivables and payables are recognized when a sale is agreed to, even though as yet, no cash has been received or paid out.
- Cash-basis accounting defers all credit transactions to a later date. It is more conservative for the seller in that it does not record revenue until cash receipt. In a growing hotel, this results in a lower incomé compared to accrual-basis accounting.

A simple example

- A small business such as a fruit stand, which buys its inventory daily for cash at a wholesale market, sells the inventory for cash, and throws away what didn't sell, can get an accurate picture of its profits or losses using cash-basis accounting.
- A remodeling business that gives customers 90 days to pay and that procures materials on account at the lumber yard, must use the accrual method to gain an accurate picture of its financial condition.
- Either business will probably get a relatively accurate picture using either method over a long period of

time, except for the transactions that have already begun that are not yet closed.

Standard accrual-basis financial statements (profit statements and balance sheets) do not indicate the cash inflows and outflows of a hotel. The Statement of Cash Flows is created to indicate that information for accrual-basis accounting. Accrual-basis accounting is more costly to maintain, because it requires the bookkeeper to record many more transactions. However, the advent of accounting software has made the difference between the reporting methods less significant.

Companies that have extended or used credit significantly should use (and in the United States may be required by the Internal Revenue Service to use) the accrual-basis method of accounting. The U.S. Securities and Exchange Commission requires that all publicly traded companies follow GAAP, thus all publicly traded companies publish their financial statements using accrual-basis method. Three kind of external stakeholders should be considered when deciding the reporting method:

- Creditors
- Stockholders
- Taxation authorities

For the creditors and stockholders of large enterprises, cash basis accounting is financially inadequate. It does not project the future cash flow of the hotel.

For tax purposes, cash basis accounting is highly favored because it defers tax burdens until the cash is received. It is often used by small businesses and organizations that are not required to use the accrual method, both for tax reasons and for its simplicity.

HOTEL REVENUE

Revenue is a U.S. business term for the amount of money that a hotel earns from its activities in a given period, mostly from sales of products and/ or services to customers. In Europe (including the UK) the term is turnover. For individuals, the equivalent term is *income*. For government, revenues refers to the gross proceeds received from taxes, fees, and the like. For non-profit organizations, revenue from products and services can be expanded to include proceeds from donations, grants, trade in lieu of cash, and other liquid assets.

Revenue is often referred to as the "top line" due to its position on the income statement at the very top. This is to be contrasted with the "bottom line" which denotes net income, revenues after all applicable costs. At times, the term "Sales" is used interchangeably, but is only accurate when the amount described is denoted in currency as opposed to units ($100,000 of iPod sales vs. 500 iPods sold).

Revenue Recognition and Unearned Revenue

Conflicts abound as to when revenue should be recognized. The Financial Accounting Standards Board's (FASB) Statement of Financial Accounting Concept 5 states that revenues should be recognized when they are "realized or realizable" and "earned". Revenues are "realized or realizable" when products are exchanged for assets (such as cash) or claims to assets (such as promises to pay). Revenues are "earned" when the entity has performed all duties necessary to the purchaser.

Oftentimes one of the two situations will arise but not both. If assets are received before revenue is earned, a liability account is created called "Unearned Revenue". An example of when this would happen is in the event of magazine subscriptions: suppose a hotel sold 12 month magazine subscriptions on July 1, 2005 for $10,000 cash. At the hotel's year end, December 31, the hotel is still obligated to deliver 6 months, or $5,000, worth of magazines to subscribers. In this case, the hotel would recognize $5,000 as revenue for 2005, and $5,000 would be seen in the liability account "Unearned Revenue."

BOOKKEEPING

Bookkeeping is the recording of all financial transactions undertaken by a business (or an individual). A bookkeeper (or accounting clerk) is a person *who keeps the books* of an organization. The organization might be a business, a charity or a local sports club. Two methods are widely in use: single-entry accounting system and double-entry bookkeeping system.

ACCOUNTS PAYABLE

Accounts payable is one of a series of accounting transactions covering payments to suppliers owed money for goods and services. The average household performs this task by writing cheques each month to such suppliers to the electric hotel, telephone company, cable television or satellite dish service, newspaper subscription, and other such regular services.

Business organisations which have become too large to perform such tasks by hand, or who prefer not to do them by hand will generally use accounting software on a computer to perform this task. Accounts payable is classified as a liability account and as such normally has a credit balance. Accounts payable is classified as a Current Liability because the obligation is generally due within 12 months from the initial transaction date. Other types of accounting transactions include accounts receivable, payroll, and trial balance.

FINANCIAL AUDIT

A financial audit, or more accurately, an audit of financial statements, is the examination by an independent third party of the financial statements of a hotel or any other legal entity (including governments and individuals), resulting in the publication of an independent opinion on whether or not those financial statements are relevant, accurate, complete, and fairly presented.

Financial audits are typically performed by firms of *practising accountants* due to the specialist financial reporting knowledge they require. The financial audit is one of many *assurance* or *attestation* functions provided by accounting and auditing firms, whereby the firm provides an independent opinion on published information. Many organisations separately employ or hire internal auditors, who do not attest to financial reports but focus mainly on the internal controls of the organisation. External auditors may choose to place limited reliance on the work of internal auditors.

Financial audits exist to add credibility to the implied assertion by an organization's management that its financial statements fairly represent the organization's position and performance to the firm's *stakeholders* (interested parties). The principal stakeholders of a hotel are typically its *shareholders,* but other parties such as tax authorities, banks, regulators, suppliers, customers and employees may also have an interest in ensuring that the financial statements are accurate. The audit is designed to reduce the possibility of a *material misstatement.*

A *misstatement* is defined as false or missing information, whether caused by fraud (including deliberate misstatement) or error. *Material* is very broadly defined as being large enough or important enough to cause stakeholders to alter their decisions. The exact 'audit opinion' will vary between countries, firms and audited organisations.

CHARTERED ACCOUNTANT

Chartered Accountant is the title of members of a certain professional accountancy associations in the Commonwealth countries and Ireland.

The term *chartered* refers to the charter under which these bodies were incorporated. Subjects examined include financial accounting, management accounting, auditing, taxation and hotel law. Chartered Accountants work in all fields of business and finance. Some are engaged in public practice work, others work in the private sector and some are employed by government bodies.

AUDIT OF GOVERNMENT EXPENDITURE

The earliest surviving mention of a public official charged with auditing government expenditure is a reference to the Auditor of the Exchequer in England in 1314. The Auditors of the Imprest were established under Queen Elizabeth I in 1559 with formal responsibility for auditing Exchequer payments.

This system gradually lapsed and in 1780, Commissioners for Auditing the Public Accounts were appointed by statute.

From 1834, the Commissioners worked in tandem with the Comptroller of the Exchequer, who was charged with controlling the issue of funds to the government.

As Chancellor of the Exchequer, William Ewart Gladstone initiated major reforms of public finance and Parliamentary accountability. His 1866 Exchequer and Audit Departments Act required all departments, for the first time, to produce annual accounts, known as appropriation accounts. The Act also established the position of Comptroller and Auditor General (C&AG) and an Exchequer and Audit Department (E&AD) to provide supporting staff from within the civil service.

The C&AG was given two main functions – to authorise the issue of public money to government from the Bank of England, having satisfied himself that this was within the limits Parliament had voted – and to audit the accounts of all Government departments and report to Parliament accordingly. Auditing of UK government expenditure is now carried out by the National Audit Office and Audit Commission.

STAGES OF AN AUDIT

A financial audit is performed before the release of the financial statements (typically on an annual basis), and will overlap the 'year-end' (the date which the financial statements relate to). The following are the stages of a typical audit:

Planning and Risk Assessment

Timing: before year-end
Purpose:

- To understand the business of the hotel and the environment in which it operates.
- To determine the major audit risks (i.e. the chance that the auditor will issue the wrong opinion). For example, if sales representatives stand to gain bonuses based on their sales, and they account for the sales they generate, they have both the incentive and the ability to overstate their sales figures, thus leading to

overstated revenue. In response, the auditor would typically plan to increase the rigour of their procedures for checking the sales figures.

Internal controls testing

Timing: before and/or after year-end

Purpose:

- To assess the internal control procedures (e.g. by checking computer security, account reconciliations, segregation of duties). If internal controls are assessed as strong, this will reduce (but not entirely eliminate) the amount of 'substantive' work the auditor needs to do.

Notes:

- In some cases an auditor may not perform any internal controls testing, because he/she does not expect internal controls to be reliable. When no internal controls testing is performed, the audit is said to follow a substantive approach.

Substantive procedures

Timing: after year-end

Purpose:

- To collect audit evidence that the actual figures and disclosures made in the Financial Statements are reliable and in accordance with required standards and legislation.

Methods:

- Where internal controls are strong, auditors typically rely more on Substantive Analytical Procedures (the comparison of sets of financial information, and financial with non-financial information, to see if the numbers 'make sense' and that unexpected movements can be explained)
- Where internal controls are weak, auditors typically rely more on Substantive Tests of Detail (selecting a sample of items from the major account balances, and finding hard evidence (e.g. invoices, bank statements) for those items)

SIGNIFICANT AUDIT FIRMS

These firms are the 'Big 4' multinational accountancy firms which audit the majority of large quoted/listed companies. In addition to providing audits, they also provide other services including tax advice and strategic consultancy.

Firm	*2005 global revenue (US dollars)*
PricewaterhouseCoopers (corporate website)	20.3bn
Deloitte (corporate website)	18.2bn
Ernst and Young (corporate website)	16.9bn
KPMG (corporate website)	15.7bn

Commercial Relationships versus Objectivity

One of the major issues faced by private auditing firms is the need to provide independent auditing services while maintaining a business relationship with the audited hotel. The auditing firm's responsibility to check and confirm the reliability of financial statements may be limited by pressure from the audited hotel, who pays the auditing firm for the service. The auditing firm's need to maintain a viable business through auditing revenue may be weighed against its duty to examine and verify the accuracy, relevancy, and completeness of the hotel's financial statements.

ACCOUNTS RECEIVABLE

Accounts receivable is one of a series of accounting transactions dealing with the billing of customers who owe money to a person, hotel or organization for goods and services that have been provided to the customer by the hotel. This is typically done in a one person organization by writing an invoice and mailing or delivering it to each customer. On a hotel's balance sheet, accounts receivable is the amount that customers owe a business. Sometimes called trade receivables, they are classified as current assets. To record a journal entry for a sale on account, one must debit a receivable and credit a revenue account. When the customer pays off their accounts, one debits cash and credit the receivable in the journal entry.

The ending balance on the trial balance sheet for accounts receivable is always debit.

AMORTIZATION (BUSINESS)

Amortization is the distribution of a single lump-sum cash flow into many smaller cash flow installments, as determined by an amortization schedule. Unlike other repayment models, each repayment installment consists of both principal and interest. Amortization is chiefly used in loan repayments (a common example being a mortgage) and in sinking funds. Payments are divided into equal amounts for the duration of the loan, making it the simplest repayment model. A greater amount of the payment is applied to interest at the beginning of the amortization schedule, while more money is applied to principal at the end.

The amortization calculator formula is: (1–vn)/r, where n = number of years, v = 1/(1+r), and r = interest rate / 100.

Divide by (1+r) if a payment is due at the beginning.

Another method of writing this kind of formula is:

where: *P* = principal amount borrowed *i* = periodic interest rate *m* = number of periods each year (vs."t"= number of periods over the life of the loan, or t=n*m) *A* = periodic payment. Negative amortization (also called deferred interest) occurs if the payments made do not cover the interest due. The remaining interest owed is added to the outstanding loan balance, making it larger than the original loan amount.

In Accounting

In accounting, amortization refers to expensing the acquisition cost less the residual value of intangible assets such as trademarks and copyrights in a systematic manner over their estimated useful economic lives so as to reflect their consumption, expiration, obsolescence or other decline in value as a result of use or the passage of time. A corresponding concept for tangible assets is depreciation. Methodologies for allocating amortization to each accounting period are generally the same as for depreciation. However, many intangible assets such as goodwill or certain brands may be deemed to have an indefinite useful life and are therefore not subject to amortization.

Amortization is recorded in the financial statements of an entity as a reduction in the carrying value of the intangible asset in the balance sheet and as an expense in the income statement.

Under International Financial Reporting Standards, guidance on accounting for the amortization of intangible assets is contained in International Accounting Standard 38, Intangible Assets. Under United States generally accepted accounting principles, the primary guidance is contained in Statement of Financial Accounting Standards No. 142, Goodwill and Other Intangible Assets.

ANNUAL REPORT

An annual report is a document which a hotel presents at its Annual General Meeting for approval by its shareholders. The report is made up of reports and of financial statements, including the following:

- Chairman's report
- CEO's report
- Auditor's report on the financial statements
- Auditor's report on corporate governance
- Balance sheet
- Statement of changes in equity
- Income statement
- Cash Flow statement
- Notes to the financial statements
- Mission statement
- Accounting policies
- Corporate governance statement of compliance
- Statement of directors' responsibilities

Other information deemed relevant to stakeholders may also be included, such as a report on operations for manufacturing firms.

In the case of larger companies, it is usually a sleek, colorful, high gloss publication. The details provided in the report are of use to investors in gaining an understanding of the hotel's financial position and future direction. The report is usually compiled in compliance with IFRSs and/or the domestic GAAP, as well as domestic legislation (e.g. the SOX in the U.S.). In the United States, a more-detailed version of the report, called a Form 10-K, is submitted to the U.S. Securities and Exchange Commission.

THROUGHPUT

In communication networks, throughput is the amount of digital data per time unit that is delivered to a certain terminal in a network, from a network node, or from one node to another, for example via a communication link. The throughput is usually measured in bit per second (bit/s or bps). The system throughput or aggregate throughput is the sum of the data rates that are delivered to all terminals in a network.

Often maximum throughput is implied by the term throughput. The maximum throughput of a node or communication link is synonym to its capacity.

The maximum throughput is defined as the asymptotic throughput when the load (the amount of incoming data) is very large. In packet switched systems where the load and the throughput are equal (where there are no packet drops), the maximum throughput may be defined as the load in bit/s when the delivery time (the latency) asymptotically reaches infinity.

Channel Utilization

The channel utilization in percentage is the achieved throughput related to the physical data rate in bit/s of a digital communication channel (also known as the network access connection speed, the digital bandwidth or the channel capacity).

For example, if the the throughput is 70 Mbit/s in a 100 Mbit/s Ethernet connection, the channel utilization is 70%. In a point-to-point or point-to-multipoint communication link, where only one terminal is transmitting, the maximum throughput is often equivalent to or very near the physical data rate (the channel capacity), since the channel utilization can be almost 100% in such a network, except for a small inter-frame gap.

For example in Ethernet, the interframe gap is 12 bytes, and the maximum frame size 1538 bytes (1500 byte payload + 12 byte interframe gap + 8 byte preamble + 14 byte header + 4 Byte trailer).

This corresponds to a maximum channel utilization of (1538–12)/1538•100% = 99.2%, or a maximum throughput of 99.2 Mbit/s in a 100 Mbit/s Ethernet connection.

In a computer network, the throughput that is achieved from one computer to another may be lower than the maximum throughput, and than the network access channel capacity, for several reasons, for example:

- The channel capacity may be shared by other users. If a bottle neck communication link physical data rate *R* is shared by *N*, every user typically achieves a throughput of approximately *N/R* if fair queuing best-effort communication is assumed.
- Flow control, for example in the TCP protocol, affects the throughput if the bandwidth delay product is larger than the TCP window, i.e. the buffer size. In that case the sending computer must wait for acknowledgement of the data packets before it can send more packets.
- Packet loss due to Network congestion. Packets may be dropped in switches and routers when the packet queues are full due to congestion.
- Packet loss due to bit errors.
- TCP congestion avoidance controls the data rate. So called "slow start" occurs in the beginning of a file, and after packet drops caused by router congestion or bit errors in for example wireless links.
- Scheduling algorithms in routers and switches. If fair queuing is not provided, users that send large packet will get higher bandwidth. Some users may be prioritized in a weighted fair queuing (WFQ)

algorithm if differentiated or guaranteed quality of service (QoS) is provided.

- Ethernet "backoff" waiting time after collisions.

Throughput, Goodput and Overhead

The maximum throughput is often an unreliable measurement of perceived speed, for example the file transmission speed in bits per seconds. As pointed out above, the achieved throughput is often lower than the maximum throughput. Also, the protocol overhead affect the perceived speed.

The throughput is not a well-defined measure when it comes to how to deal with protocol overhead. The most simple definition is the number of bits per second that are physically delivered. A typical example where this definition is practised is an Ethernet network. In this case the maximum throughput is the gross bitrate or raw bitrate.

However, in schemes that include forward error correction codes (channel coding), the redundant error code is normally excluded from the throughput. An example in modem communication, where the throughput typically is measured in the interface between the PPP protocol and the circuit switched modem connection. In this case the maximum throughput is often called net bitrate or useful bitrate.

Throughput over Analog Channels

The maximum throughput of a point-to-point or point-to-multipoint physical transmission medium, is equal to or near the channel capacity. This is affected by modulation method and physical layer protocol overhead such as error correction coding, bit synchronization and equalizer training sequences. The maximum throughput may be related to the analog bandwidth of a physical transmission medium, measured in Hertz. The link spectral efficiency in bit/s/Hz is the maximum throughput divided by the analog bandwidth. It is a measure of the efficiency of the digital transmission scheme.

In wireless networks or cellular systems, the system

spectral efficiency in bit/s/Hz/area unit, bit/s/Hz/site or bit/s/Hz/cell, is the maximum system throughput (aggregate throughput) divided by the analog bandwidth and some measure of the system coverage area.

Throughput and Latency

Normally throughput and latency are opposed goals. To improve latency you typically want to increase how much the computer checks to see if you are trying to interact. This checking overhead slows you down. However, there is one very common exception to this rule. Network protocols and programs tend to synchronize both ends regularly. If these synchronizations are slow, then throughput can suffer tremendously.

The perceived speed is mostly based on the speed of requests made or responsiveness. As such, responsiveness has far less to do with throughput than latency. To illustrate this, consider a truck full of magnetic tape en route from Moscow to Paris.

The time or latency it takes to deliver the data may be several days, but the amount or throughput of data delivered will exceed the throughput of a broadband connection. In contrast, the broadband connection, which has a throughput many times less than that of the truck, has a relatively low latency and can deliver smaller amounts of data much faster. For a user, surfing the Internet for instance, the latter which has a lower latency is perceived as "faster".

Latency is measured from the time a request (e.g. a single packet) leaves the client to the time the response (e.g. An Acknowledgment) arrives back at the client from the serving entity.

The unit of latency is time. Throughput on the other hand is the amount of data that is transferred over a period of time. For example if over ten seconds twenty packets are transferred then the throughput would be 20/10=2 packets per second. Throughput can have many units (for example: "bits/second," "bytes/second," or "packets/second"), but it is always measured in a volume-per-time ratio.

Throughput Accounting

Throughput accounting (TA) is an alternative to cost accounting proposed by Eliyahu M. Goldratt. It is not based on Standard Costing or Activity Based Costing (ABC). Throughput Accounting is not costing and it does not allocate costs to products and services. It can be viewed as business intelligence for profit maximization. Conceptually throughput accounting seeks to increase the velocity at which products move through an organization by eliminiating bottlenecks within the organization.

Cost (or Management) accounting is an organization's internal method used to measure efficiency. Since no one outside the organization uses such internal accounts for investment or other decisions, any methods that an organization finds helpful can be used. Outside parties to a business depend on accounting reports prepared by financial (public) accountants who apply Generally Accepted Accounting Practices (GAAP) issued by the Financial Accounting Standards Board (FASB) and enforced by the U.S. Securities and Exchange Commission (SEC) and other regulatory agencies.

Chapter 14

Corporate Accounting

TAXATION

Unlike India, in the U.S. Internal Revenue Code, the growth of the annuity value during the accumulation phase is tax deferred, that is, not subject to current income tax for annuities owned by individuals. The tax deferred status of deferred annuities has led to their common usage in the United States. Under the US tax code, the benefits from annuity contracts do not always have to be taken in the form of a fixed stream of payments (annuitization), and many of the contracts are bought primarily for the tax benefits rather than to get a fixed stream of income.

If an annuity was used in a qualified pension plan or an IRA funding vehicle, then 100% of the annuity payment is taxable as current income upon distribution. If the annuity contract is purchased with after-tax dollars, then the contract holder upon annuitization recovers his basis pro-rata in the ratio of basis divided by the expected value according to the IRS regulations from Section 1.72-5. After the taxpayer has recovered all his basis, then 100% of the payments thereafter are subject to ordinary income tax.

EARNINGS BEFORE INTEREST AND TAXES

Earnings before interest and taxes (EBIT), also known as operating income and operating profit, is a term used to describe a hotel's earnings. A professional investor contemplating a change to the capital structure of a firm (e.g., through a leveraged buyout) first evaluates a firm's fundamental earnings potential (reflected by EBITDA and EBIT), and then determines the optimal use of debt vs. equity. To calculate EBIT, basic expenses (e.g., the cost of goods sold, selling and administrative expenses) are subtracted from revenues. Profit is later obtained by subtracting interest and taxes from the result.

Earnings before Interest, Taxes, Depreciation, and Amortization

EBITDA *«ee-bit-dah»* or *«ee-bit-dee-eh»* is an acronym for Earnings before Interest, Taxes, Depreciation, and Amortization. The same calculation can be arrived at from "operating income before depreciation and amortization" (OIBDA). It is one measure of 'operating cash flow'.

It differs from the cash flow from operations found in the Statement of Cash Flow primarily by ignoring payments for taxes or interest. EBITDA does not add back many of the other non-cash operating expenses, like the Statement of Cash Flow does. EBITDA also differs from free cash flow because of the difference above, and also because it does not recognize the cash requirements for replacing capital assets. Although there are different POVs regarding the use of this metric by equity owners, most everyone agrees to its validity when used by debtholders, or to evaluate a business's ability to handle debt.

Use by debt holders

The holder of debt is concerned with the business's ability to pay the interest and to repay the principal when due. Since interest is paid before income tax is calculated, he has no interest in taxes. The debtholder is not interested in whether the business can replace its assets when they wear out, so he can ignore both capital expenditures and their amortization. EBITDA measures the cash earnings that he can expect to be applied to interest and debt retirement.

There are two EBITDA metrics used.

- The interest coverage ratio is used to determine a firm's ability to pay interest on outstanding debt. It is calculated : EBITDA / Interest Expense. The greater the year-to-year variance in EBITDA, the greater the multiple should be.

- The measure of the pay-back period for a debt is : Debt/EBITDA. The longer the payback period, the greater the risk.

The ratios can be customized by reducing Debt by any cash on the balance sheet or by deducting maintenance capx from EBITDA to form a measure closer to free cash flow.

STOCK

In financial markets, stock is the capital raised by a corporation through the issuance and distribution of shares. A person or organisation which holds at least a partial share of stocks is called a shareholder. The aggregate value of a corporation's issued shares is its market capitalization. In the United Kingdom and Australia, the term *share* is used the same way, but *stocks* there refer to either a completely different financial instrument, the bond, or more widely to all kinds of marketable securities.

Type of stock

There are several types of stock.

Common Stock

Common stock, also referred to as common shares or ordinary shares, are, as the name implies, the most usual and commonly held form of stock in a corporation. Shareholders' of common stock have voting rights in corporate decision matters. It is the residual corporate interest that bears the ultimate risks of loss and receives the benefits of success.

Preferred Stock

Preferred stock, sometimes called preference shares, have priority over common stock in the distribution of dividends and assets. Most preferred shares provide no voting rights in corporate decision matters. However, some preferred shares have special voting rights to approve certain extraordinary events (such as the issuance of new shares, or the approval of the acquisition of the hotel), or to elect directors.

Dual Class Stock

Dual class stock is shares issued for a single hotel with varying classes indicating different rights on voting and dividend payments. Each kind of shares has its own class of shareholders entitling different rights.

Treasury stock

Treasury stock is shares that have been bought back from the public. Treasury Stock is considered issued, but not outstanding.

STOCK DERIVATIVES

A stock derivative is any financial claim which has a value that is dependent on the price of the underlying stock. Futures and options are the main types of derivatives on stocks. The underlying security may be a stock index or an individual firm's stock, e.g. single-stock futures. Stock futures are contracts where the buyer, or long, takes on the obligation to buy on the contract maturity date, and the seller, or short takes on the obligation to sell. Stock index futures are generally not delivered in the usual manner, but by cash settlement.

A stock option is a class of option. Specifically, a call option is the right (*not* obligation) to buy stock in the future at a fixed price and a put option is the right (*not* obligation) to sell stock in the future at a fixed price. Thus, the value of a stock option changes in reaction to the underlying stock of which it is a derivative. The most popular method of valuing stock options is the Black Scholes model.

SHAREHOLDER

A shareholder or *stockholder* is an individual or hotel (including a corporation) that legally owns one or more shares of stock in a joint stock hotel. Companies listed at the stock market strive to enhance shareholder value. Stockholders are granted special privileges depending on the class of stock, including the right to vote (usually one vote per share owned) on matters such as elections to the board of directors, the right to share in distributions of the hotel's income, the right to purchase new shares issued by the hotel, and the right to a hotel's assets during a liquidation of the hotel. However, stockholder's rights to a hotel's assets are subordinate to the rights of the hotel's creditors. This means that stockholders typically receive nothing if a hotel is liquidated after bankruptcy (if the hotel had had enough to pay its creditors, it would not have entered bankruptcy), although a stock may have value after a bankruptcy if there is the possibility that the debts of the hotel will be restructured.

TRADING

A stock exchange is an organization that provides a marketplace (either physical or virtual) for trading shares, where investors (represented by stock brokers) may buy and sell shares in a wide range of companies. A given hotel will usually list its shares by meeting and maintaining the listing requirements of a particular stock exchange. In the United States, through the inter-market quotation system, stocks listed on one exchange can also be bought or sold on several other exchanges, including relatively new internet-only exchanges. Stocks are broadly grouped into NYSE-listed and NASDAQ-listed stocks. Exchanges where NYSE-listed stocks may be bought are generally not the same group as the exchanges where NASDAQ-listed stocks may be bought. Many large foreign companies choose to list on a U.S. exchange as well as an exchange in their home country in order to broaden their investor base. These shares are called American Depository Receipts (ADRs) — or, in the case of companies such as UBS and Daimler Chrysler — "foreign ordinary shares."

TREASURY STOCK

In the United Kingdom, treasury stocks refer to government bonds or gilts. The British equivalent of *treasury stock* as used in the United States is treasury share. In the United States, a treasury stock or reacquired stock is stock which is bought back by the issuing hotel. It reduces the number of outstanding stocks on the open market ("open market" including insiders' holdings). On the balance sheet, treasury stock is listed under shareholder equity as a negative number. Stock repurchases are often used as a tax-efficient method to put cash into shareholders' hands, rather than pay dividends. Sometimes, companies do this when they feel that their stock is undervalued on the open market. Other times, companies do this to provide a "bonus" or incentive compensation plan for employees. Rather than receive cash, recipients receive an asset that might appreciate in value faster than cash saved in a bank account.

Limitations of treasury stock include:

Treasury stock does not pay a dividend

Treasury stock has no voting rights

Total treasury stock can not exceed the maximum proportion of total capitalization specified by law in the relevant country

DETERMINING SHARE PRICES

Share prices in a publicly traded hotel are determined by market supply and demand, and thus depend upon the expectations of buyers and sellers. Among these are:

- The hotel's future and recent performance
- New product lines
- Prospects for companies of this type, the "market sector"
- Prevailing moods and fashions.

By dividing the price of one share in a hotel by the profits earned by the hotel per share, you arrive at the P/E ratio. If earnings move up in line with share prices (or vice versa) the ratio stays the same. But if stock prices gain in value and earnings remain the same or go down, the P/E rises. For example, if a stock price was $70 per share and it got $2 in earnings, the P/E is 35, historically high.

The Market P/E

To calculate the P/E ratio of a market index such as the

S&P500, it is not accurate to take the "simple average" of the P/Es of all stock constituents. The preferred and accurate method is to calculate the weighted average. In this case, each stock's underlying market cap (price multiplied by number of shares in issue) is summed to give the total value in terms of market capitalization for the whole market index. The same method is computed for each stock's underlying net earnings (earnings per share multiplied by number of shares in issue).

In this case the total of all net earnings is computed and this gives the total earnings for the whole market index. The final stage is to divide the total market capitalization by the total earnings to give the market P/E ratio.

The reason for using the weighted average method rather than 'simple' average can best be described by considering a recessionary period of the economic cycle, where a number of stocks would be reporting a loss. For example, a hotel with a share price of $100, may have made a slight loss of say 10 cents giving a P/E ratio of –1000 (100/0.1). In another case, a hotel with a share price of $1 may have made a serious loss of 50 cents giving a P/E ratio of – 2 (1/0.5). This mathematical anomaly would create a misrepresentation of the underlying hotel losses on the overall market index.

The P/E and Inflation

There is evidence that the P/E of the market has more to do with changes in consumer prices than any other factor. From 1900 to 2005, the highest average P/E occurred when the average change in consumer prices was 2.6%. In general, the P/E ratio is inversely proportional to the absolute value of the change in prices, in other words, the higher the price change, the lower the P/E. Some claim that the P/E ratio is mostly dictated by interest rates, but the level of correlation of P/E ratios to interest rates is much lower versus that to the magnitude of price change.

Inputs

Accuracy and context

In practice, decisions must be made as to exactly how to specify the inputs used in the calculations.

Does the current market price accurately value the organization?

How is income to be calculated and for what periods? How do we calculate total capitalization?

Can these values be trusted?

What are the revenue and earnings growth prospects over the time frame one is investing in?

Was there special one time charges which artificially lowered (or artificially raised) the earnings used in the calculation, and did those charges cause a drop in stock price or were they ignored?

Were these charges truly one-time, or is the hotel trying to manipulate us into thinking so?

What kind of P/E ratios is the market giving to similar companies, and also the P/E ratio of the entire market?

Historical vs Projected Earnings

THE P/E CONCEPT IN BUSINESS CULTURE

The P/E ratio of a hotel is a significant focus for management in many companies and industries. This is because management is primarily paid with their hotel's stock (a form of payment that is supposed to align the interests of management with the interests of other stock holders), in order to increase the stock price.

The stock price can increase in one of two ways: either through improved earnings or through an improved multiple that the market assigns to those earnings. As mentioned earlier, a higher P/E ratio is the result of a sustainable advantage that allows a hotel to grow earnings over time (ie, investors are paying for their peace of mind). Efforts by management to convince investors that their companies do have a sustainable advantage have had profound effects on business:

- The primary motivation for building conglomerates is to diversify earnings so that they go up steadily over time.
- The choice of businesses which are enhanced or closed down or sold within these conglomerates is

often made based on their perceived volatility, regardless of the absolute level of profits or profit margins.

- One of the main genres of financial fraud, "slush fund accounting" (hiding excess earnings in good years to cover for losses in lean years), is designed to create the image that the hotel always slowly but steadily increases profits, with the goal to increase the P/E ratio.
- These and many other actions used by companies to structure themselves to be perceived as commanding a higher P/E ratio can seem counterintuitive to some, because while they may decrease the absolute level of profits they are designed to increase the stock price. Thus in this situation maximizing the stock price acts as a perverse incentive.

DIVIDEND

When a hotel earns a profit, some of it is reinvested in the business and called retained earnings, and some of it can be paid to its shareholders as a dividend. The frequency of these varies by country. In the United States dividends are usually declared quarterly by the board of directors. In some other countries dividends are paid biannually, as an interim dividend shortly after the hotel announces its interim results and a final dividend typically following its annual general meeting. In other countries, the board of directors will propose the payment of a dividend to shareholders at the annual meeting who will then vote on the proposal.

DIVIDEND YIELD

Publicly traded companies often make periodic quarterly or yearly cash payments to their owners, the shareholders, in direct proportion to the number of shares held. According to US law, such payments can only be made out of current earnings or out of reserves (earnings retained from previous years). The hotel decides on the total payment and this is divided by the number of shares. The resulting dividend is an amount of cash per share. The dividend yield is the dividend paid in the last accounting year divided by the current share price.

If a stock paid out $5 per share in cash dividends to its shareholders last year and its price is currently $50, then it has a dividend yield of 10%. Historically, at severely high P/E ratios (such as over 100x), a stock has NO (0.0%) or negligible dividend yield. With a P/E ratio over 100x, and supposing a portion of earnings is paid as dividend, it would take *over a century* to earn back the purchase price. Such stocks are extremely overvalued, unless a huge growth of earnings in the next years is expected.

BOOK VALUE

Book Value is the shareholders' equity of a business (assets - liabilities) as measured by the accounting 'books'. The term is used in the context where the speaker is trying to distinguish between the accounting measures (usually historical cost) and the market value. While it can be used to refer to the business' total equity, it is most used

- As a 'per share' value': The balance sheet Equity value is divided by the number of shares outstanding at the date of the balance sheet (not the average o/s in the period).
- As a 'diluted per share value': The Equity is bumped up by the exercise price of the options, warrants or preferred shares. Then it is divided by the number of shares that has been increased by those added.

Chapter 15

The Professional Environment

IMPORTANCE AND NATURE OF CHANGE

A hotel is an establishment that provides paid lodging, usually on a short-term basis. Hotels often provide a number of additional guest services such as a restaurant, a swimming pool or childcare. Some hotels have conference services and meeting rooms and encourage groups to hold conventions and meetings at their location. There is no hard and fast rule differentiating motels from other hotels, although a "Motel" is clearly suggesting that it is aimed at motorists. This may simply mean that it is a hotel with good access to the road network (on a motorway or ring road) so that a long car journey need not be interrupted for long by town-centre traffic. In other cases the designation is simply an attempt to make the most of a poor location inconvenient for town-centre services and attractions.

Classically, though, a Motel is a hotel which is made convenient for people who, for whatever personal reason, wish to be able to have quick access from the outside world (especially from their parked car) to the hotel room - without passing the scrutiny of a receptionist or fellow guests. This is usually arranged by having rooms (sometimes in individual chalets or even trailers) arranged around the car park with room doors opening directly to the outside rather than to an internal corridor. In Australia, the word may also refer to a pub or bar. In the UK similarly, many pubs with "hotel" in their name do not offer accommodation or even food.

In India, the word may also refer to a restaurant since the best restaurants were always situated next to a good hotel. The word *hotel* derives from the French *hotel,* which referred to a French version of a townhouse or any other building seeing frequent visitors, not a place offering accommodation (in contemporary usage, *hotel* has the meaning of "hotel", and *hotel particular* is used for the old meaning).

CHANGE THEORIES

Many theories exist regarding the change process. An examination of change theories educates one seeking to implement a change within an organization. Clearly, a good manager is a successful change agent.

Literature about the management of change historically has been characterized by hypothetical practice; and in reaction to previous neglect, has overly focused on the political aspects of the change process. New interest in *the learning organization* provides an occasion to support this bias by developing a theory of change that is more congruent with the requirement to build learning capacity within organizations. The result should be the placement of learning theory centrally within a theory of planned organizational change.

A. Action Research for Change

Action research focuses on groups to effect change within an organization. This theory examines the role of a group, implicit knowledge, and the locations of learning as centre elements. Action research is a common model used in organizational cultures where participation and equality are the norm. Within this theory, learning is not a change in behaviour, as many define it, but knowledge created through the transformation of experience.

B. Theorizing about Organizational Change

A review of the diverse literature on organizational change shows the field is at an early stage of theoretical development. There is no one model of organizational change and no agreed guideline for action by change agents or practitioners who have developed frameworks for understanding and directing change based on their practical experiences in organizations. Differing theoretical approaches have been developed to analyse organizational change processes and to deal with alternate problems affecting organizational performance. Theories have been strongly affected by their socio-historical context.

THE TYPES AND PHASES OF CHANGE

Change takes place as planned, unplanned, or developmental. The first type, *planned change,* is a deliberate action undertaken by an individual or group of individuals. The goal is usually to improve an existing system. By comparison, *unplanned change* is accidental and haphazard; although after the change occurs, hindsight often reveals agents (deliberate or subconsciously) fueling the change.

Specifically, these three phases are the *threat, impact,* and *after-effect* of change. The ability of the manager to plan for change, anticipate problems before they become costly, and understand the present stage of the specific change can be a major factor in determining managerial effectiveness.

Threat Phase

The threat phase of change is that time period during which a rumor moves through informal (grapevine) or regular management channels that suggest a change is possible or likely to be imposed. A threat phase may occur even though the change *never actually happens.* If employees *believe* that such a change will happen, they can start resisting it immediately. Employees may quit their jobs or lower their productivity long before a change ever actually takes place. These negative responses by employees are a result of the fact that they believe that a change is actually coming or contemplated.

The length of time and significance of the threat phase is determined by the speed and the magnitude of the change. Changes that are made quickly obviously have a short threat phase, while changes that are large and require a considerable amount of planning usually have a threat phase of a year or more. Examples of these latter types of change include changes in building location, alterations involving technological improvements, or a major change in work procedures.

Impact Phase

The second phase of change, which is commonly referred to as the impact phase, occurs when the organizational change is implemented. Often managers get through the threat phase without difficulty because the company has a good reputation for changes in the past or they have explained the nature of the change adequately. Once the change is introduced, however, serious problems may confront these managers. Why? Many times when professionals are actually trying a new process or building new work relationships, they find that it is actually more difficult than they first realized and they then begin resisting the change.

Also, employees may find that after the change is actually introduced, many of its aspects that they thought would be insignificant in the planning phase actually turn out to be much more threatening than was originally believed. This situation calls for appropriate managerial action designed to minimize the inefficiencies due to resistant behaviour by employees. Increased attention needs to be given to communication with professionals so their true problems with the change can be fully understood and resolved.

After-Effect Phase

The after-effect phase of change can involve resistance for several months, a year, or even longer after the change has apparently been introduced successfully. Employees sometimes accept the impact phase of change simply because it is a new stimulating activity that is different from their previous work assignments. Unfortunately, however, the newness wears off, and three or four months after a change has been introduced, workers may decide they prefer to have the "old way" back again.

Resistance in the form of poor workmanship, increased conflict, or lack of tolerance for fellow workers may occur.

Thus, the change process is usually long term, particularly for larger changes. In fact, the after-effects phase may occur over a period of several years from the time the change is first contemplated until it has been fully integrated and accepted into the organization. Due to upward communication barriers, employees may not tell their managers the real problem.

CAUSES OF RESISTANCE TO CHANGE

A common cause of resistance in the professional environment is *fear,* specifically, fear of what the change will do to the individuals that have to work with the change. Managerial action that increases understanding reduces fear and increases acceptance. As was seen in the case involving office window location, changes that are perceived by professionals to lower their social status in the organization tend to be resisted. Feelings of self-worth are often influenced by subtle changes and employees vehemently resist changes that threaten their self-worth.

TECHNIQUES FOR REDUCING RESISTANCE

Considerable attention has been directed toward proper ways of introducing change so that resistance is overcome. Many of these techniques have proven value in the professional environment. Often fear of loss in status, security, or destruction of social relationships are imaginary. In these cases, introducing employee participation into the change process can be vital in reducing resistance to the change. Democratic leadership is helpful for managers when these kinds of situations are present.

Resistance to change can be reduced if the manager can "sell through participation" the idea that employees will be better off as a result of making the change. Unless the forces for acceptance are clearly greater than those for resistance, the probability of employees resisting the change is high. The extent and direction of these forces are determined by several variables. The more important of these are the manager, organizational climate, work group attitudes, employee value systems, and the change itself.

The manager can often use participation among professionals to impact favourably on enough of these variables so these employees perceive that a net gain will result from making the change. If the manager is successful with participation, the forces favouring the change would exceed the forces against the change, and resistance will be alleviated as a managerial problem. In fact, participation may be both useful and necessary in implementing change in professional environments.

ORGANIZATIONAL CRISES AND CUTBACK MANAGEMENT

Although many managers fail to plan for it and naturally avoid negative thinking, an increasing part of today's organizational life involves crises situations which include work force reductions among professional employee groups. One of the most frequent aspects of the change process is the occurrence of crisis situations.

Crises often occur because managers fail to identify the need for change or do not implement changes in a timely fashion. Slatter has identified four stages of crisis development and typical management response patterns as follows:

- *Hidden crises.* In this stage managers are unaware of emerging major problems, and the need to implement changes.
- *Crisis denial.* During this stage there are visible signs of crisis within the firm, but managers are unwilling to change. They often suggest changes that have already been implemented or state that existing problems are beyond their control or will be solved without any change. Thus, need for action is denied. Managers may sincerely believe that they are on the correct path or they may feel they are taking a position necessary for self-preservation. According to Slatter, managers often believe they will be blamed and may lose their jobs if previous actions are found to be wrong. Also, strategic change usually involves alterations in the management power structure, and

managers who currently hold power are likely to resist needed change. Managers may take action to make the firm's financial position look better than it really is.

- *Organizational disintegration.* Since needed changes are not being implemented, the organization exhibits serious problems. While some change is likely to occur, it is often too little and too late. Existing decisions makers become more autocratic, and the full and impartial assessment of alternatives does not occur.
- *Organizational collapse.* This stage is characterized by partial or total organizational failure. Effective decision making decreases and commitment to organizational goals declines. Managers become even more self-oriented and the mobile employees leave the firm.

Slatter suggests that the earlier the developing crisis is confronted, the less dramatic organizational change is necessary and the greater the chance of successful turnaround. While some managerial action may occur during the "hidden crisis" stage, more often the crisis precipitates the needed changes.

THE TASK FORCE CONCEPT

Major changes in the professional environment can often be integrated effectively with the use of the task force. This concept simply involves appointing a group of key subordinates and managers to study problems where changes are needed and to recommend the nature and content of changes to be made. Three important steps are necessary in making task forces work.

First, select key group leaders for the task force. These employees should have the respect and support of their co-workers, and should have proven performance records. Second, use democratic techniques in managing the task force so all members will become involved and committed.

Third, once the task force makes a recommendation for

change, allow it to continue as a unit to play a key role in implementation and follow-up. The positive results from following these steps will be that major changes are often integrated effectively into the organization with a minimum of conflict.

Obviously, the change must be of significant size and impact so that the cost of formulating and operating the task force will be worthwhile. Many changes that involve new technologies, work procedures, or product lines or services (where the focus of employee activities must be changed), are particularly suited for task force assignment. If the task force is formed early during major changes, especially when the change is initially contemplated, the threat phase of the change is usually minimized or eliminated.

The task force can gather data, field questions, and solicit input so that employees understand and become more involved in what is going to be done. This involvement is particularly important to professional employees because their expertise can make an important contribution to a proposed change. In addition to cutback management and cases involving disciplinary action, there are other changes that, no matter how much participation is involved, the professional employee cannot see that an improved personal position will result from making the change. In these situations there are two avenues to managers.

One is to use other compensating factors to offset the professional's perceived negative impact of the change. Some possible compensating factors are discussed. First, increase the *level of pay* to the employees affected and thereby reduces their dissatisfaction; second, increase the amount of *fringe benefits* or privileges such as travel opportunities or vacation time; and third, make changes in the physical environment, such as improved facilities or adding to support staff.

The amount of control the manager has over many of the above factors varies greatly from one organization to another and within a given firm. However, managers usually have some influence on one or more of these areas (often more than they realize), and the important point is to use it wisely.

Chapter 16

Role of Administration in Hotel Management

PERSONAL DEVELOPMENT

People are not born understanding their society's morals. Instead, these understandings develop and mature over time. Psychologist Lawrence Kolhberg's famous work has provided us with a developmental mapping of how moral understanding tends to progress through childhood and early adulthood.

- According to Kohlberg, infants have little or no moral sense, because they are not born with an understanding of the nature of human relationships. As children reach elementary school age, they enter into the first major stage of moral understanding, known as the "pre-conventional" stage. Pre-conventional children are essentially selfish in orientation. They do not think about what behaviours will serve the greater good, but rather think in terms of what will most benefit themselves. They respond primarily to power, and think of morality as a matter of following rules so as to avoid punishment.
- As children grow into adulthood, they typically enter into the stage of "conventional" moral understanding. Some children will be developmentally delayed in this regard and become adults who have the moral understanding of children; we call them sociopaths,

narcissists, and anti-social personalities. The majority of people that do make it to the conventional moral understanding start thinking in terms of duty; a duty to do what is necessary to promote the greater good. They orient towards behaviours that are most likely to gain other people's respect and admiration. Part of conventional morality is the duty to behave lawfully. Some people take this duty further and understand it as a duty to conform to what other influential people around them want.

SELF DEVELOPMENT TIPS

As long as you are still alive, you are capable of changing and growing. You can do anything you want to do, be anything you want to be. Listen to some positive thoughts on how to continue your self development and then apply them in your own life.

- Accept personal responsibility for your own growth; no one can do it for you. What you do today will determine your readiness for tomorrow.
- Take time every day to do something for yourself.
- Take classes to stay current in your field of expertise. The world is changing rapidly and you must learn to manage change to avoid obsolescence. The way Will Rogers put this was that "Even if you are on the right track, if you just sit there you will get run over."
- Listen to cassette tapes on personal and professional growth topics.
- Never look back to the past-you only can control your actions in this instant, so what should you be doing right now?
- Learn from "other people's experience" rather then having to try everything for yourself. It shortens the time needed to learn.
- Dealing with a problem helps you learn patience and strengthens your management skills; it is good mental exercise.

- Analyse, in a non-judgmental way, mistakes in which you were involved. It will help you to prevent these in the future.
- Reward yourself when you catch yourself working on the most important priorities.
- Never say something can't or won't be done. Keep looking for ways to do it.
- After attending a seminar, report to your boss or other people in your organization, what the most important things are that you learned from the programme.
- For all learning experiences, whether it is reading, seeing, thinking or attending, apply the R squared, A squared formula: Recognize, Relate, Assimilate, and Apply. These actions will help you grow in the direction of your goals.
- Eliminate one time waster a week from your life.
- Read a minimum of one chapter of a book a day.
- Read a minimum of one book a month.
- Be hungry for what life has to offer and go for it.
- Decide what you really desire to do-then do it.
- When you have the option of reading a book or listening to the cassette tape version of the programme, listen to the tape. It will be more to the point and can be done while you are driving, jogging/walking, or getting other routine things done.
- Develop a "master mind" group of four or five people with whom you can openly discuss ideas in a nonjudgmental way.
- Develop yourself as a resource for others by networking. Find out who does what, when, and for whom. You may find excellent contacts for your future needs and for the needs of others you meet.
- Work for balance in your life goals: family, financial, professional, social, spiritual, recreational.
- Always keep your goals in mind as you start a new activity.

- If you do a lot of work with the calculator, run the machine with the hand you don't use for writing.
- Do not be afraid of failing at something. You can learn and change as a result of it.
- The most difficult projects are opportunities for your biggest successes just as the most difficult people could become your strongest allies.
- Put up pictures of your dreams and goals where you will see them frequently. They will remind you and aid you in focusing and visualizing your goal.
- We all have the same 24 hours in a day. Learn from those people who get more done than you do. Perhaps you can find a way to improve what you are doing.
- Find a nonjudgmental mentor who will help you by providing feedback, suggestions, challenges and support.
- Identify some "models" and observe their style and actions. Do not copy them but learn from their experiences.
- Learn from the errors you see others make as well as from their successes.
- Fill your mind with positive ideas, thoughts and inspirations and you will have no room left for the negative.
- Trade jobs with someone so you gain additional experience.
- Ask for and accept lateral moves in the organization so you learn more about the entire operation.
- Do more than your "self doubts" say you can.
- Have confidence that you can get through and learn from anything and everything you experience.
- Reward yourself with a treat when you have completed a learning objective.
- Keep a daily journal, recording your thoughts, ideas, feelings and personal growth progress.
- Ask questions, listen, then ask more questions. You will learn as well as help others learn.

- Ask yourself, "How can I manipulate my fate?"
- Do things with someone you respect. They will be supportive of you and you will learn from interacting with them.
- Seek new information on projects for which you have responsibility. Look for new "ah ha" ideas all the time.
- Challenge yourself to learn something new every day.
- Remain flexible and constantly adaptable.
- Be open to others and sincerely interested in them. You can learn from everyone you meet.
- Mentally rehearse a new skill. Your subconscious does not know the difference between actual practice and mental rehearsal.
- Keep a record of what you accomplished the previous day(s)/week. If you did not accomplish as much as you wanted, it gives you extra incentive to do better in the next time period.
- Make notes of the questions you want answered. Then as the answers come to you, jot them down next to the question.
- Work on overcoming personal, nonproductive habits; for example: overeating, smoking, gossip.
- Keep an "Idea File" ring binder or notebook in which you record all new ideas. At least once a week in a standing appointment with yourself, review your ideas.

METHODS FOR CHANGING BEHAVIOUR AND THOUGHTS

It may help to start this section on methods you can use to change behaviours by offering a definition of behaviour. A behaviour is something that you do; some action that you take. Conventionally, a behaviour is something that you act out physically, such as taking a walk, or smoking a cigarette, or rolling your eyes when your spouse is complaining. However, behaviours can be subtle, non-physical things too. Thinking can be considered a behaviour, for instance.

The principles of learning theory apply equally well to both human beings and animals, because all animals (human beings included) share a common basic design. All animals, from the highest and most complex to the lowest and simplest, have basic needs they need to meet and are designed in such a way so that they know how to meet them. All animals get "hungry" in some fashion and search for food, and all animals know to avoid extremes of temperature, predators or other environmental threats to their continuing existence Another way of saying this is that all animals have in common that their behaviour is motivated. Any animal that can be motivated, can be manipulated according to the principles of learning theory, so as to shape the animal's behaviour.

BUILDING TRUST

Mutual trust is a shared belief that you can depend on each other to achieve a common purpose.

More comprehensively trust defined as "the willingness of a party (trustor) to be vulnerable to the actions of another party (trustee) based on the expectation that the trustee will perform an action important to the trustor, regardless of the trustor's ability to monitor or control the trustee."

"People sense how you feel about them. If you want to change their attitudes toward you, change the negative attitudes you have toward them." Building relationships requires the building of trust. Trust is the expectancy of people that they can rely on your word. It is built through integrity and consistency in relationships.

DECISIONS MAKING

In his classic work, "Think & Grow Rich", Napoleon Hill stated that 98% of people are in the jobs they have through indecision, i.e. because they never made the decision about what they wanted to do in their lives in the first place. Indecision explains why many people feel that they have a life purpose, but have no idea what it is.

Decision is the key to transformation. It is one of the key character traits distinguishing high performers from the vast ranks of the mediocre. Decision is, by definition, behind every truly great achievement anyone ever makes. Interestingly, the most successful people make decisions quickly and change them slowly. They persist with the decisions they have made. However, failures are very slow to make any decision at all (most never make any), and they change the ones they have made very rapidly indeed. Which description applies to you?

Decision making is a process of first diverging to explore the possibilities and then converging on a solution(s).

The Latin root of the word decision means "to cut off from all alternatives". This is what you should do when you decide.

The Six Thinking Hats proposal analysis tool invented by Edward de Bono is particularly useful for evaluating innovative and provocative ideas. While most of our thinking is adversarial, the six thinking hats technique overcomes these difficulties by forcing everyone to think in parallel. As participants wear each hat - white, red, yellow, black, green, or blue - they all must think a certain way at the same time.

Organizational Communications

By internal communications, we mean the steps groups take to keep their members, donors, and supporters informed about their work. Internal communications tools include newsletters, web sites, mailings, magazines and other publications, and hotlines. By external communications, we mean the publicity relations activities groups rely upon to deliver their message to their target audiences (which may include members and supporters, but also include key decision-makers, other organizations and individuals, and the media). External communications tools include news releases, media events, speaking engagements, advertising campaigns, public service announcement campaigns, brochures, fact sheets and reports. There is frequent overlap between internal and external communications, but it helps to think of them separately when developing a communications strategy or determining how to improve an organization's overall communications capacity.

- The police enter the location into a computer and look for an on-duty officer in the area.
- The police communication center sends an officer to the location.
- The officer arrives on the scene of the break-in, often five minutes or more after the alarm originally sounded.

Whether a business operates out of a factory, garage, store or office suite, good key control can protect the people, property and information inside.

The little words "Do Not Duplicate" on all of your office keys sound like good insurance against unauthorized entry. Unfortunately, they mean almost nothing in most cases, says Alan Stelzer of Antrim's Security Co. in Pasadena, California. Stelzer strongly recommends keys that can only be duplicated by the manufacturers or their agents when you present a registration card and positive identification. All of the copies should then be listed by their consecutive serial numbers and the employees who use them.

Fixing a few simple problems can go a long way in preventing crime.

Perimeter

Lighting: Do you have lights at all entrances? Are they protected from vandals and thieves?

Fences / Walls: Is it possible to get over or under them? What are they made of? Are they in good condition?

Gates: Are any left unsecured? Are they in good condition?

Storage Yard: Do you have materials next to the fence or entrance? Are the materials hidden from passers-by?

Parking Lots: Is employee parking separate from parking for the general public? How close to the building is it? Is there enough lighting?

Address Numbers: Are they legible and visible from the street?

Pedestrian / Vehicle Access: How well is it monitored? Is it in front of the building?

Chapter 17

Risk Management

The owner of a fast food franchise in East Los Angeles panicked when his drive-through cashier was robbed at gunpoint. While the criminals escaped with all the day's receipts, an even greater loss was the owner's peace of mind. Since his wife and daughter both worked at the restaurant, he stood to lose a lot more than money if the robbers returned. What could the owner have done to make his business and his family safe?

In this case, a simple bulletproof one-way drive-through window would have made the robbery impossible. More importantly, such a deterrent might make criminals think twice about their chosen target.

When looking around the inside of your building, do you see valuable equipment or merchandise that a thief could collect in five minutes or less? Then maybe your alarm system just isn't enough. Consider the steps and time involved between the alarm being triggered and the arrival of a police officer at your site.

- The alarm goes off when someone breaks in or trespasses.
- The security company must identify the location of the alarm.
- The security company calls the location to make sure the alarm was not set off accidentally by someone authorized with a special code.
- The security company contacts the local sheriff or other police communication center.

Doors

Can they be pried open? Are they solid in construction? Do they have reliable dead bolts? What kind of strike plates do they have? Are your closing procedures listed and uniform?

Windows

Are they secured with screw locks, pins or sturdy cranks? Are louvers glued shut or otherwise secured? Are there drapes or blinds that prevent would-be thieves from seeing inside your property?

Roof

Are all skylights, vents and hatchways secured or covered? Do trees, drain pipes or walls allow easy access to the roof?

Interior

Lighting: Do you have lights on after hours? Is there an emergency back-up system?

Valuables: Are they out of view of any passers-by?

Storage / Offices / Saferoom: Are they secured with high-quality locks? Are there phones in each room to allow emergency calls?

Special Areas

Loading Docks: Are they well-marked and secure?

Employee Training: Have your employees been trained in crime awareness and prevention?

Key Control: Do you have a foolproof system to keep track of key distribution? Do you know many copies have been made? Trash Areas: Are your trash bins enclosed and locked?

Security Systems

Alarm System: Is it monitored? Does it include a panic device? Do you have prominent signs announcing its presence?

Closed-Circuit TV: How is it monitored? Is there a time delay?

Guards: What kind of training do they have? Are they

bonded? How thorough a background check have you conducted on them?

Guard Dogs: How many do you have? During what hours are they present? Have you posted warnings prominently? Are you aware of your liability in case of attack?

If you are unable to answer many of these questions, a professional security consultation is in order. Remember that by investing a few hundred dollars now, you may be saving thousands of dollars in the long term.

Excerpted with permission from "Small Business Success" magazine, Volume X, produced by Pacific Bell Directory in partnership with the U.S. Small Business Administration and the Partners for Small Business Excellence.

RISK MANAGEMENT FUNDAMENTALS

Risk management is attempting to identify and then manage threats that could severely impact or bring down the organization. Generally, this involves reviewing operations of the organization, identifying potential threats to the organization and the likelihood of their occurrence, and then taking appropriate actions to address the most likely threats.

Traditionally, risk management was thought of as mostly a matter of getting the right insurance. Insurance coverage usually came in rather standard packages, so people tended to not take risk management seriously. However, this impression of risk management has changed dramatically. With the recent increase in rules and regulations, employee-related lawsuits and reliance on key resources, risk management is becoming a management practice that is every bit as important as financial or facilities management.

There are several basic activities which a nonprofit organization can conduct to dramatically reduce its chances of experiencing a catastrophic event that ruins or severely impairs the organization.

GOOD MANAGEMENT

Efforts undertaken to manage an organization well also contributes to sound risk management. For example, a fully attentive board with a wide range of skills may be the most important guard against major threats to an organization.

Careful strategic planning and effective supervision helps ensure organizational resources are closely aligned to accomplishing the organization's mission, and that staff and volunteers are treated fairly and comply with rules and regulations. Every organization must have up-to-date policies which guide the relationships between staff and management. There has been a noticeable increase in lawsuits regarding wrongful termination, harassment and discrimination, disagreements about promotions or salary actions, etc. Parties to lawsuits include the organization, management and/or board members. Therefore, personnel policies must be reviewed at least once a year by an outside advisor who is an expert about all of the employee-related laws and regulations.

RESOURCE MANAGEMENT

People

This aspect of risk management is often overlooked. Each key role in an organization should have some type of resource to back up performance of that role. For example, another person in the organization should have general understanding of another person's role in case that other person for some reason is not able to perform the role. The use of up-to-date job descriptions, todo lists and receiving regular status reports both help to ensure understanding of how others carry out their roles. Have a staff member back up another member who is on vacation. During staff meetings, have a staff member give a presentation about their role and how they carry it out. Ensure that each critical role has at least one backup person who can step in to conduct the role. The backup assignment should be part of the person's job description to help the person take the assignment seriously.

General Facilities:

- Always lock your doors. This seems obvious, but too many organizations fail to do so.

- Ensure your fire protection systems are fully functional by scheduing to test fire alarms twice a year or demanding that your facility's owner test alarms twice a year. Note that certain electrical equipment can be severely damaged from water sprinklers. Arrange adequate covering or arrangement to minimize water seepage if overhead sprinklers open up.
- Conduct inspections twice a year, including to:
  - Inspect floors for ripped carpets
  - Look for cables or wires laying on the floor (tape over them if you have to)
  - Notice any electical outlets with black soot hear outlets (this indicates electrical shortages)
  - Ask all staff if their office accommodations are sufficient, e.g., their chairs are entirely comfortable (tilted correctly for their backs and at the right heights), is lighting sufficient for desk and computer work, etc.

PROJECT MANAGEMENT

Project management is a carefully planned and organized effort to accomplish a specific (and usually) one-time effort, for example, construct a building or implement a new computer system. Project management includes developing a project plan, which includes defining project goals and objectives, specifying tasks or how goals will be achieved, what resources are need, and associating budgets and timelines for completion. It also includes implementing the project plan, along with careful controls to stay on the "critical path", that is, to ensure the plan is being managed according to plan. Project management usually follows major phases (with various titles for these phases), including feasibility study, project planning, implementation, evaluation and support/ maintenance. (Programme planning is usually of a broader scope than project planning, but not always.)

Almost any human activity that involves carrying out a non-repetitive task can be a project. So we are all project managers! We all practise project management (PM). But there is a big difference between carrying out a very simple project involving one or two people and one involving a complex mix of people, organisations and tasks.

PLANNING A PROJECT

Before describing the role and creation of a specification, we need to introduce and explain a fairly technical term: a numbty is a person whose brain is totally numb. In this context, numb means "deprived of feeling or the power of unassisted activity"; in general, a numbty needs the stimulation of an electric cattle prod to even get to the right office in the morning. Communication with numbties is severely hampered by the fact that although they think they know what they mean (which they do not), they seldom actually say it, and they never write it down. And the main employment of numbties worldwide is in creating project specifications. You must know this - and protect your team accordingly.

The agreement upon a written specification has several benefits:

- The clarity will reveal misunderstandings
- The completeness will remove contradictory assumptions
- The rigour of the analysis will expose technical and practical details which numbties normally gloss over through ignorance or fear
- The agreement forces all concerned to actually read and think about the details

The work on the specification can seen as the first stage of Quality Assurance since you are looking for and countering problems in the very foundation of the project - from this perspective the creation of the specification clearly merits a large investment of time.

From a purely defensive point of view, the agreed specification also affords you protection against the numbties who have second thoughts, or new ideas, half way through the project. Once the project is underway, changes cost time (and money). The existence of a demonstrably-agreed specification enables you to resist or to charge for (possibly in terms of extra time) such changes. Further, people tend to forget what they originally thought; you may need proof that you have been working as instructed.

ESTABLISHING CONTROLS

When the planning phase is over (and agreed), the "doing" phase begins. Once it is in motion, a project acquires a direction and momentum which is totally independent of anything you predicted. If you come to terms with that from the start, you can then enjoy the roller-coaster which follows. To gain some hope, however, you need to establish at the start (within the plan) the means to monitor and to influence the project's progress.

There are two key elements to the control of a project

- Milestones (clear, unambiguous targets of what, by when)
- Established means of communication

For you, the milestones are a mechanism to monitor progress; for your team, they are short-term goals which are far more tangible than the foggy, distant completion of the entire project. The milestones maintain the momentum and encourage effort; they allow the team to judge their own progress and to celebrate achievement throughout the project rather than just at its end.

PLANNING FOR THE FUTURE

With all these considerations in merely the "planning" stage of a project, it is perhaps surprising that projects get done at all. In fact projects do get done, but seldom in the predicted manner and often as much by brute force as by careful planning. The point, however, is that this method is non-optimal. Customers feel let down by late delivery, staff are demotivated by constant pressure for impossible goals, corners get cut which harm your reputation, and each project has to overcome the same problems as the last.

With planning, projects can run on time and interact effectively with both customers and suppliers. Everyone involved understands what is wanted and emerging problems are seen (and dealt with) long before they cause damage. If you want your projects to run this way - then you must invest time in planning.

Significant organizational change occurs, for example, when an organization changes its overall strategy for success, adds or removes a major section or practice, and/or wants to change the very nature by which it operates. It also occurs when an organization evolves through various life cycles, just like people must successfully evolve through life cycles. For organizations to develop, they often must undergo significant change at various points in their development. That's why the topic of organizational change and development has become widespread in communications about business, organizations, leadership and management.

ORGANIZATIONAL CHANGE AND DEVELOPMENT

The field of Organization Development is focused on improving the effectiveness of organizations and the people in those organizations. OD has a rich history of research and practice regarding change in organizations.

Your nature and the way you choose to work has significant impact on your client's organization, whether you know it or not. You cannot separate yourself from your client's organization, as if you are some kind of detached observer. You quickly become part of your client's system – the way the people and processes in the organization work with each other on a recurring basis. Thus, it is critical that you have a good understanding of yourself, including your biases (we all have them), how you manage feedback and conflict, how you like to make decisions and solve problems, how you naturally view organizations, your skills as a consultant, etc.

VARIOUS MODELS FOR CHANGE MANAGEMENT

There are numerous well-organized approaches (or models) from which to manage a change effort. Some of the approaches have been around for many years – we just haven't thought of them as such. For example, many organizations undertake strategic planning. The implementation of strategic planning, when done in a systematic, cyclical and explicit approach, is strategic management. Strategic management is also one model for ensuring the success of a change effort. Many people would agree that traditional models of organizational performance management are also models for managing change.

If the Project Gets Stuck

During this phase, if the implementation of the plans gets stalled for a long time, for example, many months, then you might cycle back to an earlier phase in the process in order to update and restart the change management project. Projects can get stuck for a variety of reasons, e.g., if the overall situation changes (there suddenly are new and other priorities in the client's organization), people succumb to burnout, key people leave the organization, the relationship between the consultant and client changes, or people refuse to implement action plans.

Project Termination

These activities are very important to address, even if all participants agree that the project has been successful and no further activities are needed. Project termination activities recognize key learnings from the project, acknowledge the client's development, and identify next steps for you and your client. They also help to avoid "project creep" where the project never ends because the requirements for success keep expanding.

HUMAN RESOURCE MANAGEMENT INTERVENTIONS

Performance is in regard to setting goals, monitoring progress to the goals, sharing feedback, reinforcing activities to achieve goals and dissuading those that don't. Performance also is in regard to developing employees, including by enhancing their overall sense of well-being.

Although the types of interventions selected for a project

depend on a variety of considerations and the interventions in a project often are highly integrated, the following human resource interventions might be particularly helpful in the following kinds of situations: new organizational goals have been established, a major new system or technology must be implemented in a timely fashion, many new employees, plans don't seem to get implemented, productivity is low, ineffective teams, etc.

The following activities focus especially on the organization and its interactions with its external environment, and often involve changes to many aspects of the organization, including employees, groups, technologies, products and services, etc.

Although the types of interventions selected for a project depend on a variety of considerations and the interventions in a project often are highly integrated, the following strategic interventions might be particularly helpful in the following kinds of situations: rapid changes in the external environment, rapid or stagnant sales, significantly increased competition, rapid expansion of markets, mergers and acquisitions, the need for quick and comprehensive change throughout the organization, etc.

UNDERSTANDING ORGANIZATIONS, LEADERSHIP AND MANAGEMENT

To really understand organizational change and begin guiding successful change efforts, the change agent should have at least a broad understanding of the context of the change effort. This includes understanding the basic systems and structures in organizations, including their typical terms and roles.

This requirement applies to the understanding of leadership and management of the organizations, as well. That is why graduate courses in business often initially include a course or some discussion on organizational theory. Organizational change should not be conducted for the sake of change. Organizational change efforts should be geared to improve the performance of organizations and the people in those organizations. Therefore, it's useful to have some understanding of what is meant by "performance" and the various methods to manage performance in organizations.

SYSTEMS THINKING

The past few decades have seen an explosion in the number of very useful tools to help change agents to effectively explore, understand and communicate about organizations, as well as to guide successful change in those organizations. Tools from systems theory and systems thinking especially are a major breakthrough. Even if the change agent is not an expert about systems theory and thinking, even a basic understanding can cultivate an entire new way of working.

The field of Organization Development is focused on improving the effectiveness of organizations and the people in those organizations. OD has a rich history of research and practice regarding change in organizations. Why not learn from that history? Your nature and the way you choose to work has significant impact on your client's organization, whether you know it or not. You cannot separate yourself from your client's organization, as if you are some kind of detached observer. You quickly become part of your client's system – the way the people and processes in the organization work with each other on a recurring basis. Thus, it is critical that you have a good understanding of yourself, including your biases (we all have them), how you manage feedback and conflict, how you like to make decisions and solve problems, how you naturally view organizations, your skills as a consultant, etc.

CHANGE MANAGEMENT

There are several phrases regarding organizational change and development that look and sound a lot alike, but have different meanings. As a result of the prominence of the topic, there seems to be increasingly different interpretations of some of these phrases, while others are used interchangeably. Without at least some sense of the differences between these phrases, communications about organizational change and development can be increasingly vague, confusing and frustrating. There are different overall types of organizational change, including planned versus unplanned, organization-wide versus change primarily to one part of the organization, incremental (slow, gradual change) versus transformational (radical, fundamental), etc.. Knowing which types of change you are doing helps all participants to retain scope and perspective during the many complexities and frequent frustrations during change.

Chapter 18

Off-Premise Catering

OFF-PREMISE CATERING MANAGEMENT

Off-Premise Catering Management fills you in on all crucial legal and financial aspects of the subject, including catering contracts, legal requirements, finding and working with a lawyer, preparing income statements, cost control, and much more. Off-premise catering is serving food at a location away from the caterer's food production facility. One example of a food production facility is a freestanding commissary, which is a kitchen facility used exclusively for the preparation of foods to be served at other locations.

Other examples of production facilities include, but are not limited to, hotel, restaurant, and club kitchens. In most cases there is no existing kitchen facility at the location where the food is served. Caterers provide single-event foodservice, but not all caterers are created equal.

They generally fall into one of three categories:

- Party food caterers supply only the food for an event. They drop off cold foods and leave any last-minute preparation, plus service and cleanup, to others.
- Hot buffet caterers provide hot foods that are delivered from their commissaries in insulated containers. They sometimes provide serving personnel at an additional charge.
- Full-service caterers not only provide food, but frequently cook it to order on-site. They also provide service personnel at the event, plus all the necessary

food-related equipment—china, glassware, flatware, tables and chairs, tents, and so forth. They can arrange for other services, like decor and music, as well. In short, a full-service caterer can plan an entire event, not just the food for it.

Off-premise catering can mean serving thousands of box lunches to a group of conventioneers; barbecuing chicken and ribs for fans before a big college game, serving an elegant dinner for two aboard a luxury yacht, or providing food, staff, and equipment for an upscale fundraiser with hundreds of guests. On a "degree of difficulty" scale from one to ten—one meaning "easy" and ten meaning "most challenging"—on-premise catering is a two, and off-premise would rank a ten!

Advantages and Disadvantages of Off-Premise Catering

Advance deposits Limited start-up investment Limited inventories Controllable costs G Additional revenues Business by contract Direct payment Advance forecasting Free word-of-mouth advertising Selectivity Let's discuss a few of these items in more detail. First, most off-premise caterers require some form of advance deposit prior to an event.

This deposit provides the caterer with some security if the event is canceled and also can be used to purchase some or all of the food and supplies for the party. There is no need for large amounts of capital to get started, since most off premise catering operations begin by using the existing kitchen facilities of a restaurant, club, hotel, church, or other licensed foodservice business. (It is common knowledge that many start their catering businesses in their home kitchens, but it is imperative to state that this is in direct violation of most local zoning ordinances.)

Elements of Successful Off-Premise Catering

What does it take to become a successful off-premise caterer? What experience is necessary, and what personality traits are desirable? Work Experience. Prior experience in the catering profession or the foodservice industry is important. Experience in food preparation and foodservice (both back of-the-house and front-of-the-house) helps caterers understand the procedures and problems in both areas and how the two areas interface. Those with a strong kitchen background, for example, would be wise to gain some front-of-house experience, and front-of-house personnel should learn the kitchen routine. Many successful off-premise caterers began by working as accommodators.

Accommodators are private chefs who are hired to prepare food for parties. Many assist the client with planning the menu, purchasing the food, and even arranging for kitchen and service staff. The food is prepared and served in the client's home or facility, eliminating the need for a catering commissary. Accommodators receive a fee for their services. The party staff is paid directly by the client.

Passion

Successful professionals are passionate about their work, and caterers are no exception. They love what they do! Clients and staff members will quickly detect a lack of passion, and it will cost you business and good workers. If you don't love what you do, move on and try something else. The desire to be an entrepreneur is a trait that is highly desirable for off-premise caterers.

An entrepreneur must be willing to spend extraordinary amounts of time and energy to make the off-premise catering business successful, possess an inherent sense of what is right for the business, have the ability to view all aspects of the business at once rather than focusing only on one or two parts, and demonstrate a strong, incessant desire to be his or her own boss and become financially independent.

Accounting and bookkeeping skills are necessary to understand the financial aspects of operating a catering business.

The ability to prepare and interpret financial statements is essential:

- Learn as much about computers as you can. You'll be amazed at how much you can accomplish by using e-mail, having a website, and using specialized programmes for everything from budgeting to menu planning.

- It's also important to understand the legal aspects of catering. Laws that affect caterers include regulation of licensing, contracts, liability, labour, and alcoholic beverage service. _ A caterer, like any other businessperson, must have some human resource skills. Knowing how to recruit, train, motivate, and manage personnel is critical.
- Off-premise caterers should be knowledgeable about how to develop and implement a marketing plan. Ability to Plan, Organize, Execute, and Control. These are the four basic functions of management. To plan, a caterer must visualize in advance all of the aspects of a catered event and document the plans so they are readily understood by the client and easily executed by the staff.

Open-Mindedness

Open-minded caterers read up on catering trends and try new recipes and menus. They are willing to prepare unfamiliar dishes requested by clients, after thoroughly testing and understanding the recipes.

They discover and try new dishes. They are always learning better ways to run their businesses. The needs of the client must always come first. Success in this business comes from identifying these needs and satisfying them. Unsuccessful off-premise caterers are those who get lost in trying to satisfy their own needs for money, equipment, and greater self-esteem. They forget that the primary goal is to serve the needs of the client. When a client's needs are met, the caterer's needs for revenues, profits, and positive feedback will automatically be met.

Hands-on Attention to Detail Management

The devil is in the details. Have you ever heard that old saying? Another way to put it: We've all been bitten by a mosquito or stung by a bee, but how many of us have been bitten by an elephant? It's always the little things that get us! In catering, the details are virtually endless, a stream of tiny elements that might go wrong and result in a catastrophe. One thing forgotten, misheard, or misplaced can ruin an event. So it's important to check and recheck and to be prepared for last-minute emergencies. It is simply not possible to run this kind of business from behind a desk, reading computer printouts and delegating all tasks.

Off-premise catering companies must be managed from the centre of the action, whether that is with the guests or preparing foods in the kitchen. It comes from checking and rechecking every detail to ensure that it meets the highest of standards. It comes from inspecting for the best and expecting the best. Some call this management style "management by walking around." In one sense that is true, but there is more to it than walking around.

Astute offpremise caterers must:

- Obtain feedback from clients and guests regarding the food and service.
- Oversee the catering staff to ensure they are performing as directed and as expected.
- Help out when a table needs to be cleared or when the bar suddenly becomes very busy.

Help in the kitchen during critical times such as hot food dish-up, and even help scrape, stack, and wash dirty dishes if that's what is necessary. It's a roll-up-your-sleeves kind of profession, and you should never be totally satisfied with the way things are.

Always look for new ways to present food and make it more flavorful, and for better and more efficient ways to do things. Customer-Focused Management An off-premise caterer's full-time mission must be to satisfy the needs of clients.

Mike DeLuca, editor of Restaurant Hospitality, puts it this way: Companies that are 100% customer focused make the customer's satisfaction their only goal. They do not have as goals, increasing sales by a certain percentage, raising a profit margin, or reducing debt. They believe... that if you strive to sell only the highest quality product and strive to please every customer, sales, profit and success will follow.

Leadership

There are major differences between those who lead and those who manage. Catering companies need both types of executives, and some who can do both. If a catering company is earning seven- and eight-figure annual revenues, it is most definitely being led by people with leadership skills. Leaders are able to get people to do things they don't necessarily like to do, but they do them and even enjoy them. You might say: Maintains Develops Administers Innovates Relies on systems Relies on people Counts on controls Counts on trust Does things right Does the right things Works within the system Works on the system Manages things Leads people A leader is more like a thermostat than a thermometre. A thermostat sets the standard temperature for the space it's in.

A thermometre simply records the temperature; it can't change anything. And one more important trait: Leaders take a little more than their share of the blame and a little less than their share of the credit. Professionalism and Common Business Courtesy Off-premise caterers who are not professional in their business practices will never reach the pinnacle of success in the field.

Before we address the technical aspects of catering in the succeeding chapters, it is of utmost importance that we define professionalism.

The following guidelines are adapted from an article by Carol McKibben in Special Events magazine:

- Become known for doing what you say you are going to do.
- Give price quotes and commitments only when you know everything about the event.
- Treat clients and staff members with respect.
- Build relationships with clients. Do not look at them as accounts or projects.
- Be on time, or a bit early, for appointments. Be prepared for an appointment.

- Be honest; don't play games.
- Stand behind your work. If it is wrong, make it right.
- In the face of abuse from others, don't respond by becoming abusive. Try to detach yourself from it emotionally and handle it logically. Of course, do not use your position of power to abuse others.
- Dress professionally.
- Enjoy your work as an off-premise caterer. When work ceases to be enjoyable, it is time to quit and find a new career.

Ethics in Management

The Roman philosopher Publilius Syrus said, "A good reputation is more valuable than money." This is as true today as it was in ancient times. And yet, lack of ethics is perhaps the most widely discussed topic in today's business world. We read and hear of illegalities, scandals, and other forms of questionable behaviour bringing down some of the nation's largest corporations. Off-premise caterers are in no way exempt from ethical concerns.

Even the smallest caterers deal in issues of fairness, legal requirements, and honesty on a daily basis. Examples include truth in menu, misleading advertising, unexpected and unjustified last-minute add-ons to the party price, and even underbidding a competitor when the client has disclosed your competitor's price. The truly ethical caterer will assume responsibility for the host to ensure that the host plans an event in the best interest of the guests. A host who wishes to serve alcohol to underage guests or barbecued ribs to a group of elderly people (tough to eat with dentures) is out of line and needs to be advised that this will not work. In fact, an ethical caterer will refuse to cater an event that is clearly not being planned in the best interest of the host or guests.

There are times when a caterer is given a free hand in planning a menu. Perhaps a grieving client calls for food after the funeral of a loved one, saying, "Please send over food for 50 guests tomorrow night. You know what we like!" The ethical caterer will not take advantage of this situation by either providing too much food or overcharging the client. Another temptation arises when the caterer is pressed to cater more events on a certain day or evening than he or she can reasonably accommodate. The extra money looks good.

Unethical caterers will rationalize that they can handle all the events, even if an inexperienced supervisor or staff must oversee these events, or even if the kitchen staff will not be able to prepare the caterer's usual high-quality food because of lack of time and personnel. Caterers who take on more work than they can reasonably accommodate are greedy and are considered by many observers to be unethical.

In the foregoing situation the caterer should decline the work and perhaps recommend another caterer. Some caterers refuse to recommend another catering firm because they feel that if the client is not pleased with the other firm, the caterer who turned down the business will be blamed for the recommendation. Other caterers freely recommend one or more companies when unable to cater events. There are times when it is very hard not to bad-mouth a competitor, but this is considered unethical as well as rude.

Those who are ethical would rather point out their own strengths than downgrade the competition. It can be very tempting for self-employed caterers to underreport income or overstate expenses. They rationalize that no one will know if they accept cash for a party, then fail to report it as income and pay the associated tax, or that no one will know if they happen to charge personal expenses now and then to the business. Some caterers who are licensed to sell liquor by the drink or by the bottle are tempted to bill clients for beverages that were not consumed.

These practices are not only unethical—they are illegal. Other ethical violations occur when caterers receive under-the-table cash "kickbacks" from suppliers, misrepresent their services to potential clients, or bid on party plans or ideas stolen from other caterers. Caterers also soon learn that some clients are unethical. A few are masterful at finding fault with a wedding or other important event, then demanding a "discount" based on whatever flaw they feel they have uncovered. Some will refuse to pay for linens that were damaged by candles they lit on them! You'll find people who, mid- party, will ask you to stay "a couple hours of overtime, just to wrap things up" – then not show up to pay you for the extra time the next day, as agreed.

The key to effective time management is to set goals for a lifetime, for five years, and for each year, month, week, and day. (Use some of the tips for putting SMART goals in writing–not just for "big picture" goals, but as part of your daily business.) Without written goals, off-premise caterers cannot effectively manage their time. Because time management involves choosing how to spend time, it is impossible to make proper choices without knowing your desired goals.

The captain of a ship without a destination cannot choose the proper course. He will cruise aimlessly at sea, never reaching his port of call. It is equally important to schedule "downtime" for yourself–for family, friends, hobbies, and interests other than work. You are guarding against burnout when you insist on some personal time. Off-premise caterers can choose from an array of time-saving techniques and technical advances to help them in the quest to efficiently manage time:

- Make those daily, detailed lists of goals and objectives.
- Use technical advances to speed up paper handling, such as fax machines and computers with word processing, accounting, and menu-planning software.
- For heaven's sake, if you don't have a computer, get one! You can purchase one nowadays for a monthly payment of less than $40. You can take classes to learn how to use it or hire someone to teach you individually.
- Use cellular phones to stay in touch while away from the office. These are lifesavers at off-premise catering locations when emergency and other calls are necessary, and if you have downtime, a cellular phone can make it easy for you to use this time to return phone calls.

- Handle incoming papers only once. Here's the rule: Do it, delegate it, discard it, or file it. (Better yet, hire someone else to file it!)
- Do your most important work at times when you happen to be most alert. Most of us know whether we are "morning people" or "night owls." Take advantage of your peak energy periods to handle your most challenging tasks.
- Sign up for a seminar or course in time management to learn more tips.

One of the biggest time wasters for a caterer is also the source of much business— the prospective client who calls to ask questions—so it's an interruption that cannot be ignored, but can be controlled.

Whoever answers the phone at your business should always qualify the incoming call by asking:

- The date of the event
- The location of the event
- The number of guests
- The budget for the event Why?

First of all, time can be wasted talking about an event before you ask the date and discover you're not able to do it in the first place because of a scheduling conflict. Perhaps the number of guests is too small or too large for your particular company, the budget is insufficient, or the proposed location is already booked for another event. Always focus on results by asking yourself, "Will this activity help me achieve any of my goals?" Prioritize tasks in order of their importance and know when to delegate them to others.

Most people waste countless hours, days, weeks, and years chitchatting on the phone, shuffling papers, running errands, and doing other things that are easy enough but offer little or no payoff. Learn to delegate these types of tasks whenever possible. Pay other people to do them, and don't tell yourself you can't afford it—you can always make more money, but you have only so much time.

The true achievers—in catering and in other fields—minimize their time on low priority, low-payoff tasks and turn their attention to those things that will bring the greatest rewards. These tasks are often difficult to accomplish, take a great deal of time, and involve at least some risk. For example, a caterer could spend the entire day showing prospective clients numerous suitable locations for a major event. The caterer would then spend the next three days preparing a written proposal for an event at each of the locations, with no guarantee that the event will even take place. However, if the caterer is hired, there's a five-figure profit to be made. Worth the risk? Certainly! Another high-payoff task might be to write a new catering menu.

Both this and the aforementioned task require large chunks of time and involve some risk, but more than likely will produce major rewards in increased revenues and profits. In summary, off-premise caterers who best manage their time in the long run will be the most successful. They become the leading caterers in their communities, in their states, and in the country. Getting Organized When projects, tasks, catering kitchens, and offices are organized, things run much more smoothly and efficiently. The time spent looking for things and jumping from job to job is wasted time that could be put to much better use.

Looking Ahead – Catering in the Future

What does the future hold for caterers in this new century? First of all, we know that catering is neither rocket science nor brain surgery. Change is inevitable in this business, but not at the same rate as, say, in molecular theory or medical technology. In fact, in catering, rediscovering foods of the previous century is trendy! Many caterers still feature the signature dishes – honey coconut shrimp, beef tenderloin, Caesar salad – that they've served for decades. Why? The customers demand, and enjoy, them.

This certainly doesn't mean things stay stagnant in our industry. Innovative buffet and food station décor will continue to evolve. Most catering companies will continue to build their reputations on elegant, "over-the-top" food presentations, and the healthy competition shows no signs of abating. Other caterers prize research, developing cutting-edge menu items to set them apart from the pack.

More women are entering the off-premise catering field. Paula LeDuc in the San Francisco Bay area, Katherine Farrell in Ann Arbor, Abigail Kirsch in New York, Mary Micucci in Los Angeles, and Joy Wallace in Miami are but a handful of enterprising women who have grown their companies into catering's elite. Staffing woes will continue to be monumental, as hiring, training, and retraining get tougher. Foodservice has always been a somewhat transient industry.

Astute caterers will use pre-employment aptitude and personality testing, master online staff scheduling systems, and develop their own training programmes. They will also realize, if they haven't already, that they must treat their employees at least as well as they treat their clients. Along the same lines, in a top-tier catering operation, the employees treat each other as well as they treat their clients. Caterers of the future will come to realize that bigger is not necessarily better.

Having a large volume of business is admirable—but only when the quality of your work rises to the same level. A company can grow to the point where quality slips, gross profit margins lag, more equipment is needed, overhead costs expand, and the bottom line shrinks proportionately. The intelligent caterer will downsize, watch margins and profits grow—and overall stress levels diminish—as they become more selective about the clientele they service. Caterers are realizing that "high tech" will never replace personalized service, or "high touch"—but without high tech, they'll limit their potential for high touch.

In an industry where, amazingly, some caterers still don't accept credit cards, the savvy businessperson is learning to embrace new technology, launching interactive websites and e-mail marketing campaigns. They're creating improved computer generated proposals, rental orders, packing lists, staffing schedules, and instant financial statements. And they're realizing that computer-savvy business owners have more time to do what they love—which is run their business! Competition will continue to increase.

Sales will grow, but not without some dips, because economic woes, terrorist attacks, and the resulting fears cannot help but impact the catering profession. More caterers were hurt financially by the recession at the beginning of this century than by the September 11 terrorist attacks, but both left their marks on the industry. An increased use of security cameras at high profile events (and in some cases, to thwart theft) is one result of the heightened awareness. Mega-event catering is acknowledged as an excellent way to grow business—at golf and tennis tournaments, NASCAR races, air shows, boat shows, and more.

In addition to being profitable events, they expose the caterer to a wider range of potential clients. Then again, a caterer from Augusta, Georgia, generates enough revenue from serving sandwiches and beverages at the Masters' Golf Tournament that he need not cater at all the rest of the year! The pressure experienced in servicing huge, multiday events is as big as the events themselves, but the rewards can be significant. At the end of the 1900s, B. Joseph Pine II wrote The Experience Economy, a primer about the "new rules of engagement" for businesses.

Pine asserts that a new economic model is taking shape as we move from a service-based economy into an experience-based economy, where successful vendors literally create an "experience" for clients by using props and services to engage them in an "inherently personal way." Pine claims that Walt Disney was the founding father of the "Experience Economy," and in today's restaurant industry there are plenty of examples—Rainforest Cafe, Planet Hollywood, Hard Rock Cafes, and other themed eateries that combine food, service, and atmosphere to create a more "complete" dining experience. This kind of trend is adaptable for off-premise caterers too, with elaborate themes, staff members who double as costumed performers, team-building events, and imaginative menu items presented in wild new ways to delight and entertain the crowd as well as feed them!

For those who love to have fun, and who are as adventurous as they are practical, it's a great time to be an off-premise caterer. The Seven Habits of Highly Successful Caterers Let's examine some additional techniques, philosophies, and real-life ways to be successful in the challenging field of off-premise catering. Habits are things we do automatically, like brushing our teeth, combing our hair, or straightening a tablecloth that's uneven. We hardly think about them, we just do them. Stephen R. Covey wrote The Seven Habits of Highly Effective People, which has been a bestseller for years—you should read it if you haven't already. But what are some habits that mark successful caterers? What separates star performers from the rest of the crowd? With a nod to Mr. Covey, here are seven key traits.

One of our favourite sayings is, "A turtle goes nowhere until it sticks its neck out." In order to succeed, we must be continually growing and improving, and the only way to do this is to leave our comfort zones—and stick our necks out! If you're right-handed, you feel quite comfortable writing with your right hand. Try writing with your left hand. You're definitely out of your comfort zone. But after a while, you'll find you can actually write with either hand.

Successful caterers make things happen by taking calculated risks, whether it is trying new menu items, new buffet display concepts, or accepting a job in a new and challenging off-premise location. Caterers who refuse to take risks fail to grow and learn are left behind. Sincere Concern for Others Nobody cares how much you know until they know how much you care. Empathy and genuine concern for your clients and staff are paramount to long-term success. What are their needs, wishes, and desires? What are their concerns and their "hot buttons"? By putting ourselves in their positions, we can begin to show concern for others and understand them.

When we do this, we develop meaningful relationships and, not coincidentally, loyalty. We give them what they want, and we get what we want. Keeping Up with Current Trends It's not just a matter of food and presentation and theme trends. Caterers who are not wired to do business online through the Internet and e-mail are missing out on huge opportunities. The online catering referral service, Leading

Caterers of America (founded by the book's co-author Bill Hansen), receives 5 to 20 inquiries per day from clients looking for catering services coast to coast, in Alaska, Hawaii, and occasionally overseas. People do shop for catering online, and the companies that lead the way have high quality websites and diligently reply to e-mailed requests in a timely manner.

Caterers need to get in the habit of responding to e-mail correspondence as soon as possible, as well as providing e-mailed proposals to those clients who prefer to do business via their computers.

Event planners who book caterers for their clients love receiving e-mailed proposals, because they are easy to copy-and-paste into their own proposals. If you're not in the habit of working online, you're behind the times. Excellent Priorities and Time Management You get 20 per cent of your sales and profits from 80 per cent of your clients, and 80 per cent of your sales and profits from 20 per cent of your clients. None of us ever go home at night thinking that all the work is done—it never is. It's simply a question of what's most important, as well as what's most urgent. Urgent things are never really an issue.

There's no question that if you have a catered event today, it will get done. But what's most urgent is not necessarily what's most important. You must understand the difference. For example, you could spend a day catering three small parties for 25 guests each, but fall behind on preparing a proposal for another job, in three months, for 500 guests—and lose it to a competitor whose proposal was simply submitted on time. Successful caterers spend their time in those areas that generate the biggest paybacks in terms of money, quality, and other rewards. They make a habit of planning their days, leaving time for the most important, as well as the most urgent.

At the start of each day they prepare an agenda that details both short-term objectives and long-term goals. If you're a student, you should already be using this technique to accomplish as much as you can in school.

Quality before Quantity Bigger is not necessarily better. Still, many of us get caught up in that way of thinking. If our sales are $1 million, let's go for $2 million. If they're $2 million, what's wrong with $4 million? And if $4 million is good... There's nothing wrong with building sales if quality does not suffer. However, when the quality of our products and services suffers so does the quality of our lifestyle. More business means more hours at work. And doctors will tell you they've never met a man or woman who, on a deathbed, expressed a wish that he or she had spent more time at work.

If we can grow our businesses with no adverse effects on the quality of our lives or our products, then we should go for it! But if we find profits slipping and clients complaining, and we need a letter of introduction when we stumble home at 3:00 A.M., then something's very wrong. We need to make of habit of continually asking ourselves whether we might be better off with less business and more time for ourselves and for our families.

We need to continually examine the quality of our work to ensure that it's not slipping because we've allowed ourselves to take on too much. Being Detail Oriented A baseball player who bats.250 gets three hits for every 12 times at bat. One who bats. 333 gets four hits for every 12 times at bat. The difference—one more hit for every 12 times at bat—means the difference between an average major league ball player and a Hall of Fame inductee. Do you make it a habit to continually look for the little things?

A good caterer isn't nitpicky, but is forever finding something that needs to be tweaked, adjusted, redone, or improved—little things that most customers won't notice, but that greatly impact the overall professionalism of an event. Being aware of the details in flavors, looks, aromas, and tidiness separates the average caterers from the superstars. And, by all means, check the spelling, grammar, and punctuation in all your written materials, from brochures to contracts—or hire someone to do it.

Again, the goal is to present a professional image. Remember? The devil is in the details. Setting High Standards If you refuse to accept anything but the very best, you very often get the best. Successful caterers set their standards high and expect excellence from themselves and their staff members. They're never happy with the status quo, always striving to make each party, wedding, or event better than the last.

They debrief after an event, asking staff for input and improvements. They know that if they fail to improve, they're leaving the door open for their competitors to capture a good customer or a larger share of the market.

Successful caterers also make a habit of lifelong learning. They're forever reading, attending trade shows, and exploring areas that will help them improve their own businesses with new ideas. They challenge and reward their staff members for having the same attitude.

Vince Lombardi, the late NFL coach, who during his career coached the first team to ever win the Super Bowl, put it this way: "The quality of a person's life is in direct proportion to their commitment to excellence, regardless of their chosen field of endeavor." How Does an Off-Premise Caterer Gauge Success? There are a number of signs to look for when evaluating an existing off-premise catering business. Healthy companies rate highly in all of these areas.

Those that are unhealthy, or even on the brink of failure, will not rate nearly as well.

- Management thoroughly plans, organizes, executes, and controls each catered event.
- Proper controls are in place for costs, accounts receivable and payable, and liquid assets such as cash and inventories. Theft prevention is also a priority.
- Food and service quality is well-controlled and meets or exceeds clients' approval.
- Pricing for food and services is fair and competitive with other firms in the marketplace. There is a spirit of healthy competition.
- The catering firm enjoys good working relationships with both clients and suppliers.
- Time and attention are given to food safety in storage, preparation, and display. Employees know the local health codes and follow them.
- There is sufficient working capital to operate the

business. The firm can make loan payments as they become due. Excessive credit is not extended to clients.

- Budgets are prepared and followed. Business records, insurance coverage, and licenses are kept up to date. The information derived from these records is used to provide data to help manage the business.
- Sales growth is controlled. There are sufficient financial and personnel resources to operate as business steadily grows.
- Market trends are anticipated.
- Management and staff have a good working knowledge of the off-premise catering field.
- There are solid, trusting relationships between management and staff. Staff members are well trained and feel truly appreciated—because they are.
- Management works closely with a qualified accountant to plan for payment of taxes.
- And, finally, management is willing to seek qualified professional assistance if problems arise.

The Off-Premise Catering Model is the factors that enter into the off-premise catering arena. It shows how managerial philosophies and techniques, as well as laws regarding personnel, business, alcoholic beverage service, and sanitation and safety, must all be interrelated to guide the company. It then depicts how marketing efforts produce clients, which in turn creates needs for site inspections and logistical plans, including planning in these specific areas: menus, beverages, equipment, personnel, and any other related services.

Once the planning is complete, it is possible to provide clients with written proposals, which include all the aforementioned plans along with pricing. Normally, proposals are modified somewhat. Once modification is complete and all provisions meet with the approval of both caterer and client, a contract is prepared that contains all the conditions outlined in the proposal. As the party date approaches, certain operational elements are addressed, such as:

- Hiring and scheduling staff
- Purchasing and pre-preparation of menu items

- Ordering equipment as needed from party rental companies
- Obtaining licenses and permits, as needed, for use of the site, serving alcohol, etc.
- Preparing a "pull sheet" that details all items supplied by the commissary to produce the party.
- Coordinating all beverage and accessory services with the client and the vendors.

Chapter 19

Hotel Company Practices

The importance of electronic hotel-distribution routes has grown substantially in recent years. According to statistics quoted in the Horwath Worldwide Hotel Industry Studies, direct reservations fell from approximately 39 percent in 1995 to 33 percent in 1999, with the shift in sales going almost exclusively to electronic channels. While hotels continue to make extensive use of travel-agent-oriented global distribution systems (GDSs), consumer adoption of the Internet as a reliable and secure commerce medium has prompted a change in the way in which hotel rooms are being distributed.

The Internet has dramatically changed the way people communicate, research information, and buy goods and services. Travel products in particular have proven to be suitable for sale on line. The typical Internet user—an affluent, frequent traveler who spends more than the average on leisure and entertainment—is an attractive market for travel suppliers. Furthermore, from a consumer's perspective purchasing travel products on line has, in many instances, become faster, easier, and more convenient than contacting a travel agent or telephoning a supplier directly. As a result, on-line travel-related revenues are forecast to grow sharply.

HOTEL PRICING ON THE WEB

In a 2000 study that almost six out of ten leisure travelers now actively seek the "lowest possible price" for travel services. Similarly, a 2001 Forrester Research study found that 66 percent of all buyers had used an on-line discount in the previous 12 months to buy travel on line, and a study by the Joint Hospitality Industry Congress found a real expectation among consumers that Internet prices would be lower than those available in the "bricks and mortar" world. Such a perception has developed for several reasons. First, many of the best-known Internet retailers initially competed with traditional outlets based, to a large extent, on price.

Second, savvy consumers are aware that webbased distribution costs are lower than those of other channels. As Jack Geddes, Radisson Hotels Worldwide's managing director, sales and marketing Asia, has pointed out: "Consumers now understand that suppliers are cutting costs through this channel and expect savings to be passed on to them, as well as being rewarded for making the booking themselves". Such expectations are being reinforced by the budget-airline sector, which offers substantial discounts for online bookings. Companies such as EasyJet, RyanAir, and Buzz estimate that by avoiding telesales and travel agents, they can achieve savings of up to 30 percent—which they pass on to customers in the form of lower fares. Similar or even greater levels of savings can be made by hotel companies, as can be seen from the internal, which show how an 80- to 90- percent savings in transaction charges can be achieved by selling directly to the consumer on line.

Finally, many hotels (and airlines) use the web to sell last-minute deals—packages at relatively low prices but with short lead times. While such promotions can help dispose of unsold inventory, they have also resulted in the public's associating rooms sold over the Internet with lower prices. These factors have combined to make consumers associate on-line booking with good value, which in the consumer's mind translates into low prices. However, in the case of hotel brands' own web sites, industry practice frequently seems to be the opposite of theory.

In a 1999 survey, for instance, a colleague and I found that rates obtained from the web site were usually substantially higher than those obtained by contacting the central reservations office. That study was limited, however, in that it focused only on direct sales over hotel chains' own branded web sites. Electronic distribution is rapidly evolving for hotels, and a large number of other on-line consumer focused channels are now available, with most chains using multiple routes to reach the consumer.

The availability of numerous points of sale poses some interesting questions. Foremost among these is: Is there consistency between the room availability and prices being offered over each of the channels? Unlike in the physical world, where a potential customer would have to telephone or visit several suppliers, comparison shopping on the web can generally be accomplished relatively quickly. Research has shown that consumers shopping for travel on line almost always check more than one site before purchasing. According to Jupiter Media Metrix, just 10 percent of would-be guests visit only one site to book a hotel room, another 43 percent visit two or three sites, and 22 percent visit four or more sites.

Because they check prices in several places, on line purchasers have become increasingly intolerant of inconsistent information, and may react unfavorably to a firm's disparate rates by booking with the company's competitor.

Two related questions, then, are:

- If rates are not consistent across channels, is any one route consistently cheaper?
- Is the company's approach to pricing logical from both the consumer's and the hotel's perspective?

Methodology and Limitations of The Study

Previous studies of hotels' Internet use have been limited. Murphy et al. focused on rating the content of hotel web sites, while Van Hoof and Combrink attempted to measure managers' perceptions of and attitudes toward the Internet. Web reservations facilities were investigated in detail in the co-authored paper that I mentioned above. However, the issue of pricing over several distribution channels does not appear to have been the subject of extensive systematic research to date.

The objective of this study, therefore, was to analyse the room rates being offered to consumers over multiple electronic distribution channels. An exhaustive analysis of the rates being offered by all hotels would be virtually impossible. Those rates are constantly in flux, as hoteliers project occupancy rates and open or close rate classes accordingly (according to yield-management principles).

Major international hotel chains' electronic-distribution activities are indicative of industry patterns, because recent research has shown that large companies are most active on the web—perhaps because their size often gives them an advantage in terms of technical expertise and financial resources.

Research Findings

As each of the major hotel brands uses multiple simultaneous distribution channels. The most commonly available channels were voice (via the company's CRS) and electronic. The company that did not make a CRS number available was in the economy sector. Offering hotel rooms via the company web site is almost universal, all but one of the brands surveyed offering on-line reservations in this manner. It is interesting to note that this represents a considerable advancement when compared to surveys made only a few years ago, which found that only approximately 50 percent of the major hotel companies provided on-line reservations. As hotel companies make less use of the other channels investigated.

Approximately four-fifths of the major brands used the GDS-based intermediaries Expedia and Travelocity, three-quarters used Travelweb, and barely one-third used World-Res. These findings are not in themselves surprising. Both Expedia and Travelocity draw their data from the GDSs, where the majority of the hotel brands represented in this study (being major hotel companies) can reasonably expect to be represented. Similarly, Travelweb draws its data from THISCO (The Hotel Industry Switching Company), and thus any of the hotel brands that use this as their switch service could be expected to make inventory available for sale via Travelweb. The chains' low usage of World- Res surprising.

Rates Available

Each of the electronic channels offered multiple rates. As can be seen, each channel presented an average of five rates in response to the request, with more being offered to the customer by Travelocity than by the other channels surveyed. Presenting a variety of rates to the customer has both positive and negative implications.

From a positive perspective, it offers choices to potential customers, allowing them to match their needs with the products being sold. On the other hand, presenting a large number of rates without adequate differentiation between products can confuse customers regarding what they are getting for their money.

Mean Prices

It was difficult to make a general observation about which of the several channels is consistently least expensive on average, although Expedia's rates were marginally lower than those offered by other channels and WorldRes seemed to offer consistently higher rates than did the others. Indeed, all things considered, prices across each of the channels were comparable— with the average price for the Hotel company website 444 97% Expedia 38 84% Travelocity.com 35 78% Travelweb 34 76% WorldRes 14 31% requested room being in the range of US$163. It was interesting that Expedia's mean rates were lower, because as an on-line travel agency, it has a high distribution cost, and it would be logical to assume that rates offered over this channel would reflect the higher costs.

By the same token, since WorldRes's transaction costs are relatively low in comparison with those offered by the other channels surveyed, hotels could potentially offer cheaper rates over this channel. In other words, what found is that when selling hotel products on line, there does not appear to be a relationship between the cost of using the distribution channel and the rate offered. Illogically, the electronic channels with the highest transaction costs for the hotel seem to regularly offer the best value to the customer. As will be discussed, hoteliers need to rethink their current practices and take action if they are to benefit from the increasing market for on-line hotel-room sales.

Segment Breakout

The foregoing discussion was based on an overall look at hotel room sales distribution. If the brands studied are subdivided into classifications based on their targeted market segment, a different picture emerges. As hotels at the low end of the market are far more likely to offer consistent rates across all channels used. While it could be speculated that the reason for this might be that economy properties are more likely to have a single fixed price for their product irrespective of demand, it could also be due to a more consistent pricing strategy on the part of the hotel companies involved when addressing a relatively price-sensitive market.

Furthermore it can be seen that consumers at the low ends of the market are far more likely to obtain low rates through direct (company-owned) channels. For economy brands, direct sales over the company's own web site were lowest 26 percent of the time.

When coupled with the 46 percent of cases where the same rate is offered irrespective of the channel used, that means that a consumer reserving an economy room will find the cheapest rate on the hotel company's web site nearly three times out of four. With mid-price products, the chain's web site is even more likely to give the best rate, offering the lowest rate nearly half of the time. The situation is different at the upper end of the market.

Haggling Required

It is also clear from the data that a hotel company's CRS is not the place to obtain the best rates, at least if one takes the first offer as did for this study. Irrespective of the market segment, there is a higher probability of being quoted the highest rate through this channel, and bookings through this route were almost never the cheapest available.This finding, however, is to a large extent driven by my methodology. Indeed, in many cases, as soon as indicated that did not plan to make a booking at the quoted rate, the CRS associate quoted another, lower rate. This anecdotal finding suggests that negotiation might have resulted in lower prices.

DAWN OF A NEW WAY

From the above discussion, it can be seen that both the range of channels through which hotels can be booked and the complexity of such channels have grown. This study represents a first attempt at documenting hotel companies' pricing practices over electronic routes. The study revealed that the majority of hotel brands now use simultaneous, multiple electronic channels of distribution, making their rooms available to a relatively wide audience.

While the use of CRS-based reservations has fallen slightly, there has been a growth in the availability of hotel companies' own web sites, and a vast majority of companies that studied now make their rooms available for sale in this manner. The differences between this study's findings and earlier published research indicate a major expansion in hotel chains' use of the web as a direct-sales medium, perhaps accompanied by a realization of the web's benefits in comparison with other, more traditional, electronic channels of distribution.

Most companies offer multiple rates to customers over each channel. It is interesting to note, however, the large number of companies that now offer consistent pricing across all channels. Previous research found less than 10 percent of companies had consistent pricing and cited the lack of integration among the various inventory databases used to manage inventory as a possible cause. Yet over one-third of the brands studied now offer consistent pricing across multiple channels, indicating progress in the industry's management of electronic distribution. Although no single channel consistently offers the lowest prices, in-depth analysis does reveal a link between pricing and the market being targeted.

First, the lowest prices can rarely be obtained from the CRS (absent negotiation), irrespective of market segment. As compared to the first-offered CRS price, a would-be customer can save at least 5 percent by booking over any of the electronic channels examined. From the data it can be seen that consumers are more likely to find the lowest prices on the hotel chains' own web sites in the economy and mid-price segments than will be found from those companies' CRS or third-party web sites. So-called upmarket hotel brands are, on the other hand, more likely to quote higher prices on their own web site than what they offer on other channels. Economy brands seem to be the only ones in the industry as a whole displaying a logical on-line pricing strategy (in terms of the relationship between the cost of using a channel and the rates offered there) and also in terms of actively managing their channels of distribution.

Implications

First, it is clear that for those with a taste for upscale products, the hotel brand's own web site is not the place to shop, as better value can be obtained in most cases through other channels. More interesting, however, is the fact that, in general, prices have become more or less equal across many of the channels investigated, and by implication, across many other electronic distribution channels as well. It is well established that time is a valuable commodity in today's society. Since the number and variety of ways that a consumer can book a hotel room has become undeniably manifold, the cost associated with searching through even a small number of the many consumer-focused channels currently available in the marketplace in an attempt to find a low price has increased.

Given that this study has found that many of the rates being offered over alternative channels are more or less the same for many hotels, customers should reconsider whether all that time and energy searching for the lowest rate is actually worthwhile. The implications for the hotelier are more pressing. Findings suggest that many hotel chains are not actively managing the room rates being offered in their portfolio of electronic distribution channels. Most companies offer multiple rates on each channel, which, as discussed earlier, can be beneficial as it gives a choice to the customer. Displaying too many rates, though, can be counterproductive, if the customer becomes overwhelmed.

Presenting a small number of tightly defined rates would be the most appropriate solution. However, most companies currently display about five rates in response to a customer inquiry, with others showing significantly more, usually with little or no apparent product differentiation. In addition, there appears to be inconsistency in terms of the rates being offered over electronic channels. In many cases, no clear or logical pricing strategy is apparent. The lowest prices are offered on channels with the highest transaction costs, and vice versa.

A small number of companies offer consistent pricing irrespective of the channel being used to make the booking. Informal follow up with those companies revealed that they follow this strategy as they believe in the principle of one "correct" price for each customer. In this way, they do not have to address the issue of customer dissatisfaction as a result of a person's being quoted a lower price for a room on a different channel after having already made a booking. However, such an approach ignores the issue of the cost of processing a booking over a particular channel. As was discussed earlier, such costs vary greatly depending to a large extent on the number of intermediaries between the supplier and the customer.

The greater the number of intermediaries, the greater the transaction cost and processing fees—and therefore the greater the distribution cost. This would seem to argue for having high rates on the channels that have high-cost structures and low prices on those with low cost structures. Coupled with this matter is the fact that customers have become more knowledgeable about and comfortable with e-commerce issues in general, are more aware that distribution costs are lower in the virtual world than the bricks-and-mortar one, and thus increasingly expect to find the cheapest prices over electronic, and particularly direct electronic, routes. Put simply, when they go to a hotel company's web site, they expect to find the best value there.

This study has shown that in many cases this is simply not the case, given that luxury hotels in particular tend to offer their highest rates over direct channels — and (ironically) their cheapest rates over the most expensive on-line intermediaries. Informal follow up to the study revealed that this may be due to the proactive approach of the on-line companies in contacting hotel companies on practically a daily basis and encouraging them to reduce their rates in return for better positioning on their search listings. In contrast, the rates on hotel companies' web sites go largely unmanaged, in many cases being set far in advance and not adjusted to reflect changing supply and demand. Irrespective of its root cause, the behaviour of hotel companies is driving Internet shoppers into the arms of the waiting on-line intermediaries, where in addition to consistently low prices, they also find wide product choice.

Because of this, it's likely that many hotels are losing potential bookings to competitors as a result of consumers' migration toward the on-line travel sites that offer relatively low rates from many different hotel chains. Instead of being presented with a list of a chain's properties on a company's web site, prospective guests see a much wider variety of options from the on-line intermediary and may be tempted to book a competitor's room (especially if price becomes an issue).

Once consumers conclude that they will usually find better prices on a third-party channel, they will make Expedia or Travelocity, for example, their first port of call for future bookings — threatening brand loyalty, driving up transaction fees, increasing reservation leakage, and strengthening the third parties' power to demand "special rates" or commission overrides for a company to gain premium positioning (or even inclusion) in their search listings. Hotel companies need to take urgent action if they are not to lose control over the sale of their own product. At the very least, this means offering consistent prices over all channels, but more probably means providing customers the lowest rate over their own web site. This would decrease guests' motivation to book on alternative electronic channels, would help build web-site traffic, and should help to decrease distribution costs.

Customer Relationship Management (CRM)—a managerial philosophy that enables a firm to become intimately familiar with its customers—is currently gaining widespread popularity in many industries. Firms that embrace CRM strive to provide consistent and personal customer service over time and across multiple touch points.

CUSTOMER RELATIONSHIP MANAGEMENT

Customer Relationship Management (CRM) is currently one of the hottest topics in the fields of business strategy, information technology, and marketing management. Put simply, CRM is a management philosophy that calls for the reconfiguration of the firm's activities around the customer. CRM differs from traditional marketing initiatives in that, while the latter take predominately a short-term, transaction approach, CRM focuses on maximizing revenue from each customer over the lifetime of the relationship by getting to know each one intimately. CRM is also, by definition, a cross functional philosophy that calls for substantial business integration.

Thus, to implement CRM successfully, a very different mindset is needed: The firm no longer markets to customers, but it fosters a relationship with them through programmes that span marketing, operations, information systems, accounting, and other organizational functions. One of the questions most often asked about CRM is, "why bother?" Changing an organization's philosophy and methods of operation is troublesome; developing and maintaining in-depth customer databases is expensive and the benefits of the approach are not guaranteed.

THE POTENTIAL OF CRM IN THE LODGING INDUSTRY

Lodging-industry participants face an increasingly competitive market. In addition, the basis of competition is changing. Location, a key driver of business, is fixed in the short and medium term, and attracting and retaining customers based on facilities and amenities is becoming increasingly difficult as they have become increasingly standardized across competing brands. Price competition is unattractive, even more so as consumers are able to easily find and compare prices over the Internet. As a consequence consumers are increasingly displaying less brand loyalty, and CRM is becoming increasingly attractive as a way for hotel companies to differentiate themselves from their competitors.

The lodging sector is ideally suited to applying the principles of CRM. In few other industries is there such potential to build up a comprehensive and accurate picture of the client. In few other industries do customers provide the significant amount of information hotel guests divulge when making a reservation and during their hotel stay. Every interaction between the guest and the customer is an opportunity to refine knowledge about her or him and to further build a relationship.By methodically collecting, consolidating, and analyzing both guest preferences and transactional data, hotel chains have the potential to develop a deep understanding of each customer's needs and preferences, provide substantially improved service levels, individually tailor the customer experience, and generally offer more personalized service. Providing outstanding personal service is certainly not a new concept in the hotel sector.

Companies such as Ritz-Carlton and the Savoy group historically maintained extensive manual guest-history systems recording guest preferences in an effort to better serve their best customers. However, when operated manually, such systems are expensive to maintain, are frequently inaccurate, and can only be used to track a limited number of clients at individual properties. Developments in information and communications technologies have enabled automation and efficiencies in these processes, reducing costs, increasing accuracy, and allowing comprehensive knowledge about each customer to be shared on a global basis.

The Lodging Industry's Structure

Lodging is an important component of the tourism industry, providing accommodation (and associated ancillary services) to travelers while away from home. Lodging operations are diverse, ranging from small bed-and breakfast properties in rural locations to large hotels with several thousand rooms in major cities. The majority of the world's hotel properties are concentrated in Europe (55 percent) and North America (22 percent).

The exhibit also demonstrates that the average property size in North America is larger than that in Europe (56 versus 28 rooms), with chain-affiliated properties being more common in North America. Despite controlling only a minority of room stock (approximately 30 percent of total room supply) hotel chains dominate the lodging sector and tend to exert a disproportionate influence on industry operations and performance.

THE DATA-OWNERSHIP DILEMMA

As was discussed earlier, CRM's success is predicated on the ability to collect, analyse, and disseminate large amounts of timely and relevant information for customer-service operatives to act on to improve the experience at each point of customer contact. Thus, a CRM initiative cannot be successful without commitment among a critical mass of properties. Hotel chains cannot provide a consistently high level of personal service unless customer data can be garnered from most, if not all, of the affiliated properties, organized and synthesized in one central location, and subsequently redistributed to each property on an as-needed basis.

However, we propose that (technological constraints aside) this apparently simple theoretical proposition is difficult to realize in the lodging industry due to an inherent data-ownership conflict between the major industry stakeholders. In the following sections we present the main issues facing the brand, the management company, and the owner.

The Brand

For brands, the development of an effective CRM initiative is deemed an important competitive move as it would facilitate the development of a deep understanding of customer needs and preferences, potentially resulting in a high level of personalization, thus helping to improve service levels across the brand as a whole. As a result guests would have a strong incentive to remain loyal to the brand and patronize affiliated properties, thus increasing the value proposition for owners and operators through improvements in financial performance.

The Management Company

Management companies do not appear to have strong incentives to develop a CRM initiative for themselves. As such companies tend to operate a varied portfolio of properties, each flying different flags, on behalf of different owners. By definition a CRM initiative developed across flags is unlikely to generate brand loyalty and thus is of limited interest to most management companies. The question arises, however, as to whether management companies should actively cooperate with the collection of operational guest data by brand-level CRM initiatives. As most companies operate a varied portfolio of flags, if the management company participates in a brand-based CRM initiative, it will stand to gain only in those properties that carry that particular brand.

The Owner

While owners, like operators, typically have many flags in their portfolio of properties, they have a different focus in terms of profitability. Many primarily view hotel ownership as a real-estate investment, and have a marginal interest in the question, "Who owns the data?" Where their properties fly the flag of a successful CRM initiative, they may have an advantage over other competing properties; where their properties fly competing flags, they may be at a disadvantage. Thus, the same dilemma facing the management company seems to affect the owners—whether to participate in brand level CRM initiatives, or to refuse to cooperate with the collection and consolidation of customer data.

The owners may also have interests that go beyond the use of the data strictly for operational purposes. Customer data may be used by the other entities (the brand and the management company) for marketing purposes and analyses that run counter to the owner's own interests (e.g., studying the feasibility of building new properties in the same geographical area).

Conclusions and Implications

In this paper we have drawn attention to what we term the "data-ownership dilemma"—the inherent conflict that various entities in the lodging industry face as they embrace CRM. We propose that the data-ownership dilemma represents a significant, yet often unrecognized, challenge to the success of CRM initiatives. As was discussed, CRM strategies appear most applicable at the brand level, but their success is dependent on the active cooperation of both the operator and the owner of each property. For CRM to succeed at the brand level, operators must supply the brand with in-depth customer data—a requirement with which operators in particular, and owners to a lesser extent, have little incentive to comply. Brands also face challenges in terms of maintaining control over the resulting customer knowledge and preventing its spread outside the brand network.

Health Issues and SPA Demand

Among the components one might find in a modern spa are services related to:

- Complementary and alternative medicine in mainstream lifestyles.
- Traditional Western medical and Eastern lifestyle/ wellness practices.
- A proactive approach to overall health and the quality of one's life.
- Action spas are attracting a greater percentage of men who are looking for a way to unwind and keep active. Because of this trend, an aggressive array of activities— including cardio-circuit courses, squash, racketball and tennis, free and fixed weights, jogging, and bike paths, hikes, and water spots—is still a basic spa/wellness requirement.

- As part of the wellness experience, medical affiliations are sometimes available to provide information and to check blood pressure, heart conditions, bone density, and so on.
- Exceptional food can be tailored to virtually any dietary restriction or request.
- When examining which body treatments to include, note that salt glows and exfoliant treatments are approximately four times more popular than any other body treatment. These items are a mainstay in successful spa services.
- Guests must be able to upgrade their experience with add-ons such as eye-firming therapies and mineral-enhanced hydrotherapy soaks. Further, it is important to sell services in several time blocks so guests can select services that fit their schedule and financial budget.
- Educational programmes at many levels include classes and clinics. These programmes personally empower the guest, expand the wellness center's demand base, and encourage repeat visits. Health and wellness issues encompass cardiovascular health, holistic childrearing, the integration of Eastern and Western medical practices, indigenous spiritual practices, aging, intimacy, transition/death, vitality, strength training, cooking programmes (macrobiotic, vegan, vegetarian, indigenous), women's issues, and so on. Traditionally, educational programmes at spas have focused primarily on personal health issues.
- Mind-body techniques may include spiritual and cultural instruction. Examples include tai chi, visualization, progressive muscle relaxation and biofeedback, labyrinth walking, meditating and chanting, sweat lodges, and storytelling.
- Extensive yoga programmes should include Hatha yoga for body control, Ashtanga yoga for cardio workout, Iyengar yoga for balance and alignment, and Kundalini yoga for breath work.

- Comprehensive touch/alternative manual therapies including chiropractic treatment and deep tissue massage (rolfing, myofascial release, nueromuscular massage, acupressure/ shiatsu, watsu, Trager massage, etc.) are a necessary component of any wellness clinic. This modality is an extension of the basic massage offered at all spas and wellness/healing centers. Practitioners who provide manual therapies should be cross-trained in the areas of subtle energy work such as reiki, chakra balancing, and chi gung. Offering alternative touch/energy therapy as a component of traditional massage has the potential to accelerate market acceptance.
- Ayurvedic treatments are popular and provide an additional link between the East-meets-West philosophy showcased in many day spas. Elements of ayurvedic treatments can be incorporated into most touch therapies.

SPA Classification

Spa development and its attendant popularity have deep historical roots and vast potential for the hospitality industry. The term spa was once reserved for European destination resorts where guests went to "take the waters" and restore a healthy and balanced life. However, the term now is used to describe many types of facilities and amenities in the U.S. lodging industry. At one end of the spa spectrum are dedicated destination resort spas aimed primarily at those seeking a specialized combination regime of health, fitness, and pampering. Modalities and treatments include massages, unique treatments, custom dietary plans, lectures, and adventures that can include, but are not limited to, an array of activities ranging from nonsurgical facelifts to helicopter skiing.

Destination Spas

A destination spa is one whose sole purpose is to provide programmes and facilities that support lifestyle improvements and enhance guest health. The services offered are professionally administered and include fitness, education, and lectures on lifestyle, nutrition, and disease prevention. Because of their healthful orientation, destination spas often provide programmes that support postoperative conditions, address various addictions, and provide tools to cope with serious, prolonged illness. The destination spa industry constitutes only 1.6 percent of the total spa industry, per the International Spa Association's Industry Study (Thacker, 2004). However, the growth in the development and use of destination spas reflects the market's trend toward wellness and health as a major component in spa menus.

Resort Spas/Amenity Spas

Resort spas are located on the grounds of vacation resorts where treatments for mind, body, and spirit are offered to complement other resort activities such as golf, tennis, horseback riding, skiing, and water sports. Healthful spa cuisine is on the menu as an option, complementing traditional offerings. In the evenings, guests can enjoy resort pastimes like dancing and live entertainment. Children's programmes are also offered.

According to the ISPA Spa Industry Study, the resort spa represents 14 percent of spa locations in North America but accounts for almost 41 percent of the total industry revenue, 27 percent of all spa visits, and 26 percent of the industry's employees. A luxury resort spa has the ambience of a secluded retreat on the grounds of a first-class resort. Set in beautiful surroundings, these resorts commonly have world-class golf courses and other excellent recreational facilities. Gourmet dining and exceptional spa therapies are not only expected but demanded.

Day Spas

Day spas are designed to provide a healing, beautifying, or pampering experience in a short period. Guests may book individual treatments that last as little as an hour or a package of treatments that take up to a whole day. Found throughout

North America, day spas are freestanding or located in health clubs, hotels, and department stores. The day spa industry constitutes 72.2 percent of the total industry revenues, per the International Spa Association's 2004 Spa Industry Study.

The large percentage of day spas and their growth pattern reflect spa goers' time crunch. Day spas can be owner-operated or chain affiliated. Preliminary data from ISPA's 2004 survey show that industry growth is still robust. As of midyear 2004, there was a total of 12,000 spas nationally, of which 8,700 were day spas. These numbers reflect 25 percent growth in the industry in general and 20 percent growth exclusively in this market. The total number of day spa visits in 2003 was 81.2 million. However, only 13 percent of the general population had used a spa in the prior three-year period, indicating that the industry still has large growth potential.

Medical Spas

Medical treatments in various spa environments represent a significant trend in the scope, depth, and inclusiveness of numerous spas. Medical spa treatments can range from elective, reconstructive surgery to noninvasive Eastern modalities incorporating elements of Eastern philosophy that draw on the body-mind-spirit connection to create positive, measurable changes in the client/patient.

Slightly over half (51 percent) of the medical spas in North America have a partnership with a medical doctor, and 26 percent have a doctor on staff. The remaining configurations include being located in a doctor's office or having licensed staff members. Botox and microdermabrasion are the two most popular treatments, followed by chemical peels and laser hair removal. In North America, allopathic or Western medical procedures found in medical spas often incorporate Eastern-based treatments.

Mineral Springs Spas

Many mineral springs spas are considered to be the original spa prototype, where guests go to "take the waters." Mineral springs spas, by definition, are located at naturally occurring mineral springs, and by number of locations represent 2.8 percent of the total spa industry, or 1.3 percent of the total industry revenues, making this one of the more modest income producing segments of the spa industry.

The popularity of mineral springs spas is reflected in a cumulative growth from 1999 to 2004 of 143 percent. Growth from 2002 to 2004 represents only 15 percent, implying that the number of sites available directly affects the growth in this segment.

Club Spas

Club spas lack a lodging component, and their primary objective is to facilitate daily fitness activities. Many club spas' services complement the primary fitness component of the club by offering sports massage (deep tissue), chiropractic services, physiotherapy, and related treatments that address issues of pain management, flexibility, and mobility. By location, club spas represent 5.8 percent of the total spa industry in North America and account for approximately 3.7 percent of the industry's revenues. Growth in the club spa portion of the spa industry is the lowest of all spa segments. Between 2002 and 2004, cumulative club spa growth was only 3 percent.

SPA OPERATIONS

Spas as an Operating Department Historically, spa operations were treated by management similarly to other revenue departments, like catering and restaurants. These departments were simply perceived as an amenity needed to attract guests to the hotel. As long as the department broke even, or didn't lose too much money, their ability to increase occupancy was deemed sufficient justification for their existence. However, in the late 1990s, hotel spas followed the path of other operating departments and transformed from support facilities to profit centers. This trend is strong and continues today. In 1999, PKF Consulting identified only 30 hotels in the United States, thousands that report data to the PKF, extensive spa facilities and analyzed the financial performance of those properties and their spa departments.

Dedicated destination spa resorts were not included in the analysis due to an insufficient sample. While spas were a relatively small source of revenues for the sample properties, spa revenues grew at a relatively strong pace. In 1999, spa revenues for the subject sample represented just 3.3 percent of total sales.

Customer Service Training

A spa's reputation is easily made or destroyed by its level of customer service. Guests can forgive an occasional shortcoming if the level of service is exceptional. For this reason, it is essential that all spas have an integrated quality management programme that provides ongoing training to assist its employees in addressing customers' expectations. Customer service training (CST) helps ensure that guests' expectations are exceeded. In a spa environment, expectations are usually very high, and a trusting bond can be quickly established if the spa employees are sensitive to guest needs. The guest's arrival sequence, starting at the front desk, initiates the spa ritual that brings the spa guest to a place of trust, relaxation, and rejuvenation.

Provide Value, Create

Value Spa aficionados are savvy. They are looking to be indulged, pampered, and nurtured, not fleeced. Setting price points with market sensitivity can create tremendous customer loyalty. Because spas are no longer a one-time indulgence but rather a lifestyle choice, it is important to price services competitively and provide incentives for customers to return regularly. Numerous variables are involved in the development and operation of a spa as part of a hotel or resort. Doing one's homework is essential to success.

When a spa is developed or repositioned correctly, it can be a lucrative and rewarding experience. When it is not developed correctly, it can be a financial liability that haunts the spa director and jeopardizes the hotel's market position. If spas and their programming are not an integrated part of the hotel's future development, the property may lose a significant competitive opportunity. Spa-less hotels or poorly run properties have an inherent competitive market disadvantage. Not only do they find it more difficult to penetrate the market but they also often lose market share.

Resort Spas

The ratio of guest rooms to treatment rooms is based on many factors, including the anticipated return on investment to the owners, the topography of the site, the scope and theme of the spa, and the competition. In a destination resort, where the reason for the spa facilities is the reason for the trip, there should be an average of 1 treatment room for every 4 to 5 guest rooms. At the other end of the spectrum, such as a casino hotel, the spa is definitely an amenity, and 1 treatment room should be built for every 50 to 100 guest rooms. The spas at lower-end hotel properties normally are limited in scope and are often between 3,000 and 6,000 square feet, whereas luxury spas at full-service, high-end resorts average between 10,000 and 35,000 square feet. These ranges vary based on each hotel's specific circumstances, including seasonality, accessibility, meeting space, fill patterns, and local demand. Each market and each lodging product must be individually evaluated to assess the appropriate ratio of treatment rooms to guest rooms.

Another matrix that measures the viability of a resort or hotel spa is the cost to build the facility. Once again, a number of factors support various outcomes in this process, including the amount of available land, the finishes of the spa, the finishes of the hotel (these should be compatible), and the need to develop a spa either vertically or horizontally.

SPA TRENDS

On-Site Industry Trends Anti-aging treatments and products are driving much of spa menu and retail development. This calls for devoting a treatment room to outpatient medical procedures. Programming and spa menu items include sun damage treatments, chemical peels for skin renewal, and other rejuvenation techniques that build on repeat procedures. Commensurately, spas are developing retail product lines that can take the spa experience home and continue the wellness regime. Gift card sales are driving new users to spas. In the friends and family sector as well as the corporate gift-giving world, day spa certificates are creating demand that is not directly user driven. Third-party purchasing brings to spas clients who may not normally have chosen the location or treatment, creating a large but undefinable market demand.

Impulse appointments

"Life is uncertain, but I want a massage (reflexology appointment, yoga class, etc.) now!" This trend may result in developing adjunct programmes for oncall staff resources. The as-needed portion of the programme limits a hotel's payroll burden and other related fixed costs. Of course, this implies existing core programmes and facilities where these programmes can be developed and supported.

Shift in perspective

Self-indulgence, pampering, and luxury are being reevaluated and repackaged with a new, broader emphasis on self-care, stress relief, and emotional balancing. This is reflected in spa programming, the menu of services, food and beverage outlets, and spa-related retail. The retail positioning and spa programming components represent huge untapped revenue opportunities.

Changes in demographic use profile

Historically, the greatest segment of spa goers was women between the ages of 35 and 55. More couples and families are expected to visit the spa together as an alternative social/recreational activity. This trend has the potential to extend business-related stays, fill business hotels on the weekend, and create demand for destinations. It is important to understand this trend when evaluating ways to increase market penetration in a down market.

Medical affiliations

For some markets, an affiliation with a medical centre or

group in the area can be established to provide treatments such as acupuncture, nutritional assessment, laser therapies (hair removal and wrinkle reduction), Botox injections, collagen treatments, chemical peels, laser resurfacing, body contouring, microderm abrasion, and vascular procedures. When creating these types of relationships, it is essential that spa owners thoroughly investigate the legal disclosure and liability implications of being an affiliated medical service provider.

Index

D

E

T

U

V

W